Social Theory and Social Change

Also by Trevor Noble

Modern Britain: Structure and Change

SOCIAL THEORY AND SOCIAL CHANGE

Trevor Noble

palgrave

Published by
PALGRAVE
Houndmills, Basingstoke, Hampshire RG21 6XS and
175 Fifth Avenue, New York, N. Y. 10010
Companies and representatives throughout the world

PALGRAVE is the new global academic imprint of
St. Martin's Press LLC Scholarly and Reference Division and
Palgrave Publishers Ltd (formerly Macmillan Press Ltd).

Outside North America
ISBN 0–333–91238–1 hardcover
ISBN 0–333–91239–X paperback

Inside North America
ISBN 0–312–23328–0 cloth
ISBN 0–312–23329–9 paper

This book is printed on paper suitable for recycling and made from fully managed and sustained forest sources.

A catalogue record for this book is available from the British Library.

A catalogue record for this book is available from the Library of Congress.

10	9	8	7	6	5	4	3	2
10	09	08	07	06	05	04	03	02

Printed in China

Contents

Preface   viii

1 Introduction: Dimensions of the Debate   1
Social change and social theory   2
Key issues for theory   4

**2 Structural Effects: Adam Smith and the Unintended
 Consequences of Human Action**   17
Adam Smith's influence   17
Structural individualism   20
The division of labour and the market   24
Conflict and classes   30
The invisible hand and the evolution of commercial
society   36

**3 Evolutionary and Neo-Evolutionary Theories:
 Necessity and Possibility**   40
Evolution and progress   40
August Comte: the law of progress   42
Herbert Spencer: survival of the fittest   48
Some neo-evolutionists   57
 Sahlins and Service: general adaptive capacity   58
 Smelser: uneven structural change   59
 Parsons: structural differentiation   60
 Rostow: the stages of economic growth   65

4 Theories of Revolutionary Change:
  Marx and Contradiction 71
Marx's legacy 71
The intellectual background 72
The materialist conception of history 77
Base and superstructure 83
Contradictions of the capitalist mode of production 87
Contradictions of Marxist theory 91
  Unfulfilled prophecies 91
  Problems with the past 94
  System inconsistencies 96
  Marxist ideology 99

5 Reactionary Theories: The Loss of Community:
  The Persistence of Elites 101
Tönnies: *gemeinschaft* and *gesellschaft* 102
  Conservative romanticism 106
Pareto: rational and non-rational action 108
  The circulation of elites 111
  Conservative cynicism 115

6 Social Action Theory: Weber 118
Weber's methodological individualism 118
Ideas and social change 122
Power and authority 130
Rationalization and the modern world 138

7 Sociological Realism: Durkheim 145
Social change and the emergence of individualism 145
Pathological forms of the division of labour 151
Social facts as things 157
Religion and the categories of thought 161

8 Systems Theories: Functional Integration and
  Global Convergence 172
The functional analogy and the interconnectedness of
change 172
Parsons and the social system 176
Dependency theory: Frank and Wallerstein 187
Convergence theory: Kerr and Galbraith 194
How much more than the sum of its parts? 198

9 Modernity, Postmodernity and Postmodernism 202
Modernity, crisis and change 202
  Jürgen Habermas: the legitimation of capitalism 203
  Daniel Bell: cultural contradictions 207
  Anthony Giddens: consequences of modernity 213
Postmodernity, postmodernism and after 221
  Jean-François Lyotard: language and paralogy 226
  Jean Baudrillard: postconsumerism and hyperreality 231
Postmodernist theory and continuing change 235

10 Continuing Change and Continuing Theory 238

Bibliography 245

Index 255

Preface

In this book I have tried to portray, in bold outline, some of the major concepts and debates in sociological theory in the context of a single major theme: the exploration of the causes and consequences of social change. This has played a predominant role in the development of sociological thought from its eighteenth-century origins, through the work of the major nineteenth- and twentieth-century theorists to the more recent discussion of modernity and postmodernity. The conjunction between social theory and social change can be looked at from several points of view: as the primary substantive issue for theory to address; as common ground where theories can be compared; as the external conditions generating the ideas theorists articulate; or, finally, as a continuing sociological challenge.

Most of what follows here concerns a variety of attempts either to identify the principal causes of social change or to explore its consequences for those of us caught up in the process. And, inevitably, we all are. Whether you can take it in your stride or secretly tremble, wondering if you'll ever be able to cope, social change is something we all are aware of. New faces, new places, new gadgetry are all fine and exciting if you can choose when and how much of them you will have to deal with. But the changes over which we have no control, over which nobody seems to have any control, while they may present us with new horizons and new opportunities, at the same time confront some of us with serious problems of adjustment and loss. These apparently impersonal processes cannot be easily explained in terms of the will, or the whims, of individual political leaders, businessmen, generals, inventors or writers, however ostensibly powerful or prominent they might be in their own spheres. Why is it that not just individuals, but whole populations, whole societies, abandon traditional values or begin to seek their livelihoods in new ways? Social change is the greatest challenge for social theory. It is an issue about which different theorists have come to very different conclusions. Furthermore it is one which sharply reveals the very different starting points from which they have begun their discussions.

For all this diversity, which will become evident as we go through the rest of the book, the writers to be considered have all had important and original ideas to contribute, but these have been neither additive nor substitutable. None of them, that is to say, can be taken as subsuming any of the others. They have different things to tell us and help us to understand that none of the different ways of thinking about social processes has a monopoly on validity or truth.

This brings us to another aspect of the relationship between social theory and social change. Social theory is a response to social change. Its origins lie in the political, economic and cultural upheavals of the eighteenth and nineteenth centuries, and its development reflects the perception of new straws in the wind of continuing change since then. The development of social theory has been discontinuous, experimental, a series of fresh starts, each embodying a new conception of the changing social world. Sociological theory has, in this way, more in common with the history of the novel than the systematic, linear and cumulative growth of the natural sciences. In physics, chemistry or the biological sciences, each new insight has been built upon the achievements of its predecessors. By contrast, current social theory often seems not so much a matter of 'standing upon the shoulders of giants' as of chipping away at their ankles in the general attempt to topple the founding fathers from their pedestals. In presenting them in an approximately historical sequence, each new perspective might be seen as in some sense rooted in its historical circumstances and that the changing directions of social and cultural change over the past two centuries are to some extent mirrored in the shifting emphases of their paradigms. But the literature of social theory is more than a mere reflection of its original historical context. The great innovators of sociological theory were inspired, creative thinkers responding to their own times and situations to produce original ideas of lasting, general significance. They are not just historically limited figures in an evolving tradition, but survive as still significant participants in a continuing discussion about the driving forces in human society and the widening repercussions of social change.

Each point of view which I have tried to explore in the following chapters is presented as mainly the conception of one major writer rather than in more formally abstract terms or as the common ground of a school of thought. This is, therefore, neither a detailed history of all the varied contributions to the sociological tradition nor a comprehensive review of every topic of sociological concern and inquiry. Admittedly, this procedure disguises the diversity of emphasis and shades of academic interpretation amongst those who identify themselves as critics or exponents of any given perspective. My aim, however, has been to try to present them relatively free of scholarly quibble and therefore in a way which is more accessible to the new student (whether of sociology, politics, development studies, cultural studies or social policy) and, at the same time, to show the basic ideas as essentially the work of writers engaged in lively and still relevant exploration of issues which still matter to us all. Social theory has this further connection with social change – one, however, that we must each make for ourselves. In so far as we are not just helpless victims but are active participants in the process, the better understanding of the complexities of social change, which this rich endowment of theoretical argument and commentary can provide, may help us to adapt more effectively where we have to and, where we can, to shape its outcomes with greater insight and to more humane ends.

1

Introduction: Dimensions of the Debate

Change is everywhere. The births, marriages and deaths of friends and relatives, the crises of schooling or the stages of a career, weave the fabric of our individual life-worlds. In the wider world we move in too, there are new ideas to assimilate, new procedures, new technologies, fresh opportunities to grasp or ignore. And even the apparent absence of change, in the community, the family or the organization where we work, is subject to development and transformation as experience accumulates; the newness of relationships turns into familiarity and the innovative becomes the taken for granted. It is true that beneath the constant activity of daily events and the cyclical changes of a lifetime or a career lie all the enduring ties of kinship and nationality, the persistent inequalities of fortune and power, and the remorseless exigencies of market forces. Deeper still, however, there are currents reshaping and rearranging even these abiding coordinates of the social map. The comings and goings of everyday life, that is to say, take place within a framework of basic assumptions, settled relationships, familiar patterns of behaviour and an established division of resources. But it is less immovable than it looks. The framework itself may be subject to alteration, adaptation, slow erosion or radical upheaval. It was the causes and consequences of changes at that level, of what we can call structural change, that concerned the major social theorists whose work we shall consider in this book – and that, indeed, greatly fuelled the impetus driving the development of sociology as a discipline.

Social change and social theory

The industrialization, political revolutions, civil changes, commercial development, population growth and, not least, the artistic and intellectual creativity of the eighteenth and nineteenth centuries gave rise to modern social theory. Thinkers sought to apply to society the scientific temper of natural history and so explain the rapidly and visibly changing world around them. This did not lead, however, to a consensus of view about the nature of the historical processes at work or about where they were leading us all. Some welcomed what they saw, some were pessimists; some saw great impersonal forces unfolding in the course of history, some saw individual men acting rationally in the light of their moral understanding; some thought the new world emerging was utterly unlike anything that had gone before, some thought new styles merely served to disguise the same harsh old realities. Little has changed when we look at sociology today. Social change and its consequences remain key themes for contemporary social theory. In fact, I'd argue that other issues – the problem of social order, for example, the relationship of agency and structure and of the global and the local, or the social dimensions of identity – while important in themselves, can be seen as subsidiary to this theme of social change.

This book therefore is about both sociology and change. In looking at what has been said about structural change and what kinds of repercussions it has upon the lives of ordinary people or the fate of nations, at the same time we shall have to make some appraisal of the strengths and weaknesses, the plausible and implausible features of these diverse contributions to the debate. Debate can sharpen our understanding of the different strands of a complex subject. The arguments we shall examine in the following chapters may not give all the answers we might like, but I hope they will improve the quality of the questions we can ask about society: how social change comes about, what its effects are, and where it is leading us.

The various theoretical perspectives are presented here in a broadly chronological sequence, starting with Adam Smith in the eighteenth century and ending with the postmodernist theories of the late twentieth. This has the advantage of revealing how some later theorists have sometimes drawn upon and, more rarely, taken further ideas first advanced by earlier writers. I have been concerned to give credit where credit is due, but this broadly chronological approach also allows us to see how far ideas can be adapted in different contexts or how far there may be further implications to an argument, which a writer may not have made explicit.

This is not the principal rationale for ordering the discussion in this way, however. It is also intended to represent the logical structure of the debate about social change. Thus Chapters 2, 3 and 4 look at pioneering theoretical work which established some of the basic concepts necessary for the analysis of social change. In Chapter 2 we can identify a specifically sociological level of analysis, before the term itself had been coined, in Adam Smith's work on the division of labour in society and the social and cultural, economic and political consequences of the market. Smith draws our attention to the emergent and systematic effects, larger but unforeseen, arising out of people's purposive activities, but independent of their intentions. Sociological theory, in contrast with, say, metaphysical, psychological or theological explanations, might be defined by this concern with the coherent, but unintended consequences of human actions. The evolutionary theories discussed in Chapter 3 represent a further step in the analysis of social change. They suggest that change can be seen as a progressive, linear series of stages which can be ordered as part of an evolutionary sequence. The dynamics of the transition from one stage to the next is the focus of Karl Marx's theory of revolutionary change discussed in Chapter 4. Influential for many reasons and in countless ways, a major part of the importance of Marx's theory is his analysis of how each stage grows out of, and is shaped by, the contradictory character of the one before.

There are, however, counter-currents in the theoretical discussion of social change and the following three chapters, 5, 6 and 7, deal with some of these. In contrast with the generally optimistic theorists of evolutionary progress, there is also a strong tradition of criticism pointing out, on the one hand, the damaging costs of change and, on the other, the superficiality of ideas of progress while the brutal realities of power and domination persist. Chapter 5 discusses early and profoundly influential statements of these positions developed by Tönnies and Pareto.

The question of what are the generators and what the outcomes of social change remains at the heart of what has become a long-standing division in sociological theory and the chapters on Weber and Durkheim set out their groundbreaking attempts to elaborate the two sides of this debate. While Weber argued that ideas and values are crucial in shaping human action and can thereby bring about change, in Durkheim's view, changing ideas and values are themselves the product of social change.

The next two chapters, 8 and 9, on systems theories and theories of modernity and postmodernity, show that this concern with cultural factors as cause or consequence continued in the dominant theories of the later twentieth century. A number of powerful theories using systems models, however, focus particularly on the interconnectedness of all change in maintaining the homoeostasis of successful, that is, surviving, social systems. Nevertheless, the main theme in discussions of the economically developed world is the critique of contemporary culture. Theories of modernity, that is, of the shaping and continuing development of the advanced industrial countries, have been preoccupied with what have been perceived as crises of political legitimacy and personal identity. With postmodernist theory, the reflexive element in cultural critique – the argument that theorists too are but creatures of their times and circumstances – has come to challenge the possibility of theory itself and in a concluding chapter, we must confront the question of what, if anything, can follow the postmodern.

Key issues for theory

The score or so of theories of social change reviewed here are diverse and incompatible. They do not converge towards a happy synthesis. Those which have proved most stimulating, either to those who have found them persuasive, or to those who have been provoked into criticism and attempts to confute them, have started from often radically different assumptions. Apart from their different insights and idiosyncrasies, however, there are a number of generic questions that they all confront, issues about which each of them has necessarily had to adopt a position. These not only define their different starting points, but provide a comparative understanding of why they have proffered such different interpretations. Amongst all the other similarities and differences, affinities and divergences, there are six dimensions which distinguish the distinctive approach of each of these theories. Two concern the nature and character of structural change; two concern the character of social phenomena in general; and two address issues concerning what sort of knowledge is possible and what sort of statements about the social world can therefore be regarded as acceptable. (These questions are *epistemological* in character.)

There are, of course, many more than six issues which might distinguish one theoretical argument from another, but I would argue that the others are much less fundamental to the architecture of the theories which result and, some at least, are merely special cases or corollaries of the principal half dozen.

Six key issues for theories of change

[handwritten annotations: direction is inevitable, governed by laws, linear progress, historical cycles]

(a) The character of change
1. Change is Endogenous vs. Exogenous.
2. Change is Inevitable vs. Contingent. (e.g. The idea of progress vs. the rejection of metanarratives.) *[handwritten: No pattern]*
(b) The character of the social
3. Sociological Realism (Structure) vs. Methodological Individualism (Agency). *[handwritten: individual, society]*
4. Materialism vs. Idealism.
(c) The character of explanation
5. Possible Objectivity (Science) vs. Inescapable Commitment (Ideology).
6. Rationalism vs. Empiricism.

Let us look at each of these positions in more detail:

1. Endogenous vs. exogenous change

The first issue for theories of change is where to look for its causes. Is change primarily *endogenous* – that is, generated within the social system itself by the cultural and structural processes at work within it – or is it mainly *exogenous*, that is, the result of external factors intruding so as to destabilize an existing situation? You might think the obvious answer would be to say that it is sometimes the one and sometimes the other. But, as we shall see, theorists have mostly tended to be either interested only in those changes which were primarily exogenous or, conversely, have focused almost entirely on endogenous change.

The reason for these contrary views is that they mostly reflect a more profound disagreement about the predominance of conflict or consensus in human affairs. This difference of perspective has long predated modern sociological theorizing. Without going all the way back to classical Greece, we can find the basic opposition in the views of philosophers such as Thomas Hobbes (1588–1679) in the seventeenth century and Jean-Jacques Rousseau (1712–1778) in the eighteenth. Hobbes held that the natural condition of mankind is a war of all against all. Society exists to superimpose some degree of order on us and without the discipline maintained by the power of the state, the life of man would indeed be 'solitary, poor, nasty, brutish and short' (1968, p. 186). Modern versions of this view, that life is naturally a competitive struggle for dominance, appear in neo-Darwinian theory, which is sometimes interpreted by biological scientists as having sociological implications (Wilson, 1975; Dawkins, 1976). The view of social relations as naturally harmonious and the nature of mankind as self-reliant, peaceable and cooperative, but enslaved and corrupted by society was expressed notably by Rousseau in *The Social Contract,* which had a powerful influence on those intellectuals who helped to make the French Revolution of 1789. Of course, consensus theorists are aware of wars and persecutions and the many confrontations of life, but they view them as unnecessary and avoidable. Similarly, conflict theorists are not blind to the collaborative achievements of mankind, but view conflict as an 'endemic but intermittent feature of collective action' (Collins, 1975).

Marxists have tended to regard society as a matter of the inevitably conflicting interests of lord and peasant, capitalist and worker, but other socialists like the followers of Fourier (1772–1837), or anarchists like Peter Kropotkin (1842–1921), have argued that class struggle is a historical aberration which can be replaced by a return to a society of mutual aid. Equally, some politically conservative thinkers from Machiavelli (1469–1527) or in twentieth-century sociology, Vilfredo Pareto (whose work we will look at in Chapter 5), have stressed the need for hierarchy and the concentration of power in order to contain the irreducibly conflicting interests of the more and the less privileged. But others, of a less reactionary but still conservative inclination, have argued for the complementarity of interests within society's division of labour, the idea of mutual obligation between the ranks of society and the integrating functions of hierarchy. The latter idea has been developed by René Dumont in his discussion of the Indian caste system as explaining the long endurance of traditional Hindu society over centuries of political upheaval (Dumont, 1972). Consensus and conflict orientated theories, then, are associated with political points of view, but not in the simple way that is sometimes suggested.

As for social change, conflict theorists regard the momentary equilibrium which may be attained in a society at any given period as essentially precarious. The potential for endogenous change is always there in the struggle to reallocate the distribution of social advantage. Consensus theorists are likely to see change as exogenous, originating as an adaptation to culture contact, invasion or changes in the economic environment. The common interests of the members of the group, or the component elements of the wider society, then need to adjust in the light of the changing circumstances. In this way change is, on the whole, regarded as a reaction to events elsewhere.

2. Inevitable vs. contingent change
Is there a direction to history? In all the apparent contingencies and upheavals evident in the historical record, can we see the unfolding of some larger pattern? There are those who see human history, like other natural processes, as governed by laws of development which are accessible to scientific discovery. Most nineteenth-century sociology reflects this preoccupation under the two powerful influences of Hegelian and Darwinian ideas – Hegel's theory of the progress of the human spirit towards the final full realization of positive freedom through reason had widespread influence upon Marx's dialectical theory of history, as we shall see in Chapter 4. A recent manifestation has been Fukuyama's argument that history has now come to an end (Fukuyama, 1991). The idea of progress in the work of St Simon in the 1820s, and the more systematic theories of Comte (1798–1857) in France and Herbert Spencer (1870–1903) in England (both discussed in Chapter 3), reinforced the popular impact of the Darwinian theory of the evolution of animal species in a progressive chain of evolution, from the protozoa right up to the Victorian man of letters (Burrow, 1966; Bowler, 1983). The laws of historical motion may be linear, through a progressive succession of stages, or cyclical, as the historian Toynbee (1961)

and the philosopher Spengler (1918) argued.

Other theorists, however, have rejected both linear progress and historical cycle. To borrow some pre-sociological rhetoric, their view of history is of 'a tale told by an idiot, full of sound and fury, signifying nothing'. In the eighteenth century Montesquieu (1689–1755), reflecting on the diversity of human societies, how they flourish, how they decay, concluded that there was no pattern to the process. More recently, Karl Popper (1902–1996) attacked the belief in an underlying and inevitable direction to historical evolution, what he called historicism, especially as exemplified in the theories of Marxism and Hegelianism. The main thrust of his study, *The Poverty of Historicism* (1957), was that there is a logical flaw in claiming to explain the past and the present in terms of the destination towards which it is leading, such as analysing the dynamics of capitalist society in terms of its inevitable revolutionary overthrow. He argued that whatever we can say about the future, at best uncertain, can only come from our knowledge of the past and present. Therefore, to explain the past teleologically, that is, in terms of its contribution to the realization of what still remains, the future is an obvious case of entirely circular reasoning. In other words, it doesn't explain anything at all.

In recent times Krishnan Kumar has again emphasized the unpredictability of change, of discontinuity in history (Kumar, 1978). He has also drawn attention (1995) to the widespread loss in recent years of any belief in what certain theorists, among them Lyotard and Baudrillard, describe as the 'metanarratives' of history (1995; Lyotard, 1984; Baudrillard, 1976). By metanarratives we mean the basic underlying assumptions of historical writing, such as the belief in progress or the increasing rationalization of the world, or perhaps the succession of historical eras leading ultimately to the replacement of capitalism by socialism. Of course, the rejection of historical inevitability, of metanarratives or historicism, need not make historians redundant or entail abandoning all attempts to understand the processes of historical change. But we may have to recognize that the trends we tentatively discern, the sequences we believe we can trace, the configurations of apparently related events do not represent the discovery of the secret pattern of history.

3. Methodological individualism vs. sociological realism

This is a very familiar paradox masked in possibly rather daunting sociological terminology. Ordinary common-sense thinking has a proverbial capacity for accommodating apparently quite contradictory things: for example, too many cooks spoil the broth, but many hands make light work. Sociologists theorizing in a more systematic and rigorous way have tended to find it harder to integrate two apparently contradictory lines of thought. The first of these asserts that, for all the routine and ritual, the rankings and regalia, all the authority, all the money, all the ceremony and rules, what we call society is only a facade behind which are people much alike in their wit and strength, their weaknesses and hopes. There is no such thing as 'society', it is only an abstraction, something that exists solely in our continued belief in the conventions and the day-to-day practices through which we relate to one another. These are not facts of nature like the laws of chemistry; they are neither inevitable nor necessary. Life, in essence, is what we make it.

This form of individualism implies that social scientific analysis must begin with what is intelligible at the level of individual experience. Its approach, described by Popper (1945) as *methodological individualism,* is characterized by a commitment to what has meaning for those directly involved, and is generally associated with the work of Max Weber, whom I shall discuss in Chapter 6. It has mainly been influential, however, in the work of writers like the interactionists, followers of George Herbert Mead (1863–1931); the phenomenologists since Alfred Schutz (1899–1959); and those generally concerned with face-to-face interactions, like Erving Goffman (1922–1982), who have had little or nothing to say about social change.

On the other hand, common sense also tells us that we are only what society has made us. We are the creatures of our era, of our class, our culture, our gender or place. 'What can you expect of anyone with such a background?' It is society that makes us what we are; French speakers, Martiniquaises, Catholics or whatever. What choice we have is restricted, and the views and preferences we have are only those we were brought up to have, or have since learned to have. On this view it is society that is real, and our analysis therefore must begin at the level of the social whole. This is the view labelled *Sociological Realism*. The perspectives of Marx and Durkheim, and of the structural functionalists like Talcott Parsons, are all alike in this respect, in that their analyses begin with the social system and individual actions are to be understood only within that wider context.

At a common-sense level, both views seem plausible enough, at one time or another. For social theorists however, with their self-imposed obligation of consistency, they present an unavoidable dilemma. The debate about the reconciliation of these two approaches continues very actively in terms of the relationship between *agency* and *structure* or 'the individual and society', and various arguments that there isn't really a gap between them at all. For some writers (Scotford Archer, 1988; Giddens, 1984; Layder, 1994; Scott, 1995), this is the central issue for present-day sociological theory.

4. Materialism vs. idealism

The debate between materialist and idealist theorists has very long philosophical roots and only some aspects of the controversy figure directly within social theory. Materialist sociological theories are those that argue we must begin with the conflicts and collaborations of men and women who work and fight and procreate in order to survive. Everything else is essentially epiphenomenal, that is to say a matter of rationalization, justification, window-dressing. Idealist sociological theories begin with the premiss that social interaction is essentially meaningful. We behave as we do because we interpret our situation in a particular way. So the first things we need to understand will always be the ideas, the rules and assumptions which guide people's behaviour. Thus, as materialists, we might stress the needs, desires, opportunities and resources that determine our behaviour in the tangible world of flesh and blood people at large in a material environment. On the other hand, as idealists, we may want to focus on the phenomenological context. That is to say, you may take the view that the material world is effectively inert until we give it meaning. A piece of rock can be an element in an admired landscape, a potential sculpture, an obstacle to travel, building stone, mineral ore, protected habitat for rare lichens, cover for a marksman; any or several of these at once. But it is only when we attribute meaning to the world that it acts upon us or we upon it. And that goes for the world of our fellow human being too. If you have ever fallen over a piece of furniture you didn't realize was in the way, the materialist view would seem to have some strong arguments on its side. However, in sociological matters the question is far from clear-cut. Six people in a room could be there for all sorts of reasons. They constitute a committee because they are designated as such and act as they believe they accordingly should. If they turn you down for the job or approve your application for a grant, they can have a real and material impact on your prospects, even though the committee exists, in some sense, only because the relevant people believe it to exist. Its rules and its powers are not imaginary, but you can only bump into them metaphorically. This sort of idealist perspective in social theory develops the view that cultural factors; values, meanings and beliefs, are what make the world intelligible and are ultimately what shape human action. Functionalists like Kingsley Davis (1948, 1959), Edward Shils (1981) or Robert Nisbet (1969), as well as the interactionists like G. H. Mead (1934) and Herbert Blumer (1969), or Alfred Schutz (1972) and the phenomenologists have, in their different ways, developed their arguments within this general perspective.

In contrast, materialists have stressed the determination of social development by the practical necessities of procuring a subsistence. For most versions of Marxist thought, and for many non-Marxist materialists, how people gain a livelihood has been the central issue in social history. Marxists have generally emphasized the importance of who owns or otherwise controls the means of subsistence in a society, that is, the land and the commercial and industrial infrastructure. Some have emphasized technological developments (Gordon–Childe, 1958), as have non-Marxists like St Simon, who stressed the importance of industrial technology, Aron (1964), or Fernand Braudel (1976) who has shown the profound and far-reaching effects of growing trade and commerce in medieval and Early Modern Europe and Asia. The American geographer Ellsworth Huntington (1945), in the 1940s revived ideas first outlined by Montesquieu 200 years earlier about the critical importance of soil and climate on social development. More recently, Leonard Dudley (1991) has argued that historical change can be explained in general terms as a result of major developments in the delivery of information: the invention of writing, printing, the mass media and information technology; and in the delivery of violence: the invention of metal weapons, artillery, steam transport and heavy cavalry (including tanks). These have transformed the scale and effectiveness of the state in controlling larger and larger populations. All these writers were materialists in the sense we are using the term here.

Although they are quite distinct issues, there tends to be a congruence between writers' views on this question of materialism and idealism and their sociological realism or methodological individualism. On the whole, most materialists have been sociological realists, while the majority of methodological individualists have stressed the importance of ideal factors in their theory. The notable exceptions have been very influential, however. Hegel's philosophy of history (G. W. F. Hegel, 1770–1831) is concerned with the evolution of whole societies through the progressive transformations of the spirit of the age. On the other hand, materialist methodological individualists have been less concerned with questions of social change. Probably the best examples of this type of theorizing in sociology are those who have been strongly influenced by the psychological theory of Behaviourism first developed by J. B. Watson (1878–1958), and subsequently evolved almost into an academic orthodoxy in the 1950s and 1960s by B. F. Skinner (1904–1990) and his followers. This approach, which regarded only observable behaviour as relevant to scientific inquiry and all subjective experience as conjectural and not to be relied on, had a particular influence in the 1960s on what was described as Exchange Theory, but it is of only marginal relevance here (Homans, 1961; Blau, 1964).

5. Objectivity vs. commitment

This, the first of the two epistemological issues we identified in our six basic positions, concerns whether objective knowledge of the social world is possible. In its strong form, this debate is about whether, on the one hand, sociology can be regarded as a science or whether, on the other, it is impossible to avoid being ideological whenever we say anything about society.

Science aspires to be a neutral body of objective truth that is equally true for everybody regardless of their wishes, motives or the benefits such knowledge might give or deny them. It is true that scientists sometimes get things wrong and have to revise their opinions, but that is precisely what the system of scientific thought and procedure is about: to test our views of the world and to provide for their correction when we discover something new or find errors in what we thought before. By ideology, we mean a set of beliefs organized in such a way as to justify the best interests of the group who hold to them. Thus the view that all change is invariably for the worse makes good sense as part of the ideology of those who benefit most from the present order of things. The feeling that any change is better than none is perfectly intelligible as part of the ideology of those with nothing to lose.

Those who believe that sociology could never be an objective science argue that ideological thinking is unavoidable. We cannot help but see the world from our own point of view, however much we may try to sympathize with others. It is a problem of values rather than facts. Facts do not speak for themselves. The meaning they have for us is coloured by the emotional, moral or political commitments which make the framework of our understanding. These values are shaped by our socialization into a culture, a class position, a religious community, a gender role. It is not possible to step back from society for an objective view. We are inextricably part of it, permeated by it through our loyalties and prejudices, our livelihood and our sense of personal identity. How can we be dispassionate about what we are so intimately involved with? Isn't a study of society necessarily going to be biased by our own allegiances and material interests? Isn't the attempt to be scientific about what most people are irretrievably committed about itself an expression of values?

In a well-known article first published in 1970, but often reprinted, Alan Dawe argued that there were two sociologies, namely, one ostensibly scientific but concerned with the problems of order and control in society and therefore ideologically conservative; and the radical, especially Marxist, sociology politically committed to liberation from prevailing social forms, especially those characteristic of capitalist society (Dawe, 1970). Thus one sociology is, in fact, no more 'scientifically' neutral than the other. Those who claim to be 'objective' are merely making a debating point.

This point of view has been criticized for its oversimplification and for the relativism that follows from it (see Ryan, 1970; Peel, 1978; Flew, 1985). Martin Hammersley has more recently made similar criticisms of those feminist arguments which propose that all thought is necessarily 'gendered' (1992). Basically, if all sociology is ideological, then there could be no common understanding between those whose interests divided them, between revolutionary proletariat and bourgeoisie, between men and women. If we exclude the possibility of a common understanding, then, except when exhorting those who already agree with us, all argument and discussion is really a waste of breath or paper. If what Dawe claims is true, not only would it be impossible to convince anyone who disagreed, but his own argument is relativized. That is to say, it is only 'true' because it seems to be so from his point of view. It cannot be equally true for anyone who has a different opinion because if it were *really* true for all of us regardless, then objectivity *is* possible and his argument falls down. In other words, if he convinces me, it means his argument is false. Such are the trials and absurdities of the relativist position.

An absolute faith in the truth of one's own convictions is not the only alternative to ideological relativism. Instead we may argue that ideas about the social world are not wholly determined by our circumstances and that it is possible to change our minds in the light of experience and observation. Thus objectivity can be constructed in the course of our investigations. It is a way of dealing with evidence by empirical inquiry and logical criticism. Even if we cannot attain the precision and the experimental rigour of the natural sciences, it may still be possible to aspire to their neutrality. Even if sociology cannot qualify as a science in the strictest sense, it might still be possible in this way for it to be an objective account of the world. Weber's distinction between being value-free and value-relevant is a helpful one for those who strive to achieve objectivity in their methods. Sociologists' work is value-relevant in that, being only human, mostly, they also have their personal commitments, allegiances and prejudices, and these make some of the issues they study more personally important to them than others. But these feelings and commitments need not, Weber argued they should not, determine their findings. Their work, to that extent, is value-free. They may conceivably be surprised by their results or disappointed about the conclusions their studies lead them to. Of course, truth and objectivity are also values, socially achieved and defended all too rarely and with great difficulty. But they do not necessarily entail any other values. They simply make the pursuit of other values possible.

6. Rationalism vs. empiricism

The final dividing line I want to draw amongst the theorists I propose to consider is based on how they envisage a satisfactory explanation. These differences have their modern (that is, as opposed to ancient Greek) philosophical roots in the seventeenth century, in the systematic rationalism of René Descartes (1596–1650) and the empirical philosophy of Francis Bacon (1561–1626). Both were passionately concerned with understanding the phenomenal world, but their conceptions of the place of theory and how it orders observation are radically different. Descartes sought to establish rational thought on logically impregnable foundations. Bacon believed that understanding must be grounded in observation of the real world. (It is said that as an old and sick man, he insisted on getting out of his carriage one wintry day to stuff a dead chicken with snow to see if the refrigeration would preserve it from decay. Unfortunately, as a result, he caught a fatal chill, so one could say he died for his beliefs.)

Rationalist explanation proceeds by logical deduction from first principles. So an adequate explanation of some observation or event would show how it follows as a result of the consistent application of the basic rules of a coherent theoretical system. History is explained when it can be accounted for within a structure of logically related ideas. Thus, for example, the collapse of capitalism can be explained rationally in Marxist terms by our understanding of the contradictions inherent in the system itself, which must inevitably destroy it since, in the last analysis, the law of the accumulation and concentration of capital is clearly incompatible with the persistence of market relations which necessarily requires a distribution of capital.

As we have seen in the case of Bacon, empiricism contrasts with rationalism in that, instead of deriving explanations from already understood principles, empiricism seeks to build its theory upon observation and experience. While the empiricist tradition has been particularly important in the natural sciences, particularly in Britain and America, rationalism has played much the greater role in the European tradition of social thought and philosophy (see Hawthorn, 1976). As Kumar has noted, Francis Bacon '... leads us away from the abstract, ahistorical Platonic concern with "clear and distinct ideas" to the actual technological, social and political accomplishments of modern

societies, and the blessings and headaches they have brought'
(Kumar, 1995; and see Rorty, 1985). But while the rationalist
perspective has played much the greater role in sociological
theorizing from the nineteenth century onwards, empiricism has
continued as a less explicit *modus operandi* in the procedures of
a great deal of the investigation of specific issues that also goes
under the name of sociology. Thus a lot of what one might call
'practical sociology' seems to have but slight connection with
the preoccupations of the theoretical literature, and may be
subject now and then to derisive comment from those interested
in the central issues of contemporary theory. This does not,
however, mean – cannot mean – that such work is 'theory free',
mere description. It is rather that the theory involved proceeds
in a tentative, provisional and piecemeal manner.

When we turn to examine the actual theories which follow, it
is endlessly intriguing, if sometimes bewildering, to consider the
sheer variety and fecundity of ideas produced by all these people
trying to make sense of the changing times they were living
through. There is much we can learn from each of them and,
perhaps, more still from thinking about how, for all their
originality and powerful arguments, they have reached such
different conclusions. The diversity of these perspectives
illustrates the creativity of the continuing controversy which has
come to comprise the sociological tradition and suggests that it
is not too late, there is still room for us to join in.

2

Structural Effects: Adam Smith and the Unintended Consequences of Human Action

Adam Smith's influence

Some of Adam Smith's (1723–1790) ideas were later incorporated as central elements in the theories of Marx and Durkheim, among others. But it is not just as a precursor whose work profoundly influenced the subsequent development of theory that he is worth our present consideration. His work remains a distinctive response to the dilemmas of theory, an original and still stimulating sociological synthesis of individual action, the critical role of structural relationships, conflict and sympathy. His sensitivity to the psychological, economic, moral and political factors also at work strengthens his claims for the pivotal function of the specifically structural characteristics of a society.

It was already becoming apparent in the eighteenth century that countries where trade and commerce were well developed were beginning to prosper even more than those whose climate, fertile soils, mineral deposits and large populations might seem a richer natural endowment. In these trading nations it was increasingly evident that changes were taking place. The general level of prosperity was rising, populations growing, innovation in manufacturing, changes in manners and beliefs and in the social order of wealth and rank, as well as political ideas and relationships – all were changing as apparently never before. Nowhere was this more obvious than in England, but nowhere was it more keenly observed than in Scotland, England's poorer, smaller neighbour, politically weakened by recent civil war and

17

religious divisions and newly joined with its richer and thriving southern neighbour in a United Kingdom. Scottish writing in philosophy, history, theology, jurisprudence, fiction, poetry and political economy was astonishingly prolific and outstandingly original at this time. Adam Smith, one of the most distinguished figures of this flowering of creative thinking, was not, then, an isolated figure in his own time. In this 'Scottish Enlightenment', the scientific outlook of many of its thinkers was applied in particular to questions of history, of human nature and the nature of human society. Thus John Millar addressed the origins of social inequality and of social classes and Adam Ferguson (1767) set out a comparative examination of the variety of cultures. Smith had read David Hume's major study, the *Treatise on Human Nature* when studying at Oxford. The discovery of such a heretical work in his rooms almost got him expelled. He later made friends with Hume when teaching in Glasgow. Hume's continuing importance in moral philosophy, the philosophy of religion, the theory of mind and scientific method is hard to match among British philosophers, and he also wrote a widely read *History of England*. Though much less prolific, Adam Smith was almost as versatile and in no way less subtle or original in his thinking. His influence, however, has mainly been confined to a most selective reading in the early development of classical economics. I want to argue here that his originality is in his anticipation of a fully developed sociological theory before any such discipline had even been named, and that his greatest importance lies in his sociological understanding of the processes of economic growth and social change.

Smith's published works are few. He produced two major books: *The Theory of Moral Sentiments* (1759) and *An Inquiry into the Nature and Causes of the Wealth of Nations* (1776). In addition there are some essays, notably a 'History of Astronomy' (1758) and his *Lectures on Jurisprudence,* given while Professor of Moral Philosophy at the University of Glasgow, in which he first set out the ideas later developed more fully in his published work. The lack of any institutionalized academic interest in social science in Britain 200 years ago meant that, after its favourable initial reception, Smith's analytic approach to social change was generally forgotten there, and later tended to be dismissed in caricature as the crude precursor of the dehumanized calculations of classical economics. This discontinuity has led to the general exclusion of Smith's work from the canon of theory which students are routinely taught in sociology courses even in his own country, and elsewhere he is represented as worth no more than a dismissive footnote to the work of others.

His reputation has suffered sadly from two sources; his ostensible enemies and his seeming friends. Those who have taken his name as an emblem for *laissez-faire* political economy have mainly derived their enthusiasm via the work of Ricardo and James Mill who, in the early nineteenth century, established classical economics. But in drawing inspiration from Smith, they largely abandoned the sociological content of his arguments and focused narrowly on the marginal choices of a decontextualized economic man, entirely disregarding Smith's moral and historical discussion of change, power and values.

From the opposite direction ideologically, some of Adam Smith's detractors have often sought to ignore the many debts Marx owed to the analysis in *The Wealth of Nations* and have attributed to Marx an originality for ideas extensively borrowed from the Scot. Marx himself in the *Grundrisse*, the great ground plan for the work of which *Capital* is only the incomplete introduction, was himself not above misrepresenting Smith when appropriating his ideas. But few readers of Marx apparently check up on the accuracy of his accounts of the writers whom he criticizes. The word of Marx is enough. The emergence of classical economics as a distinct discipline and the profound influence of Marxist thought in European social theory in the late nineteenth and throughout the twentieth centuries have led to a regrettable neglect of Adam Smith's own writings. The monopolization of the name without the substance, on the one hand, coupled, on the other, with the selective appropriation of his arguments without attribution represents not only a historical injustice, but has discouraged the attention of others from a wealth of original thought and insight into issues which continue to preoccupy us.

In what follows I have attempted neither a full critical discussion of Smith's potential contribution to modern social thought nor a thorough scholarly critique of his thought in its historical context. But in outlining his arguments on social change, it seemed necessary to attempt to characterize his general theoretical perspective in terms accessible to the present-day reader. Issues which were of central concern to his eighteenth-century readers, such as his religious beliefs – Dr Johnson and Boswell condemned him as an unbeliever (see Boswell (1791), 1992, p. 712), though some modern commentators have argued for the religious context of his thought (e.g. Campbell, 1981, p. 97) – may be of less interest for the majority of those considering his ideas for the first time today. The accessibility of Smith's literary style may also count against him with modern or postmodern academics, but even more than is generally the case with sociological theorists, the original texts are generally more intelligible than most accounts of them turn out to be.

Structural individualism

[handwritten margin note: Benthamite Utility]

[handwritten margin note: Maslow's hierarchy]

The purely rational consumer, coolly optimizing marginal utility is not a creature to be found in Smith's thinking. Adam Smith believed that we are primarily driven by private, human considerations: 'hunger, thirst, the passion which unites the two sexes, the love of pleasure and the dread of pain'. The pleasure and the pain include the pleasure of being thought well of, or deserving to be thought well of, by our fellows and the shame or embarrassment of earning or deserving their unfavourable opinion. Nor are our actions directed by any impersonal historical force or Divine purpose shaping them to its own ulterior or predestined ends (*Theory of Moral Sentiments*, Part I, Ch. V). He argued that, on the whole, individuals tend to pursue their own self interest without much sense of any larger plan:

> It is not from the benevolence of the butcher, the brewer, or the baker that we expect our dinner, but from their regard to their own interest. We address ourselves not to their humanity but to their self-love and never talk to them of our own necessities but of their advantages.
>
> (*Wealth of Nations*, Book I)

Men in a similar class position (he was after all writing at a time when feminist consciousness was only beginning to enter intellectual discussion) – be they landowners, merchants, manufacturers or the numerous members of the propertyless poor – tend to <u>act in similar ways because</u> their interests are similar. But it is as individuals that they act, or fail to act. There is no suggestion of a collective will or superorganic identity. The individuals who comprise a class are naturally influenced, socialized by their similar experience, similar material interests, and similar opportunities and resources so as to arrive at similar views, similar opinions and so to act in similar ways.

> People of the same trade seldom meet together, even for merriment and diversion, but the conversation ends in a conspiracy against the public, or some contrivance to raise prices. (*Wealth of Nations*, Book I)

But these individual actors on the social scene are themselves the product of their time, their upbringing, their social origins. We are moral beings not mere automata, we make choices and we try to do what is right, as well as what is opportune. Our moral ideas are not merely learned, but have their origins in the processes of interaction and our need to live together in society. In *The Theory of Moral Sentiments*, Smith argued that morality itself has social origins. The general rules of what is held to be good or bad, of right or wrong conduct, emerge out of interaction. We soon become aware of how our actions appear to others in our immediate circle. In widening experience beyond the partiality of family life, however, each individual begins to discover how his or her behaviour is judged, regardless of particular feelings of sympathy or antipathy. We are able to become an object for ourselves as we learn to anticipate the possible praise or blame that we might expect for our intended behaviour. We learn to estimate how far our own actions are likely to arouse the esteem, affection or dislike of others in general, and thus how our behaviour is likely to appear not just in the eyes of those that we know and who know us personally, but how it would look to any impartial observer. To that extent, we learn that what we do or fail to do is not only likely to be praised, but to be judged by any potential witness as in itself praiseworthy (*Theory of Moral Sentiments*, Section III, Ch. II). This hypothetical impartial observer, whose potential praise or blame in our monitoring our own behaviour is the medium and arbiter of moral reflection, is essentially what G. H. Mead, much later, was to call the 'generalized other' (1934).

That moral sentiments are unquestionably a real and important feature of civilized society should not, of course, be taken to imply that they are equally highly developed in everyone, nor that they are never overridden when moral scruple seems to conflict with an opportunity for personal advantage. Smith's comments on the capacity for violence of the poor, the rapacity of the rich, and the perennial violence and injustice of rulers will readily disabuse any reader of the mistaken view that he saw society as composed of oversocialized conformers. On the other hand, frugality and trustworthiness, reliability and hard work are important in the operations of the economic market, as are tolerance and charitableness in the continuity of the social order. Society does not have its origin in ideas, but beliefs, even mistaken beliefs, play an undeniable role in maintaining its day-to-day activities.

Religious beliefs differ greatly from one society to another, but in every society there are moral rules of right and wrong, though what they specify may also differ. And, of course, faithfulness to their observance can vary quite a lot too. In Adam Smith's view, it was from the consciousness of what could be seen as praiseworthy or blameworthy, rather than the other way round, that the discovery of general rules of morality must have emerged. In other words, his argument in *The Theory of Moral Sentiments* goes further than the social origins of the individual conscience to suggest that the rules of morality themselves were socially generated rather than being there aboriginally since the beginning of human society, or given complete in some heroic or divine revelation.

Smith's purpose then, was to find a human and social explanation for human social facts:

> ... the present inquiry is not concerning a matter of right ... but ... a matter of fact. We are not at present examining upon what principles a perfect being would approve the punishment of bad actions, but upon what principles so weak and imperfect a creature as man actually and in fact approves of it.   (*Theory of Moral Sentiments*, Part I, Ch. V)

People act from many motives then, including moral principle and vanity, as well as for material gain. But their intercourse may have results they did not intend or never envisaged. As Adam Ferguson noted in his *Essay on the History of Civil Society* (1767): ' ... nations stumble upon establishments which are indeed the result of human action but not the execution of any human design.'

Of the division of labour itself, the specialization skills and separation of trades which is such a central element in his analysis, Smith writes:

> This division of labour, from which so many advantages are derived, is not originally the effect of any human wisdom which foresees and intends that general opulence to which it gives occasion. It is the necessary, though very slow and gradual consequence of a certain propensity in human nature which has in view no such extensive utility. The propensity to truck, barter and exchange one thing for another.
>
> (*Wealth of Nations*, Book I, Ch. II)

This tendency to exchange, to barter, is a natural, but specifically human attribute which Smith believed to be a necessary consequence of the faculty of speech and the human capacity to reason. Of course, once the advantages of specialization became obvious in the highly differentiated division of labour of his time, it was actively developed by merchants and manufacturers seeking to gain from those advantages. But to begin with, and through most of human history, there was no such exploitation of the system. In other words, though the relations and interactions themselves were originally each separately entered into for private reasons, the resulting pattern of relationships itself has consequences deriving from its structural properties. Thus the division of labour may have begun in simple societies merely as a convenience to individuals with different skills to barter, but its persistence and development has profound effects on the opportunities available to, as well as in the demands made upon, the people whom it encompasses.

Each individual in pursuit of his or her own objectives, is unconcerned with the general consequences of his or her activities and, indeed, is very unlikely to have the least notion of the general picture. As at the moment of conception few are likely to be thinking of the effect of their activity upon the birth rate, so too in seeking to make a living, no-one has the promotion of the public interest in the forefront of his mind (*Wealth of Nations*, Book IV, Ch. II). Change is brought about or prevented through individual activity, but as a result of the structural properties of the system within which they act rather than as an intended or deliberate consequence. The extensive discussion of this issue, of the relationship of agency and structure, in the 1980s and 1990s has become voluminous and, of course, much more sophisticated than Smith's incidental treatment of the issues appears (but see Raphael). To this reader, however, it does not seem to have got much farther, if as far. However, the matter is only discussed here in order to show some of the essential theoretical underpinning to Adam Smith's more general concerns with the emergence and development of civil society. It is now time to take a more detailed look at Smith's discussion of the division of labour for a fuller understanding of how he saw the dynamics of social change.

The division of labour and the market

The main determinant of the cost of things is the direct or indirect labour component in bringing them to market. The astonishing increase in productivity brought about by the division of labour lowers the real cost of goods and services, and so raises – though never equally, however – the general standard of living in society. This is brought about neither by the character of the individuals involved nor as a product of the material conditions they have to endure, but because of the structural features of the society they generally unwittingly embody in the course of their various personal pursuits.

In Smith's analysis the central structural factor is the division of labour. That is to say it is the subdivision and specialization of skills, and the separation of trades, that has increased the productivity of work out of all comparison with what any one of us could achieve if we were to attempt to provide for our own needs and those of our immediate household. There are three ways in which specialization increases the efficiency of work. Firstly, each individual can become more proficient in performing the narrowly defined task which he or she specializes learn by doing

Jack gell take

in. Instead of at best doing a lot of different things moderately well, by concentrating on a single activity he or she can become much more skilful, and thereby not only produce a less crude, more serviceable, product, but produce it in much greater quantity in less time. Secondly, the worker who concentrates on doing one thing saves a great deal of time which is otherwise spent in going from one task to another, perhaps in a different place and requiring different tools, or equipment which has to be got out and put away. Specialization means that this time can be used in productive activity. Thirdly, the simplification and separation of operations into their component activities encourages the use of machines which enable one worker to produce the output of many.

Smith illustrates his argument with the manufacture of pins. Even after the many operations involved in mining, transporting and smelting the ore, when the metal has been drawn into a wire of suitable thickness, it must be cut into appropriate lengths, pointed, silvered, the head shaped and affixed, the pins gathered, sorted, packaged and distributed to wholesalers and retailers before they are available for use in tacking up a hem. No-one could sensibly attempt to do all that for themselves. Without the subdivision and specialization involved in this division of labour, a single pin would cost the wages of a multi-skilled, highly versatile worker over many days of unremitting work. Throughout, mechanization can improve the consistency of quality, the regularity and quantity of output. While the use of machines enables one worker to match the output of many working by hand unaided, Smith argues that the general consequence is not, however, to displace labour, but rather, by increasing the supply which the same number of workers produce, to lower the price of the product (*Wealth of Nations*, Book I, Ch. I). It is in this way that the growth in productivity leads to a general reduction in prices.

There are three main factors which encourage and accelerate the division of labour. As Smith noted, the process was at first very slow where it occurred at all, so slow that over centuries, it might scarcely be noticed. However, the first factor we can identify is the size of the market for the goods or services produced. In a society of hunters and gatherers a man who was particularly adept at making arrows might supply his fellow hunters in exchange for the surplus of their kill. But since such societies usually consist of only 20 or 30 families, he is unlikely to have enough demand to keep him fully occupied or his household fully fed. Where there is a large level of demand for a particular product or service, a man or woman can devote themselves to it as a full-time livelihood. The second factor reinforces this argument. Smith notes that the division of labour is increased by population density. In a city a tradesman is more likely to find enough customers for his specialist services. In remoter, rural areas a plumber or joiner would have to range far afield to find enough business to pay him. He is more likely to turn jack-of-all-trades for the populace within reach – one of the reasons why services are likely to end up costing more in the country than in town. The third factor encouraging the division of labour is rising labour costs. The system, as it were, feeds upon itself. In the larger market the greater productivity of labour increases the accumulation of capital by the successful traders. It also tends to push up wages as a result of the demand for labour and the generally more prosperous conditions of trade. Together, these provide a powerful incentive for employers to use their capital so as to enhance the productivity of their workers still further, and so protect the profitability of their investment. And the further the process goes, the stronger the incentive. So the larger the amount of capital involved, the more important to the employer is the productivity level of his employees and, consequently, the greater the division of labour and the greater the degree of mechanization is likely to be. Smith puts it, as usual, more simply and clearly:

> The person who employs his stock in maintaining labour necessarily wishes to employ it in such a manner as to produce as great a quantity of work as possible. He endeavours, therefore, both to make among his workmen the most proper division of employment, and to furnish them with the best machines which he can either invent or afford to purchase. His abilities in both these respects are generally in proportion to the extent of his stock, or the number of people whom it can employ.   (*Wealth of Nations*, Book II, Introduction)

Frederick Taylor or Henry Ford were not therefore the first to note the importance of the subdivision of tasks and their mechanization in the pursuit of profitability. Closely related to the division of labour, growing out of it but providing for the full realization of its productive potential, is a further structural pattern, the market. The free market, Smith argued, provides for the <u>most effective allocation of scarce resources</u> and therefore for the most efficient exploitation of the possibilities of the division of labour. The structural development of a progressive division of labour is fostered by the structural relationships of the market and, where these have coincided, the <u>consequent growth</u> has demonstrated the intimacy of the relationship between them. But it must not be assumed that this will always be the case. In the Introduction to the *Wealth of Nations*, Smith noted that:

> Nations tolerably well advanced as to skill, dexterity and judgement in the application of labour, have followed very different plans in the general conduct or direction of it; and those plans have not all been equally favourable to the greatness of its produce. (*Wealth of Nations*, Introduction)

<u>Limitations on the freedom of trading relationships</u> within the division of labour <u>prevents</u> the allocation of resources finding an optimum level where supply matches demand. The market achieves this by operating as <u>a self-regulating system, but only in ideal circumstances</u> (*Wealth of Nations*, Book I, Ch. VII). For it to work in practice, knowledge must be freely available, particularly knowledge about prices, but any information which may be relevant is significant. Monopolies and restrictive practices of any kind also interfere with the processes of the market. Such obstructions limit the effectiveness of the market as a <u>feedback mechanism continuously adjusting</u> supply to demand. The optimal exchange of goods and services cannot occur if, through <u>interference</u> with the market or through the inadequacy of the <u>information</u> available, prices are kept artificially too high or too low. If prices are higher than they would be in a fully effective market, then fewer consumers will be able to afford to satisfy their needs. Smith believed that: '<u>consumption is the sole end and purpose of all production</u>; and the interest of the producer ought to be attended to, only so far as it may be necessary for promoting that of the consumer' (*Wealth of Nations*, Book IV, Ch. VIII). If prices are

kept below what a free market would have made them, then resources will be allocated wastefully. Either producers will be driven out of business so that the supply of consumer needs may dry up, or material and effort will be devoted to providing the commodity where it could have been more usefully deployed elsewhere.

This account of the efficiency gains deriving from the division of labour and a free market gives us a description of the structural basis of high economic growth rates, of 'The causes of the Wealth of Nations'. It is far from the case, however, that these conditions are to be found everywhere. The growth in national wealth which Smith observed in eighteenth-century England was notably absent in other potentially rich and powerful countries elsewhere. He discusses the case of contemporary Imperial China:

> China seems to have long been stationary, and had probably long ago acquired that full complement of riches which is consistent with the nature of its laws and institutions. But this complement may be much inferior to what, with other laws and institutions, the nature of its soil, climate and situation, might admit of. A country which neglects or despises foreign commerce, and which admits the vessels of foreign nations into one or two of its ports only, cannot transact the same quantity of business which it might do with different laws and institutions. In a country too where, though the rich or owners of large capitals enjoy a good deal of security, the poor or owners of small capitals enjoy scarce any, but are liable, under the pretence of justice, to be pillaged and plundered at any time by the inferior mandarins, the quantity of stock employed in all the different branches of business transacted within it, can never be equal to what the nature and extent of that business might admit. In every different branch, the oppression of the poor must establish the monopoly of the rich who, by engrossing the whole trade to themselves, will be able to make very large profits.
>
> (*Wealth of Nations*, Book I, Ch. IX)

The historical accuracy of this account is not what concerns us here, though it is persuasive and offers interesting parallels for the situation in a number of third-world countries today.

The important point for our present discussion is to see the kind of factors which Smith believed to be responsible for inhibiting economic growth. First of all, we should note that there is no inevitability about growth. The factors which have prevented growth are institutional, that is to say characteristic of the social and political structure. The role of the state and its legal system cannot be overlooked, that is to say the distribution of power is the critical factor in fostering and obstructing growth (cf. Needham, 1954). Lastly, the role of monopolies in keeping prices artificially high reinforces the generalization that great inequalities tend to be self-perpetuating and tend to sustain a degree of economic stagnation. The positive influence of such structural features on economic development can be reinforced by the effects of urbanization, which favours manufacturing and commerce and thereby tends to boost the division of labour (*Wealth of Nations*, Introduction and 'Plan of Work') and the role of ideas, which perhaps more often in practice tend to hinder growth than otherwise, as J. M. Keynes was to note many years later in his comment that 'practical men, who believe themselves to be quite exempt from any intellectual influences, are usually the slaves of some defunct economist' (1936). Smith himself commented on the impact of earlier theorists:

> Those theories have had a considerable influence, not only upon the opinions of men of learning, but upon the public conduct of princes and sovereign states. I have endeavoured, in the Fourth Book, to explain as fully and distinctly as I can, those different theories and the principal effects which they have produced in different ages and nations.
>
> (*Wealth of Nations*, Introduction)

To summarize briefly, at the centre of Adam Smith's theory of social change are the structural properties of the social system, the division of labour and the degree of market relations. These are critically determined by the degree of inequality of power, especially within the state and its associated legal system. Additional sociological factors, such as population density or urbanization, can also be important. The actions of individuals within this institutional framework may be influenced for good or ill by the ideas, including the theoretical ideas, current

amongst them. It is, however, the structures that make the
difference between growth and stagnation. The market operates
to allocate resources of time and effort, as well as of material
commodities. Potentially, at least, it can also serve to unify
society across the differentiations of the division of labour.
Through the market we are brought directly and indirectly into
an interdependency with all the other diverse and equally self-
interested participants with whom we share only our common
need for the support and provision of the wider society. The
individual ' ... in a civilized society ... stands at all times in
need of the cooperation and assistance of great multitudes,
while his whole life is scarce sufficient to gain the friendship
of a few persons' (*Wealth of Nations*, Book I, Ch. II).

In those societies which have prospered economically then,
we can discern, in Smith's view, two emergent structural
patterns. The first is the progressive division of labour which
has increased productivity and the generation of wealth. The
second is the growth of the market which integrates the
activities of the increasingly differentiated, but increasingly
interdependent population. But this has not been a once-and-
for-all development. It is a continuous process, sustained by
the fact that the market relationships are unequal and lead to
the intensification of the division of labour while, at the same
time, the increasing specialization of the division of labour
makes us all the more interdependent upon one another in the
complex whole. The processes of differentiation and
interdependency, in other words, have fed upon one another,
in what we might nowadays think of as an accelerating chain
reaction.

Conflict and classes

The operations of the market hold society together across the
divisive differentiations of the division of labour by providing
for the needs of each person through their common dependence
upon the more or less unintentionally concerted efforts of all.
But that provision is far from equal. To Smith, people seemed
moral beings, though basically inclined to follow their own
best interests. In a simple society their personal interests are
likely, very generally, to coincide, but with the increasing

division of labour these personal interests are increasingly likely to become distinct and to differ from one another.

While the division of labour increases the accumulation of wealth, this is not evenly distributed. Though wages tend to rise with economic growth, the greater share, Smith appears to have believed, goes to the owners of capital who are able to arrange the employment of labour in the most productive way. The division of labour itself proceeds very slowly at first, until accelerated by the sectional interests of these owners and employers. '[T]ill some stock be produced there can be no division of labour', Smith argued, 'and before a division of labour takes place there can be very little accumulation of stock' (*Lectures on Jurisprudence*). There is thus a slowly emerging division of interests among different sectors of society. It may be true that: 'All for ourselves, and nothing for other people, seems in every age of the world, to have been the vile maxim of the masters of mankind' (*Wealth of Nations*, Book III, Ch. V). However, apart from this perennial divide between the rulers and the ruled, Smith identifies <u>three principal grouping</u>s. These are: the merchants and manufacturers whose capital enables them to employ the larger class of propertyless wage labourers of varying degrees of skill; and the third group consists of the declining class of landowners, once in feudal times the rulers of society but with much reduced influence in civil society. These three cl<u>asses are based on the different</u> <u>resources upon which they rely for their livelihood</u>s. The merchants' and manufacturers' incomes derive from the profitable investment of their stock of capital. The propertyless workers depend upon the wages earned by their own labour, and the landowners live on the rents they receive from letting their property to tenants.

Among these groups, it is the merchants and manufacturers who, pursuing profit, have in their own interests sought out markets and accelerated the division of labour. It is they particularly who have been instrumental in generating economic growth. Their arrival at this position in society can be attributed to their overtaking the power of the landowning aristocracy in the Early-Modern period. The landowners, according to Smith, set about converting their feudal dues and power into money rents, which th<u>ey could spend on themselves</u> rather than on maintaining a large household of dependent followers and retainers. Their 'childish vanity' in seeking their own personal comfort, plus the merchants' 'peddler principle of turning a penny wherever a penny was to be got', led to the decline of the large retinues of servants and men at arms of the feudal magnates, weakening their local territorial power and increasing both the independence of their tenants and facilitating the spread of centralized royal power throughout the provinces (*Wealth of Nations*, Book III, Ch. IV). 'Neither of them had either knowledge or foresight of that great revolution which the folly of one, and the industry of the other, was gradually bringing about' (ibid.). The interests of wage earners and of the manufacturers and merchants who employ them are by no means the same either: 'The workmen desire to get as much, the masters to give as little as possible' (*Wealth of Nations*, Book I, Ch. VIII). But the balance of power lies with the employers. Even without the legal discrimination which has, from time to time, put into law various limitations upon the rights of workers to organize in defence of their own interests, the economic balance of power always lies with the employer: ' ... in the long run the workman may be as necessary to his master as his master is to him; but the necessity is not so immediate' (ibid.). In any dispute the employers will almost always be able to outlast striking workers. Yet although the owners of capital have promoted the general level of manufacturing and commerce, this has never been their intention so much as an unintended consequence of them looking after their own interests. Paradoxically, while rising levels of economic activity benefit landowners by making it possible for prosperous tenants to pay higher rents, and wage earners by increasing the demand for labour so that in the market wages tend to rise, the rate of profit on capital investment falls in times of growth and rises in times of economic decline (*Wealth of Nations*, Book I, Ch. XI). In their class interests, therefore, the manufacturers and traders constitute: '... an order of men, whose interest is never exactly the same with that of the public, who have generally an interest to deceive and even oppress the public, and who accordingly have, upon many occasions, both deceived and oppressed it' (ibid.).

It is hard to find, in reading Adam Smith's own words, the ideologist and apologist for the capitalist class which he is

conflict of interest in "competition"

frequently represented to be in dismissive comments by those who appear to know of him only at second hand. Smith is generally claimed by economic liberals as the progenitor of *laissez-faire* economics (the term and the principle, that the state should not interfere with market forces, was introduced in the 1750s by the French economic theorists known as the physiocrats because they believed economic policies should be governed by natural resources). But although Smith emphasizes the critical role played by the free market in the generation of economic growth, his account is more broadly based than that and, as we have seen, also emphasizes the institutional context. Furthermore, he did not restrict his approval to an acquiescence in the outcome of market forces regardless of their human effects.

> No society can surely be flourishing and happy, of which the far greater part of the members are poor and miserable. It is but equity, besides, that they who feed, clothe and lodge the whole body of the people, should have such a share of the produce of their own labour as to be themselves tolerably well fed, clothed and lodged.
> (*Wealth of Nations*, Book I, Ch. VIII)

↝ Heilbronner, however, regards Smith as essentially a conservative theorist (1986) and, clearly, he was no revolutionary. Smith saw no hope for the amelioration of the human condition in the overthrow of the prevailing social order. Indeed, the increase of prosperity in commercial society had generally been beneficial to all. Wages had risen and real prices had fallen, raising the standard of living of the majority of the population. After the preceding century of civil war and political revolution in Scotland and in England, only precariously stabilized within his own lifetime, he believed that: 'The peace and order of society is of more importance than even the relief of the miserable' (*Theory of Moral Sentiments*, Section II, Ch. I).

That 'even' is significant. The improvement of the conditions of the poorest was important, but the gains to be made required a practical programme and political realism if they were to be secure gains. Among the objects of his scorn he included 'the man of system', the scheming idealist or promoter of political

panaceas which all too often do more harm than good (ibid.,
Section II, Ch. II). Donald Winch (1978), on the other hand,
has drawn attention to some of his more radical views. Between
The Theory of Moral Sentiments of 1759 and the *Wealth of
Nations* published in 1776, the conservatism of Smith's views
appears to have lessened. The system seemed to spread out the
necessities of life comparatively equitably in 1759:

> When providence divided the earth among a few lordly
> masters, it neither forgot nor abandoned those who seemed
> to have been left out in the partition. These last too enjoy
> their share of all that it produces. In what constitutes the
> real happiness of human life, they are in no respect inferior
> to those who would seem so much above them.
>   (*Theory of Moral Sentiments*, Part IV, Ch. I)

After leaving his professorship in Glasgow four years later to
accompany, as paid mentor, the young Duke of Buccleuch to
France and Switzerland, he returned home to Kirkcaldy in 1767
and remained there until the publication of the *Wealth of Nations*
nine years later. This presents an altogether less optimistic, more
ironic and more critical account of the unequal relations between
the different classes. In the earlier work he sets out the usual
eighteenth-century view that the distinction of ranks serves to
maintain the peace and order of society (*Theory of Moral
Sentiments*, Part IV, Section II, Ch. I). In the later work there is
more emphasis not only on the material inequalities of society,
but a concern for the moral consequences of the increasing
division of labour which anticipates the young Marx's writing
on alienation half a century later. The narrow specialization of
the division of labour might increase the productivity of labour,
but at a human price paid wholly by the workers themselves. A
working lifetime devoted to the endless repetition of a
mechanical operation reduced to its simplest, Smith feared, must
lead to 'parts of the human character (being), in great measure,
obliterated and extinguished in the great body of people', leading
to a 'drowsy stupidity, which, in a civilized society seems to
benumb the understanding ... The state into which the labouring
poor, that is, the great body of the people, must necessarily fall,
unless government takes some pains to prevent it' (*Wealth of
Nations*, Book V, Ch. I, Art. II.) These measures, including the

extensive <u>provision of education</u>, including adult education, cannot be left to the operations of the market, but must fall to the responsibility of government (ibid.). The role of government in maintaining the competitive framework of the market itself, and in preventing the emergence of monopolies, is also evident, though one should not perhaps set too high one's expectations of '... that insidious and crafty animal, vulgarly called a statesman or politician, whose councils are directed by the momentary fluctuations of affairs' (*Wealth of Nations*, Book IV, Ch. II). Indeed, he goes on in the following chapter:

> The violence and injustice of the rulers of mankind is an ancient evil, for which, I am afraid, the nature of human affairs can scarce admit a remedy. But the mean capacity, the monopolizing spirit of merchants and manufacturers, who neither are, nor ought to be, the rulers of mankind, though it cannot perhaps be corrected, may very easily be prevented from disturbing the tranquillity of anybody but themselves. (*Wealth of Nations*, Book IV, Ch. III)

That hardly reads like pro-capitalist propaganda.

Given the inequality of power between them, <u>the conflict of class interests is more effectively contained within a growing economy.</u> When growth levels out, or economic decline sets in, we move to what today would be called a zero-sum conflict, and for everyone the struggle for resources is intensified, and the poor lose out:

> ... it is the progressive state, while the society is advancing to the further acquisition, rather than when it has acquired its full complement of riches, that the condition of the labouring poor, of the great body of the people, seems to be the happiest and the most comfortable. It is hard in the stationary and miserable in the declining state. (*Wealth of Nations*, Book I, Ch. VIII)

In Smith, then, we find advocacy for economic growth, the distrust of revolution, the concern for the disadvantaged in the struggle between the social classes. If his work does not wholly conform to the programmes of liberal, conservative or radical theory, although it contains elements that have been appropriated by each of these ideologies, it may be that after reading Adam Smith for ourselves, it is evident that he cannot readily be identified as a partisan of any of them. Instead we have to consider his work as that of an authentically original and independent thinker.

The invisible hand and the evolution of commercial society

In Smith's inquiry into the nature and causes of the wealth of nations, there is no necessary law of development all societies must obey, no irresistible impulse leading inevitably to growth. Instead, what he proposes is a theory of the structural conditions which have led to the transformation of some societies, while others have stagnated or decayed. The nature of his inquiry is an empirically based theoretical model which aims to explain equally what has actually happened, and what elsewhere has not happened. Looking back from the evident prosperity of his own time, he suggests, it is as if some 'invisible hand' had guided the process. This metaphor has been much discussed and parallels the later debate following the publication of Darwin's *The Origins of Species* (1859) about biological, as distinct from social, evolution. Here the argument has also been about whether complex systems could evolve blindly, as it were, 'naturally', or whether they demonstrate some purposive design. Mid-twentieth-century discussions about the development of the eye are an example of this (Dawkins, 1986). Smith's writings are consistent with the deism of many of the intellectuals of his time, the belief that the benign intentions of the 'Great Author of Nature' were realized only through the operations of the laws of nature. In this context the image indicates the unplanned, but intricate integration of the activities of ordinary mortals myopically pursuing no more than their own self-centred ends. The phrase is used only once in the *Wealth of Nations* and once in *The Theory of Moral Sentiments*. In the earlier, more optimistic work it refers to how, notwithstanding the indifference of the rich, a nearly equal distribution of 'the necessaries of life' is arrived at:

The rich only select from the heap what is most precious and agreeable. They consume little more than the poor, and in spite of their natural selfishness and rapacity, though they mean only their own convenience, though the sole end which they propose from the labours of all the thousands whom they employ, be the gratification of their own vain and insatiable desires, they divide with the poor the produce of all their improvements. They are led by an invisible hand to make nearly the same distribution of the necessaries of life, which would have been made, had the earth been divided into equal portions among all its inhabitants ...'

(*Theory of Moral Sentiments*, Part IV, Ch. I)

In the later, more critical work the image relates only to the ignorance of any general effects on the part of the entrepreneur going about his private business. Since to speak of the revenue of the whole economy is only another way of describing the value of the annual produce of its industry and trade, as each individual businessman seeks to make a profit for himself simultaneously he is contributing to the growth of the economy as a whole: '... he intends only his own gain, and he is in this, as in so many other cases, led by an invisible hand to promote an end which was no part of his intention' (*Wealth of Nations*, Book IV, Ch. II.) The image of the invisible hand is another way of presenting the idea that society itself, social institutions and social structures are not deliberately contrived arrangements set up in some immemorial social contract, but are the more important but, none the less, unintended consequences of mundane human activity. Nowadays, we should probably talk about emergent social morphogenesis, but it is far from obvious that we should understand the idea any better.

In his *Lectures on Jurisprudence* given in Glasgow in the 1750s, Smith proposed a still useful (and possibly the first) classification of human societies. The simplest and earlier type was the *Society of Hunters* consisting of small groups of no more than 20 or 30 families, sometimes smaller, having no regular form of government and with so little beyond the merest subsistence that their general poverty produces virtual equality. The second stage *Pasturage*, represented by such peoples as the desert Arabs or the Mongols of the central Asian steppe, is followed by that of settled *Agriculture*, while the fourth stage

is that of commercial or *Civil Society*, that is, societies
dominated by town dwellers.

> Among the hunters there is no regular government; they live
> according to the laws of nature. The appropriation of herds
> and flocks, which introduced an inequality of fortune, was
> that which first gave rise to regular government. Till there
> be property there can be no government, the very end of
> which is to secure the wealth, and to defend the rich from
> the poor.   (*Lectures on Jurisprudence*, Vol. IV)

It is the accumulation of property, as we have seen, that is the
essential basis of trading between those with different assets,
and therefore of the foundation of the market and the
development of the division of labour. The state and its
institutional framework of law originated for the regulation
and protection of property.

> Laws and government may be considered in this, and indeed
> in every case, as a combination of the rich to oppress the
> poor, and preserve to themselves the inequality of goods,
> which would otherwise be soon destroyed by the attacks of
> the poor, who, if not hindered by government, would soon
> reduce the others to an equality with themselves by open
> violence. The government and laws hinder the poor from
> ever acquiring wealth by violence, which they would
> otherwise exert upon the rich; they tell them they must either
> continue poor, or acquire wealth in the same matter as they
> have done.   (*Lectures on Jurisprudence*, Vol. IV)

This is, in essence, a conflict theory of law and the state. The
evolutionary sequence of societies, however, from small-scale
hunters and gatherers to urbanized, commercial society with
its large accumulations of capital stock and elaborate political
and legal structures of authority, represents only a schematic
arrangement and not a programme through which all societies
necessarily progress. Nor will every society develop in the same
way. In the overall scheme of things: '... the greater part of the
capital of every growing society is, first directed to agriculture,
afterwards to manufacture, and last of all to foreign commerce.'
But, *Smith* points out: '... though this natural order of things

must have taken place in some degree in every such society, it has in all the modern states of Europe been, in many respects, entirely inverted.' That is to say, it has frequently been the growth of trade and urban development which has led to the improvement of agriculture instead of the other way round (*Wealth of Nations*, Book III, Ch. IV).

History, then, is a complex process, not a simple unfolding of a preordained pattern as evolutionary theorists in the nineteenth century were to make it appear. Smith's inquiry was founded upon an empirically based model of economic growth and the social developments which it provided for and which, in turn, constrain it. These structural conditions, notably the market and the progressive division of labour, together with high population density and so on, may be necessary for growth, but are not sufficient to bring it about by themselves. Legal and sociopolitical circumstances, the steady application of businessmen to their trade, even the personalities and whims of rulers, all play a part in the eventual outcome of the complex interplay of all these factors.

Methodologically then, Smith's structural individualism embraces a model of endogenous change within a framework of emergent institutions, through which conflicting interests are mediated. There is no immanent and unfolding pattern to history. Epistemologically, as we have described the terms in the preceding chapter, Smith was an empiricist rather than a rationalist, and believed in the objectivity of knowledge rather than in irredeemable ideology.

We shall now turn, in the next chapters, to some major nineteenth-century theories which, in contrast with Adam Smith, and differing amongst themselves about the mechanisms involved, have argued that the development of human society from its simple origins to complex modern forms has, in fact, followed [rationally coherent immanent laws of evolutionary development.]

3

Evolutionary and Neo-Evolutionary Theories: Necessity and Possibility

Evolution and progress

An obvious way of getting to grips with historical change is to contrast how things were before and after it. Most evolutionary theories of social change have adopted the approach of identifying a succession of stages through which human societies have progressed, from the supposedly relatively simple patterns of our remote ancestors to the complexity and diversity of the present day.

Though the terms evolution and progress overlap a good deal, in social theory there is an important distinction to be made. Evolution refers to a gradual development, usually from simpler to more complex forms. It is essentially a descriptive term, that is to say it carries no implication that the end of the process should be preferred to the beginning. Progress, on the other hand, with its suggestions of embetterment, implies a value position. 'The forward advance of social progress' suggests an improvement on an unsatisfactory past and a process of evaluation that has come to this conclusion. From the 1820s at least, the development of science and engineering was evident to all eyes in the rapidly expanding railway system demonstrating ever new prodigies of civil engineering, speed of travel, and almost unbelievable quantities of goods and people transported. But the spread of literacy and the achievements of fiction and poetry, political reform and the moral achievements of the Factories Acts in Britain and the abolition of slavery (full emancipation throughout the British Empire was completed in 1838), together with the prevailing

40

interpretation of history as the advance of political and civil liberty, all confirmed the general view of the time, that the nineteenth century was the age of progress (Burrows, 1966; Pollard, 1968; Bowler, 1983).

The intellectual underpinning for the idea of progress was the concept of evolution. The discovery of geological time and the growth of palaeontology (the study of the fossil record of extinct life forms) clearly underpinned the development of theories of biological evolution, as did, crucially, the work of Lamarck (1744–1829) and of Darwin (1809–1882). Lamarck believed that species, slowly adapting to their environments over many generations, had thereby gradually diverged as their environmental conditions differed. Darwinian Theory argued that a process of natural selection, through a competitive struggle for survival, eliminates genetic variants not well suited to the conditions of their habitat, while those variants better able to thrive multiplied. Again environmental differences favoured different characteristics and so species evolved different characteristics. Darwin and Alfred Wallace independently published their almost identical theories more or less simultaneously. However, Darwin's *Origin of Species* (1859), which appeared to challenge the then widely accepted biblical account of a once-for-all week of creation, made the greater popular impact. The idea that all the species and varieties of plants and animals we can see around us descended over the course of millennia from simpler, lower forms of life created enormous popular interest. The public controversy, notably the celebrated debates in England in 1860 between T. H. Huxley (pro-evolutionist) and Bishop Wilberforce (pro-Genesis) were widely reported and made for much hilarity in the comic papers of the time. The application of evolutionary ideas to mankind's biological heritage seemed threatening and controversial. But the idea of progress from the heathen and brutish dark ages of history to the present Victorian age of trade, respectability and science was rather more palatable. Thus the idea took hold that human society had evolved, whether or not our ancestors swung about in the trees.

In this chapter I want to look first at two nineteenth-century evolutionist theorists, Comte (1798–1857) and Spencer (1820–1903). Comte, though perhaps too much of a pioneer to acknowledge any great debt, might be broadly assigned to the Lamarckian way of thinking about evolution. Herbert Spencer, on the other hand, may be closely identified with Social Darwinism.

Both were enormously influential in their own time. Though less regarded in the twentieth century, I believe they are both worthy of some attention today because, in their different ways, they show, more clearly than later derivative work, the value and the problems of thinking about social change as progress through a sequence of evolutionary stages. Current concern with the apparently irreversible and ever-widening process of development from local and small-scale cultures to the more complex societies and global social order of today gives the evolutionary ideas they first outlined a continuing relevance (Lenski and Lenski, 1987; Giddens, 1999). After some neglect, which would repay a historian's thoughtful consideration, evolutionary theory was revived by neo-evolutionist writers in the 1960s and 1970s, and some of these are briefly examined in the final part of the chapter in order to show something of how evolutionary theory has been adapted to changing historical circumstances and how some of the problems it has thrown up have been addressed.

August Comte: the law of progress

From a minor aristocratic family in Montpellier in southern France, Comte was given a first-class scientific and technical education at the Ecole Polytechnique in Paris in the years after the defeat of Napoleon. For a time he worked enthusiastically as secretary to Henri Saint-Simon (1760–1825), the founder of French socialism, who had argued that the *ancien régime* of court and church politics – dominated by landed interests, the idle rich of the 'unproductive classes' – should be replaced by the newly emerging industrial classes of entrepreneurs, engineers and workers. He had collaborated with Saint-Simon in the development of a utopian plan, in which rational administration would remove the sources of social conflict and eliminate the need for the state. Inheritance of property would be abolished. But, after the defeat of the revolutions of 1830 and 1848, Comte became disillusioned with the prospects for revolutionary action, which seemed capable only of bringing about ever more reactionary restorations. He came to reject and oppose those ideas which had inspired the great Revolution of 1789 and the later unsuccessful attempts which had brought France little but bloodshed and disorder. In his view, the doctrines of egalitarianism, individualism and political sovereignty had not, in the event, led to justice or peace or prosperity. What was necessary was a scientific understanding of social order and social change, which could be applied to society in the same way that the natural sciences were being applied to the physical world in the development of industry, leading at last to *real* social progress.

August Comte invented sociology, or at least he gave it its name, though really it was a matter of naming a kind of theoretical discourse which had been going on in France, and elsewhere, for at least a century before him. But he believed he was creating something new, a crowning achievement of the sciences which would prepare the way for a new society. The progressive growth of the sciences had begun with the study of the inanimate world. Astronomy and, subsequently, physical and chemical sciences were the first fields to which scientific method was systematically applied, emphasizing the importance of empirical observation, careful and systematic comparison of phenomena and experimentation. Then, through the development of the biological and medical sciences, the focus became ever more closely centred upon issues related to the nature of humanity, till, finally, with the advent of the social sciences, and of sociology in particular, questions hitherto exclusively the province of metaphysical speculation or religious moralizing were to be studied scientifically. Comte's new science of sociology represented the application of his new philosophy of Positivism to human affairs. The basic theme of Positivism is that only science, firmly grounded in non-metaphysical fact and the discovery of the laws of cause and effect which explain the observable universe, can finally liberate the world from ignorance and disorder. Positivism is a philosophy of progress through the advance of scientific knowledge, and its ultimate embodiment, the science of sociology, would reveal, indeed has already revealed, the key to understanding that progress in the Law of Three Stages (Andreski, 1974).

Comte's sociology distinguishes between Social Statics and Social Dynamics. Social Statics is concerned with the social nature of mankind and with discovering the laws governing social order. The subject matter of Social Statics includes: work, family patterns, property, language and the state. Social Dynamics is concerned with the laws of social evolution. The principal overarching conceptualization here is the *Law of Three Stages*. These three stages relate both to the development of human thought from primitive superstition to modern scientific reason, and to the changing social order which the evolution of consciousness gives rise to. They are:

1. The **Theological** stage;
2. the **Metaphysical** stage;
3. the **Positive** stage.

In the Theological stage human thought is dominated by the supernatural. The world is understood as subject to the direct intervention and whims of the gods, or whatever other supernatural agencies may be about. Religious ideas themselves develop through three stages; beginning with the stage of fetishism, when powers are attributed to features of the natural world, through polytheism, where a variety of gods and goddesses exercise the powers of life and death, war and love and fruitfulness, and so forth. In the third stage, monotheism, a solitary but still personal deity is both creator and the governor of human affairs though, in his omnipotence, he is usually less arbitrary and capricious than the impulsive beings who inhabit the pantheons of polytheistic religions. The Theological stage of thought is superseded by the Metaphysical stage. Here supernatural beings give way to more abstract principles of philosophical destiny. A personal god is replaced by the deism of a first, uncaused cause, the architect of the universe who does not intervene in the laws of nature he has set in motion; or by philosophies like Hegel's philosophy of history, where the progress of pure spirit serves to make the advance of reason, or the struggle for liberty, and even the concrete events of the past, seem more intelligible to people. In the third, Positive stage, these metaphysical abstractions will be replaced by positive, that is, factual, scientific knowledge.

These three epochs in the evolution of human thought correspond to, and indeed account for, three stages in the evolution of human society. In the first, the theological era of history, societies were dominated by priests and warriors. With the metaphysical stage, societies come to be governed through the apparatus of the centralized state and, in practice, fall under the domination of lawyers and theologians, who articulate the principles upon which government is conducted and pursue the involuted intricacies of their administrative implementation. In the third *Positive stage* of society Comte rediscovered St Simon's socialist vision. Thus, he argued, with the full development of an industrialized system of production, the state with all its legalistic ramifications will wither away, as the scientific understanding of the practical needs of social management will eliminate the conflicts and disorders which require the intervention of governments. Instead of the rulers of the state, power will be in the hands of engineers and scientists. Comte believed that the world in the mid-nineteenth century was on the threshold of this new Positive Era!

Comte's law of three stages

Stages of Development	Dominant Mode of Thought	Dominant Social Groups
Theological	Supernatural/ religious	Priests and Warriors
Metaphysical	Philosophical/ theoretical	Lawyers and Theologians (the state)
Positive	Scientific	Scientists and Engineers (industry)

These stages are a unilinear and necessary sequence of development. Comte's notion of science was a mechanistic, deterministic one of invariant causal laws. Any given social state therefore is the inevitable outcome of the preceding one in the chain: 'Sociology has for each epoch in turn exhibited the present as the necessary outcome of the past' (1876, Vol. III, p. 535). The singular importance of sociology is that it will make apparent to everyone the inevitability of the development towards the Positive Stage of society. When that arrives society will be under the benevolent guidance of a scientific and industrial elite, concerned for the welfare of all, because concerned to anticipate and resolve any problems that could present themselves. Progress is evident in the growth of social order. 'When society is finally organized no other disturbance can arise' (1875, Vol. II, p. 338).

The unit of analysis in Comte's sociology is not the individual actor, or even the rise and fall of particular societies. His concern was with nothing less than understanding the history of all mankind. In the mid-nineteenth century, when he was writing, he was, he believed, witnessing the birth of the new positive, scientific age of human society. This sense of being at the beginning of a new era, of reading straws in the wind is characteristic of a great deal of social theory. It gives it a sense of excitement, the glamour of being ahead of the others. The hazard of at least intellectual adventurousness. To Comte's terminological inventiveness, optimistic spirit and sensitivity to human idealism, we owe his coinage of the term altruism to denote the transcendence of the self-seeking pursuit of private interests and concern with the interests of others as a principle of action, which would characterize the scientific or technical elite of the positive era of society. It is a little startling that no-one had felt the need for such a term before. We also owe to Comte the admirably candid principle of 'cerebral hygiene', which many students might find reassuring and may vindicate their own practice in relation to theoretical sociological issues. While working on his six-volume *Cours de Philosophie Positiv*, which he began at the age of 32, Comte declared this further methodological innovation. Timascheff describes it with great tact and brevity: 'This discovery ... meant that he stopped reading in order to keep his mind uncontaminated by the thoughts of others' (1957, pp. 17–18).

Comte was no mere theorist, no mere academic contemplating history from his library. He was a charismatic figure, the founder of an international social movement: *Positivism*. The philosophy of Positivism was the view that science could tell us the final truth about the world, and the newest of the sciences, *sociology* – which he had newly established – had its first milestone in his discovery of the law of Progress – the law of three stages. The application of scientific knowledge to the management of society would eliminate confusion and conflict, the upheaval, poverty and bloodshed so characteristic of early-nineteenth-century history. The slogan of Positivism, *Order and Progress*, was the ideal of a movement which inspired many, who thought that science could replace prejudice, superstition, blind tradition and the intolerant conservatism of the *ancien régimes* everywhere, and, equally, the blind utopianism and mindless savagery of the revolutionary masses which had been so destructive in Comte's own lifetime. An educated elite applying the science of society would bring about practical order and progress for all (Feuer, 1975). Many saw themselves playing a role as a member of such an elite, particularly amongst the professional classes and those with a technical education, building a new social order, especially in the newly independent countries in South and Central America, notably in Mexico and Brazil where the Positivist slogan, 'Order and Progress' is inscribed in the national flag. Comte's belief in science was perhaps more of a blind faith itself, scientistic rather than scientific. He affirmed science rather more than he practised it, and believed that laws were established by asserting them and piling up illustrative examples from history. Of course, he was by no means unusual in such a misconception of scientific method and the pseudo-science of his sociology has been followed by many more pseudo-sciences since then, making the same claims to scientific legitimacy and not dissimilar claims to have a privileged access to ultimate truths. Comte was the founder of an ideology, of a social movement, a man of originality and flair.

If we refer back to the six key issues identified in Chapter 1, Comte's work can be summarized as follows:

1. The evolution of human thought is an <u>endogenous process</u>, but the prevailing ideas of each era prescribe the social order, and social upheavals and disorders are contained within its dominant paradigm. Comte does not emphasize conflict and he anticipates that in the final Positivist stage of history, a consensus on the basis of technical, scientific knowledge will prevail.
2. The <u>inevitable progress</u> from the Theological to the Positive era as a result of the law of progress makes this an example of historicist theory. The future state, according to Comte, is known and, once attained, will not change.
3. Comte's analysis of change was <u>sociologically realist</u> as the unit of change was all human society or mankind in general.
4. It was <u>idealist</u> as he believed that it was the dominant <u>ideas</u> of the era which <u>shaped the social</u> structures and determined the pattern of domination. Though it was the <u>development of ideas</u> which brought about social change, for example the pursuit of scientific Positivism which was ushering in a new age, he did not explain why either thought or society should develop along the particular lines that they have done.
5. Notwithstanding the pivotal role given to science in Comte's

sociology, and in his Positivist philosophy generally, it is, however, essentially ideological rather than objective. Only Positivism can reveal the inevitable future. Science is invoked as the legitimating ideology of the Positivist movement.

6. Finally, though influenced by the scepticism of David Hume, and by British empiricism, in his criticism of metaphysical thinking and in setting out the tenets of philosophical Positivism, his argument is essentially a rationalist one in structure. Given the law of progress, his discussion of social statics, as well as his account of the emerging Positive era, is deducible from the basic idealist assumptions.

Comte's evolutionary theory has much to teach us, a sort of third way between revolutionary and reactionary perspectives, even if few now have much time for Positivism. His theory shares many characteristics with other, better remembered theories and, besides the sweep of his ideas, his sense of being at the beginning of a new era and his belief in the critical role of sociology in the transition have many resonances when we come to consider the aspirations of present-day social theorists.

Herbert Spencer: survival of the fittest

The old photographs one sometimes sees of Herbert Spencer do not do him justice. They show a rather dry, elderly man in old-fashioned clothes and very old fashioned whiskers. But Spencer was a man very much up to the minute of his time. As a young engineer involved in building the fast-growing railway network in the 1840s, he had been a technician personally engaged in the latest, leading-edge technology. He was also deeply interested in the development of the new and exciting ideas in the newly developing subject of economics. His first article, in support of *laissez-faire*, was published when he was 22 and, when he was only 28, he became editor of *The Economist* in the revolutionary year of 1848. He was also actively interested in, and his most widely influential work was in, the philosophical revolution of evolutionist thought and the challenge of applying a scientific outlook to the issues of human society that in Victorian England were still heavily wrapped in religious and culturally traditional assumptions.

His great vision of the unity of all the theoretical sciences was based on the conviction that the laws of nature were ultimately the same throughout the natural world. That is not to argue that he believed the different sciences are all reducible to a single set of propositions. Among the physical sciences, chemistry is not reducible to physics, nor are the biological sciences reducible in their turn to physics and chemistry. Though biological processes unquestionably are physical and chemical, that is not all they are. Similarly, while the biological sciences deal with organic matter, the social sciences deal with the superorganic and, while the men and women who are the agents of social life are unquestionably biological beings, social structures and human culture cannot be reduced to purely biological processes. But though the different sciences have their distinctive subject matter, the principles of natural law are common to all and the most immediately obvious of these is the law of evolution, which has clear relevance in the world of inanimate matter, in the ordering of the organic or biological world and also in the progress of the superorganic world, the history of human society. The law of evolution, he argued, determined that everything was evolving from *Uniformity* of spatially diffused, unstructured material, towards *Heterogeneity* of spatially concentrated structures. In his *First Principles* (1862) he described the 'inherent instability of the homogeneous'. The universal pattern is one of undifferentiated diffused matter becoming organized into more complex and more stable structures. The increase in the complexity of forms in the natural world, from interstellar dust clouds to planetary systems, or in the organic world from protozoa to professors, corresponds to the evolution of societies from a *Uniform* state with similar component parts performing similar functions, like the peasant households of simple agriculture or the wandering family groups of hunting and gathering societies, to the *Differentiated* state with dissimilar institutions performing distinct and complementary functions.

Spencer offers two, slightly different, accounts of the evolution of societies. The first relates to the type of social coordination by which societies are structured. This evolutionary scheme is essentially an illustrative contrast of what he described as *Militant Societies*, based on compulsory coordination, which in the course of evolution are superseded by *Industrial Societies*, based on voluntaristic cooperation. Victorian, *laissez-faire* England in his view represented this highest stage of development (1873). Militant societies, as the name suggests, are organized with a view to defensive or offensive war. Examples of such militant societies might include classic military feudalism in Europe, Tokugawa Japan or the Aztec empire in sixteenth-century Mexico. The individual is subordinated to the imperatives of the society, with limitations imposed by law and custom on personal property, liberty and mobility. Individual enterprise and private associations are not permitted. Power is centralized, often in the person of the ruler. Society is rigidly stratified according to rank; with social standing, occupation and residence determined by inheritance. Economically, militant societies aim at self-sufficiency or plunder, with little external trade. The values of militant societies are those of obedience, discipline, loyalty and faith. Industrial societies are dedicated to the peaceful processes of production and trade. The state apparatus exists to guarantee individual freedom and property rights and to uphold the principles and practice of justice. Power is decentralized and private enterprise and voluntary associations are encouraged. The rigid divisions of social rank give way to widespread social and geographical mobility. An industrial society has an open economy dependent on free external trade. Respect for others, trustworthiness, initiative and independence are the values which guide the life of industrial societies.

The second schema is more compatible with Spencer's formulation of the general law of evolution. It is based upon the degree of internal structural differentiation which any given society has attained. This classification produces a hierarchy of social types beginning with: (i) *Simple Societies* based on the family unit, which develop into; (ii) *Compound Societies* based on the clan; (iii) *Doubly Compound Societies* based on the tribe; and (iv) *Trebly Compound Societies* based on the nation. In Simple Societies a ruling family begins the process of differentiation; gradually, a division of labour between men and women, then the specialization of working skills, followed by the distinction of ranks, including enslavement, and the institutionalized enforcement of the ruling power emerge, together with specialized systems for the production of food and the conduct of trade. These stages of increasing structural complexity represent the broad evolutionary history of human society, with the great historic civilizations of Egypt, Mesopotamia, Mexico and Peru, Greece and Rome, and modern European nations like Britain, France, Germany, and so on, trebly compound, '... or perhaps, in some cases, a still higher stage' (1899, p. 554). Within each stage of

evolutionary development, however, Spencer noted there was a
diversity of social forms of comparable structural complexity.
Nomadic peoples or societies of settled agriculture, maritime empires
or city states may be compound to comparable degrees, but have
followed different evolutionary paths: '... social progress is not linear
but divergent and redivergent ...' so that 'there have arisen genera
and species of societies' (1899, p. 3; and see Peel, 1971).

The apparently Darwinian element in Spencer's thinking about
social evolution had roots in his early advocacy of *laissez-faire*
economics written 16 years before he had read Darwin. It is in
competition that the most efficient peoples – those best adapted
to the prevailing conditions and those best able to seize the available
opportunities – survive, while the inefficient and unadaptable are
eliminated. At each evolutionary stage there is a struggle for
survival, both in relation to subsistence within the physical
environment and in competition with other societies. The struggle
for survival is unremitting at the macrosocial level, and also within
each society through economic and political competition. In the
interests of the cohesion and adaptability of the social organism
as a whole, this internal competition is regulated by morality, law
and enlightened self-interest, but without it stagnation and decline
would soon ensue. Not only between societies in rivalry for political
domination or economic markets, but within each society the ruling
principle and the law of nature must be, in Spencer's phrase, 'the
survival of the fittest' (1865, Part III, Ch. 12). That is to say, the
intelligent, the industrious and the healthy, who benefit the race
biologically and through their efficiency benefit the social order
as a whole by contributing to its capacity to adapt and survive,
will themselves survive. The idle, the chronically sick, stupid,
crippled, the poor and the criminal, all in their different ways
only handicap the social organism and should be allowed to die
out. Presumably, even for a utilitarian like Spencer, since they are
not wilfully responsible for their condition, traditional moral
considerations would rule out their deliberate elimination.

There are other ambiguities in Spencer's view on the survival of
the fittest. The first is the questionable evaluative assumption that
because the most evolved, the trebly or quadruply compound
societies, are at the top of the evolutionary hierarchy, then they
must be the fittest. But, of course, the most evolved are not the
only survivors from the past, flat worms are not a highly evolved
species but they have outlasted the dinosaurs. The second problem

to some extent applies to evolutionary theories in general. This is the <u>problem of circularity</u>. What or who is fittest will survive and – because they have survived – that proves they must have been fittest. The <u>argument justifies itself by assuming the truth of its conclusion.</u> We may, in any case, wonder whether the survivors weren't just lucky, or more treacherous; but in Spencer's evolutionary scheme, maybe luck and ruthlessness are what fit us for survival. On the other hand, who or <u>what was</u> fittest in the past may not be fittest in the long run. The notion of absolute fitness has evaluative overtones, it is seen as generally admirable, sometimes even glamorous. Situational fitness, however, means only what best matches the requirements of the occasion. The criteria for what constitutes fitness may be different for a brigand than for a bishop, very different in a foundry and a florist's shop, surely not the same on Omaha Beach in 1944 as on Copacabana in the 1980s. In the Darwin/Wallace theory of natural selection this situational fitness is all that is entailed, but in Spencer's application of the theory to the social organism, allied to the notion of progress, current situational fitness takes on a moral overtone which it is hard to like.

It is true that only the at least relatively successful are in any position to adapt to changing circumstances, but, in some cases, <u>the very completeness of their adaptation may handicap their further adjustment in the face of extraneous change.</u> As in biological evolution, it is unlikely to be the dominant species in one epoch which is best able to take advantage of the different possibilities of the next. So the great civilizations of the past were unable to survive in changing times in the face of competition from more adaptable barbarians, with less to lose and better able to exploit the possibilities of changed circumstances. Alexander's defeat of the Persian Empire, the fall of Rome to the Goths and Vandals in the west and the loss of Constantinople to the Ottomans in the East, or the Arab conquest of Egypt, all illustrate the point. In modern times and among Industrial Societies, Spencer points out that it is often the late developers, not the industrial pioneers, that achieve the most rapid growth. He gives the example of railway development which, since it first took place in Britain, committed Britain to a heavy capital investment in relatively primitive equipment, while countries whose railway building was slow to start could learn from Britain's early mistakes and plan for a much more efficient system. Later industrialization meant that inefficient leap-frogging

and small-scale technology could be by-passed, while the pioneering efforts of the early days tied up capital in costly and obsolete plant (1873, pp. 59–60). It is surprising how often this point has to be rediscovered (see, e.g., Veblen, 1915; Bell, 1979), but Spencer made it first.

Thus social progress is neither a linear nor a continuous process. Different societies have adapted to the struggle in different ways and there is no uniform ascent 'from lower to higher', there is 'retrogression as well as progression where the conditions favour it' (1899, p. 609). But while that is true for particular societies, Spencer, if not wholly optimistic, was guardedly optimistic that the overall tendency was progressive (ibid.). On the other hand, although he was concerned with the progress of human society in general as part of a cosmic process of evolution, the unit of his analysis, in contrast with Comte, was the historically particular society.

What he regarded as the competitive struggle within each society, he conceived in terms of a competition between essentially rational individuals, each maximizing their separate interests, but generally guided by an enlightened self-interest, where collective action and the observance of law and the rules of morality was clearly to the benefit of all. A society is, to that extent, analogous to an organism with differentiated elements fulfilling the needs for subsistence, reproduction, regulation and decision making. These are functionally integrated to ensure the progress and survival of the whole. There is no necessary contradiction between his view of the functional adaptation of the component institutions of the social organism, and the Benthamite utilitarianism of his discussion of the actions of, and relations among, individuals. The superorganic has its own distinctive emergent properties and the structure, integration and evolution of a society cannot be accounted for in terms of the laws of individual psychology, utilitarian or otherwise.

To summarise:

1. Though adaptation in the face of external competition is crucial, change is generated within societies which are, to that extent, successful. In Spencer's theory the progress of evolution leads to the external adaptation of a society to its environment and a functional internal adaptation within the social organism of its component elements. Those theoreticians (mostly Marxist) who therefore classify Herbert Spencer with the Functionalists

for stressing social harmony and integration as the principal features of human society are, however, mistaken. They disregard the fact that his theory of evolution was about the survival of the fittest. The progressive change and adaptation of social forms is the result of the struggle for survival. Spencer was a conflict theorist, a Social Darwinist before (as well as after) Darwin. However, in his view, not classes but rather whole peoples were the most important actors in the unrelenting competition to survive and adapt. But human beings can cooperate with one another as well as fight and, the more effective their collaboration, the better their collective adaptation to the demands and the dangers of their social and material circumstances is likely to be. In this respect Spencer differs little from what Marx believed to be true, or at least possible, within classes. For Spencer, however, the last analysis was not the economic one, but concerned the destiny of the whole society.

2. Although there will always be some unpredictability about the future of particular societies, there is a clear linear progression in human history from Simple to Trebly Compound Societies, and perhaps beyond. The uncertainties of history may bring about stagnation or regression in some cases, and not all societies will progress up the evolutionary ladder, but there remains an overall pattern of change from uniformity to heterogeneity. At a global level, then, this is a historicist theory.

Though warfare played an important role in the consolidation of larger states and in encouraging industrial progress (1873, p. 176), Spencer believed that at the end of the nineteenth century, a war between the major industrial societies could only be harmful (1898, Vol. II, pp. 664–5). Even the Franco-Prussian War of 1870, though humiliating to the French and politically destabilizing, had not had a major impact on France's commercial and industrial character. But, by the end of the century, the progress of civilization and the intensification of trade and commerce among the most advanced states made a war between any of them unthinkable. The Great War of 1914–18, however, brought an end to this optimistic view of social evolution as progress. The subsequent rise of Nazism and the Second World War shattered any remaining illusion that social change could be identified with a growing human moral progress.

3. Though individuals' identities and actions are not explained as socially determined, it is the society with its own evolutionary dynamics that is the primary unit of Spencer's analysis. His theory of social progress is, then, a form of sociological realism, but with the potential of specifically social processes limited to the level of the social itself.

4. Again in contrast with Comte, Spencer, at least in his later classification of social types, held it was not ideas and values that give societies their different characters, but the complexity of their structural form. Certainly his earlier contrast between Militant and Industrial societies has a strong element of Idealism in making the distinction on the basis of the ruling principle, but this is absent from the later categorization. On the other hand, material factors are equally more evident in marking the contrast between Militant and Industrial than in distinguishing the Simple from the Compound and Doubly Compound. But if this classification is structuralist, the evolutionary imperative is survival and thus Spencer's ontological assumptions may be regarded as a modified materialism.

5. Like Comte, Herbert Spencer believed in the unity of all the sciences as a distinctive form of knowledge, but was more scrupulous in his use of evidence and his employment of theoretical ideas in developing his account of the evolution of human society. The survival of the fittest, however, has ideological overtones and obviously lends itself to use as a justification for existing inequalities or as a reason for disregarding any argument for the amelioration of the condition of the unprivileged. Spencer's sympathy for these unsympathetic views may compromise, but does not fundamentally change the objectivity of his theoretical perspective. Except in the general, and absurd, theory of ideology – where all ideas are ideological because they are influenced by the social context within which they were conceived – because an argument has an appeal for the sectional interests of some particular group does not mean the argument itself is automatically ideological. That would be the case only where the argument is constructed for the purpose of serving those interests. In this sense, given the diversity and uncertainty of evolutionary outcomes he identified, Spencer's

theory would seem to fall short of an ideological commitment.

6. Spencer clearly adopts a rationalist rather than an empiricist approach in his application of evolutionist theory to social change. From the first principle of the cosmic trend from uniformity to heterogeneity, the whole compounding, doubly and trebly compounding of social order is a rationally deducible consequence. The empirical concession of divergent and retrogressive development in particular cases merely dilutes the theory, without either effectively accounting within its own terms for the diversity of outcomes or modifying the theoretically specified trend.

For more than 30 years Spencer popularized the concept of evolution with especial reference to social development and gained a wide popular, as well as an academic, readership. But after his death, he was little regarded. In the new century, events soon rendered the optimism of the general theory implausible and the idea of progress lacked ideological appeal for any subsequent social or intellectual movement. Even with the revival of interest in evolutionary theory in the 1960s and 1970s, many of his most important insights, for example the distinction between global and particular national development, the diversity of local evolutionary outcomes and the significance of structural differentiation, were newly proposed by neo-evolutionists as though for the first time. Apart from the modernist and postmodernist rejection of the idea of human progress, perhaps the main theoretical flaws in Spencer's theory are the poverty of his utilitarian motivational theory for the individual actors in the social process and, secondly, the lack of theoretical specificity in causal explanations of the apparently accidental pattern of observed historical change. On the other hand, at the end of the twentieth century, with signs of reviving Social Darwinism in discussions of economic and welfare policy, there may be a revival of interest in Spencer's evolutionist ideas suitably transmogrified into the language of globalization and the era of information technology. From an academic point of view the single-mindedness of his application of Darwinist evolutionary theory will continue to be both challenging and instructive.

Some neo-evolutionists

There is less to the distinction between Evolutionist and Neo-Evolutionist Theory than you might think. Neo-Evolutionism revived many of the old, apparently abandoned, ideas, but justified its 'Neo' label by exaggerating the contrast with the past and, partly, by oversimplifying what earlier writers had actually said. A certain amount of simplification, however, may be welcome if it puts life back into unjustly neglected ideas and, more important, the neo-evolutionists were, in some cases at least, able to raise significant issues for the first time, leading to research which has given us a much better understanding of social change.

Earlier evolutionism, like nineteenth-century social theory in general, was principally concerned with the transformation of European societies as a result of their industrialization. For writers like Comte and Spencer, a new kind of society was emerging around them, unlike anything encountered before in the history of human societies. They were dealing with what was happening at the crest of a historical wave sweeping away the taken-for-granted world of traditional beliefs and obligations, mainly rural economy and monarchical authority. The neo-evolutionist theory of the second half of the twentieth century was primarily concerned with the less economically developed Asian and African countries of the so-called Third World. These countries mostly had newly achieved independence from the former European colonial empires, and were struggling to establish coherent social and political structures with little in the way of the administrative, urban and industrial infrastructure necessary to sustain growth. Newish countries like Australia (an independent Dominion since 1912), Canada (self-governing since 1867) or Norway (independent since 1905) were not included in this interest. The focus was almost entirely upon the struggle for modernization by non-European populations and modernization, for all intents and purposes, meant Westernization.

Neo-evolutionist analysis is essentially political rather than social or cultural. That is to say, they do not seem to be concerned how in the long-run, even the very long-run, the Wai Wai of the Rupununi might one day evolve their own version of Chicago, always supposing that in the meanwhile, they haven't all emigrated there anyway. As with Spencer, the unit of analysis is the national state, even though some colonial boundaries forced together peoples of distinctive cultures, different ethnicity and diverse languages, and independence often opened up serious problems of national identity, of economic cohesion and political stability. Social evolution therefore was predicated upon a territorial unit rather than a cultural or even ethnic identity, and the prospects for the Wai Wai were not considered, except as part of a larger, heterogeneous political state. Neo-evolutionist analysis, in other words, operated in terms of the problems which might arise within the then prevailing political order. The problems of modernization and development were those problems which might upset the political apple-cart.

Sahlins and Service: general adaptive capacity

Neo-evolutionist theory re-emphasizes the distinction Spencer had made between: (a) the evolution of particular societies, which may flourish for a time or languish and decay; and (b) the broad evolutionary history of mankind in which the cumulative breakthroughs, such as the establishment of settled agriculture, the invention of writing, the codification of law or the advent of bureaucratic administration, are not confined to a specific culture. These great discoveries spread through cultural diffusion. In the course of general evolution, therefore, it is not necessary for every particular society to follow an identical path or for each one to recapitulate the whole process for themselves. As Ginsberg commented in his 1965 Introduction to the reprint of a 1916 study of preliterate societies: 'why anyone ever thought that a theory of social evolution must necessarily assume that all peoples developed in a uniform manner is now difficult to say' (1965). Steps can be omitted by late developers adopting 'state of the art' technologies from the innovating pioneers. Of course, some countries may fail to do this and, as a result, instead of catching up, can stagnate or go into a decline and become vulnerable to competition, conquest and incorporation, or extinction. Neo-evolutionist theorists have generally tried to avoid the explicitly evaluative identification of evolution with progress; the idea, in other words, that Westernization should be the aim for everybody. This has not been altogether convincing and the definition of evolutionary markers in most cases remains culture bound. There are probably still many Iranians who believe that the development after the 1977 revolution of an Islamic state was a positive evolutionary development, though it would be hard for a Western theorist to reconcile it with neo-evolutionary criteria.

Sahlins and Service's efforts to suggest a value-free definition of social evolution have been among the most successful (1960). They defined it as the increase in 'the general adaptive capacity of society.'. Though not that far from Spencer's ideas, they were more original in suggesting this capacity might be assessed partly in terms of ecological criteria. Thus a society's 'general adaptive capacity' would be demonstrated: (a) by its relative autonomy from conditioning environmental forces; and (b) what would seem to be a particular instance of the same autonomy, by its 'more varied and more effective capacity to use the energy resources of a wider variety of environments' (cf. Lenski, 1976). In addition, Sahlins and Service suggest the general adaptive capacity of a society is indicated by (c) its 'ability to dominate and replace less advanced types'. The environmental autonomy (a) and energy adaptability (b) criteria clearly apply at both the local specific-society level and at the general human level, at least so far. Environmentalists argue, in a sort of Malthusian way, that there must eventually be a limit to the planet's resources, but up to the present, these measures would distinguish societies at different levels of technology and capacity for innovation. The final consideration (c) in the context of the other two (a) and (b) is not entirely circular, in that less-advanced types are presumably also less independent of their local environmental resources. It raises the central Darwinist issue of survival and replacement, but begs the crucial question of 'how do they do that?'. In other words, is it possible to specify what the ability to dominate and replace other societies is?

Smelser: uneven structural change

Neil Smelser (1964), like Spencer too, identified the process of structural differentiation as the central and critical evolutionary trend increasing adaptive effectiveness. For example, family and kinship relationships provide for the economic, political, health care, leisure and religious needs of people in simpler societies, as well as for the socialization and education of children, the psychosexual and other emotional needs of adults, their sense of identity, what guarantee there is of their rights and physical safety. With the development of non-family institutions providing for most of these needs, schools, democratic representation, police and so forth, family involvement may remain important. But the kind of provision available in a hospital intensive care unit considerably enhances the life-support system based on granny's traditional remedies; or the levels of financial provision available through a modern insurance fund considerably augments the powers of what most families can do from their own resources alone. Still, insurance funds, hospitals and families need to operate in harmony. Smelser draws attention to the frictional difficulties of integration, where uneven development among differentiated institutions within a social structure may generate serious social problems. With the development of market-orientated industrial economies, the rapid urbanization and increasing population may put unbearable pressures upon the more vulnerable sections of society. Displaced peasant farmers and the new urban proletariat have to cope without either traditional rural subsistence systems or adequate urban infrastructure and welfare systems. Political unrest and extremism is the hardly surprising symptom of the alienated, and often criminal, underclass that is brought into being by uneven and unintegrated structural change. Social evolution in rapidly developing societies, therefore, is frequently a far from smooth process and, even when it is effectively adaptive at a collective or societal level, one that is paid for by its victims.

Parsons: structural differentiation

Talcott Parsons's (1902–1979) views on the modernization of society are extremely abstract and concern the general case rather than any given historical sequence in particular. They are Lamarckian rather than Darwinian. That is to say, modernization is the result of an endless series of functional adjustments among the component subsystems of society. He makes no mention of struggle, competition or extinction. His earlier ideas on the topic were expressed (1951) in terms derived from Tönnies's analysis of modernity (see Chapter 5), of a shift from social life characterized by Particularism to the predominance of Universalism and from Ascription to Achievement. These are two of the pairs of 'pattern variables' he identified as basic cultural dilemmas confronting any and every social system. Thus we can distinguish those societies or cultures in which people are treated particularistically, that is to say, because they are who they are, the nephew of my friend, from my home town, a pupil at my old school, someone whom, in other words, I know. In contrast, there are those where the norm is to deal with everyone universalistically, as, say, another candidate for this job, one of many with similar qualifications and experience whom, in all fairness, I must treat like all the others. The doctor does the best she can for you regardless of whether she likes you as a person. The teacher gives you a D for your assignment because it is a poor piece of work and not because of the things your mother said about his dahlias at the flower show last year. Ascription and Achievement is a closely related distinction, first proposed by the anthropologist Ralph Linton (1936), to distinguish societies where your status is ascribed to you because of your parentage, sex, age, religious affiliation, and so on, in contrast with those where you are what you make yourself. Individuals achieve what they do via the examinations they pass, the qualifications they acquire, the opportunities they seize.

These dimensions; universalism-particularism and ascription-achievement are independent and any combination of alternatives is possible. Particularist-Achievement could describe the message of many a Presidential electoral campaign or the outcome of the Miss World competition. Universalistic-Ascription would apply to the view that all members of a given ethnic group are alike and you can't trust any of them. But it is the contrast between the other two pairs and the greater emphasis on Universalism and Achievement that, for Parsons, was indicative of modernity. Modernization reduces ascription and particularism, it represents the growth of universalism and achievement. The kind of situation in which the boss's son inherits the business while, with a private word to the foreman, the sweeper's son might be taken on as a sweeper, is replaced by the kind of bureaucratic recruitment policy that selects personnel in accordance with their accredited competence. Thus, in this version of his theory, Parsons views evolutionary social change as, in essence, a change in cultural values.

In his later work (1966, 1971) Parsons proposed a five-stage classification of societies on a sort of evolutionary scale. Each stage has a characteristic combination of a new level of structural differentiation and a distinctive means of social integration.

Parsons's Evolutionary Scheme

Increasing Structural Differentiation	Stage of Development	Type of Integration
	Primitive	a) **Baseline Society,** undifferentiated, no fixed territory, kinship dominated (e.g. Australian Aborigines, Kalahari Bushmen)
		b) **Advanced Primitive,** settled territory, kinship and property more differentiated. Kingship (e.g. Ashanti, Baganda, Maori society)
	Intermediate	Emerges with written language
		a) **Archaic,** more advanced agricultural basis, centralized governmental structures (e.g. dynastic Egypt, Mesopotamia, early feudal Europe)
		b) **Advanced Intermediate,** historic religion and imperial organization. Full upper-class literacy, distinction between natural and supernatural (e.g. T'ang China, Mogul India, Islamic Caliphate, Imperial Rome)
	Modern	**Industrialized production,** common citizenship and democratic institutions, rational legal process, open intellectual culture through renaissance (e.g. capitalist Western Europe, USA. and modern Japan, plus USSR and Eastern Europe)

Adapted from Parsons, 1966, 1971.

This outline of social evolution is not directly keyed in to the earlier contrast of 'pattern variables', but the picture it presents is broadly consistent with the earlier account. It would be interesting to know whether the universalism-achievement/particularism-ascription balance is only supposed to shift at the transition from Intermediate to Modern societies or if, and how, it might tilt in earlier transitions.

Alongside the progressive structural differentiation, the step from *Primitive* to *Intermediate* societies occurs where integration relies, at least in part, on the production of written records. The medium of writing provides for the ordering coordination of more diverse systems over greater distances and with greater continuity over time. Modernity takes this process much further, with the systematization of law and administration made possible and reinforced by the spread of literacy to the whole population. Closely associated with mass literacy is the emphasis on equality and the emergence of democratic values and representative institutions. The rapidly increasing dispersion of these character-istics to a widening range of societies, particularly after the Second World War, has brought about the existence of a single 'modern world system'. The persistence of premodern loyalties and divisions among religions, ethnic and regional groups in some societies may, however, sometimes generate serious tensions where they come into conflict with the rights of common citizenship (1971). It is important to recognize that this is the chart of an evolutionary hierarchy (not) of an evolutionary path. It represents the pattern of evolution of human societies in general, but not the historical path followed by any one of them. It is not just that some people might get stuck along the way, for one reason or another. The modern USA never was an archaic empire, nor was the Caliphate ever likely to evolve into a modern capitalist or communist society.

Parsons's evolutionism isn't really much of an advance, if any, on what had gone before, though it has been extensively referred to and needs to be considered before we look at his structural-functionalist systems theory in a later chapter. Part of the problem is the generality of the argument. Parsons refers to particular societies as illustrative examples, but does not examine the actual process of evolution in any one of them. The contrast, for example, of the primitive and the modern is, as a result, overdrawn. Thus Mary Douglas writes:

The idea that primitive man is by nature deeply religious is nonsense. The truth is that all the varieties of scepticism, materialism and spiritual fervour are to be found in the range of tribal societies. They vary as much from one another on these lines as any chosen segments of London life. The illusion that all primitives are pious, credulous and subject to the teaching of priests or magicians has probably done even more to impede our understanding of our own civilization than it has confused the interpretations of archaeologists dealing with the dead past.   (1973, pp. 36–7)

Again the assumption of an antithesis between traditional values and economic modernization is a questionable one. Empirical studies of development, in Japan (Vogel; Davis) or Hong Kong (Wong) for example, have shown that traditional religious and family values have often been helpful to the development of a modern economy rather than obstacles to it (see also Noble, 1998). Where evolution is defined primarily in terms of value shifts, these findings constitute a more serious objection than they would for an analytic contrast based on purely structural or technological criteria.

The emphasis on cultural diffusion in neo-evolutionist theories means that, for individual societies, change is generally exogenous. Conflict is a side-effect of change rather than a primary determinant of it so, one can conclude, these neo-evolutionists are consensus orientated. Though not obviously historicist in relation to specific societies, there is a strong element of historicism at the very abstract level of discussion about the general evolution of human societies. Neo-evolutionist theorists are sociologically realist and idealist in stressing cultural values as the critical factors in change. Their epistemological perspective, particularly in the case of Parsons, is essentially rationalist and ostensibly objectivist. The frequent Marxist accusation that Parsons defined modernity in terms of what are essentially American values, and therefore his account of social evolution is an ideological one rather than scientific, may be countered by drawing attention to his inclusion of the USSR and communist Eastern Europe in the category of modern societies. Whether the accusation or the rebuttal are worth worrying about at this stage is doubtful.

Rostow: the stages of economic growth

I want to turn now to a much cited, but apparently little read, book by W. W. Rostow. Possibly because of his concluding critical review of Marxist theory, Rostow's argument has often been disparaged as ideological and his book *The Stages of Economic Growth* (1960) has almost equally often been misrepresented either as arguing for a uniform and inevitable development for all, or as proposing a crude kind of economic determinism. Having pointed out that, if the seedcorn is not all to be eaten up, for economic growth to be sustained, investment must exceed the rate of population growth, he has been caricatured as suggesting that all that is necessary is to push the investment rate up to 10 per cent of Gross National Profit (GNP).

Though an economist, concerned with the explanation of economic development, Rostow recognized a need to go beyond the purely economic conditions of traditional, non-industrialized societies and also examine the whole range of psychological, cultural, political and social factors which help to determine a country's history. The sociology he developed to this end was not therefore a merely off-the-peg functionalism, but stresses the importance of both material and cultural factors, and is alert to the significance of conflict within and between societies. His open-ended view of history is far from historicist and his argument is both empirically based and objective in orientation. The argument of the book amounts to a summary of how societies have in the past evolved from traditional, preindustrial origins, in some cases to reach their mid-twentieth-century state of high mass consumption; a formal analysis of the practical conditions which must be met if other societies are to undergo the same change; and an outline assessment of the prospects for newly independent, non-industrial countries making the transition in the foreseeable future.

He identified five stages of economic growth, of which the first and last are Before and After states. Unlike other evolutionary schemes we have considered, the importance of his examination of the middle three stages is that it is explanatory. They show us how a society gets from one stage to another. The five stages are as follows:

1. **Traditional society**: societies in this category are very diverse, but are mainly agricultural and prescientific in culture. They may experience all sorts of changes and upheavals, but these are non-linear, non-cumulative changes, and the changed society remains predominantly agricultural, prescientific and traditional.

2. **Preconditions for takeoff**: at this point both exogenous and endogenous factors play an important role. The stimulus which breaks the continuity, or merely cyclical variation, of the traditional society has to come from outside. It may be the external political context where military and political rivalry with economically more-advanced powers has been the major factor in encouraging a deliberate policy of development, as in the industrialization of most of the industrialized nations in the nineteenth and earlier twentieth centuries. In other cases it was imperialist intervention and conquest, or large-scale economic investment by overseas interests taking advantage of previously unexploited local natural resources, that have disturbed traditional structures and the existing balance of interests. Perhaps only England, the first country to industrialize, did not, to begin with, confront such a situation, and the historical circumstances of its long-drawn out industrial revolution may be of little relevance for the later cases of economic development elsewhere.

It is, however, the internal changes in response to these external influences that determine whether or not a society takes the evolutionary path. For those moving toward economic takeoff, Rostow argues, the precondition of economic change is a shift in the cultural, or psychological horizon of expectations. But: (a) *Cultural Changes* in, for example, religious or other values so as to encourage profit-maximizing activities (see the discussion of Weber in Chapter 6) are insufficient by themselves to bring about an economic transformation. This requires (b) *Social Changes*, especially the emergence of new elites. To be effective, however, a new elite must not only feel itself denied access to power and status within the existing traditional social structure, but that social structure must be flexible enough to allow them to achieve power and personal advancement instead of conforming to traditional patterns, or be incapable of stopping them from doing so (op. cit. p. 51). There must thus be (c) *Psychological Change*, whereby these new cadres come to regard further change as both possible and necessary. Fourthly, for the implementation of change, there must be (d) *Political Change*, with the growth of a movement amongst the rising members of the society aiming at national, and not merely personal, objectives. The ideology of nationalism is often the potent motivating factor in instigating this series of changes:

> ... a reactive nationalism – reacting against intrusion from more advanced nations – has been a most important and powerful motive force in the transition from traditional to modern societies, at least as important as the profit motive. Men holding effective authority or influence have been willing to uproot traditional societies not, primarily, to make more money but because the traditional society failed – or threatened to fail – to protect them from humiliation by foreigners.   (ibid., pp. 26–7)

To overcome the resistance of traditional political and social groups, usually with their roots deep in regionally based agriculture or allied to the established colonial administration, there needs to be effective collaboration amongst the diverse elements of the new elites. The typically successful pattern involves a coalition or coalitions among the intellectuals – teachers, technologists, lawyers, and so on, with commercial and military interests.

> The merchant has always been present, seeing in modernization not only the removal of obstacles to enlarged markets and profits but also the high status denied him – despite his wealth – in the traditional society. And there have almost always been intellectuals who saw in modernization ways of increasing the dignity or value of human life, for individuals and for the nation as a whole. And the soldier – an absolutely crucial figure of the transition – often brought much more to the job than resentment of foreign domination and dreams of future national glory on foreign fields of battle.   (op. cit. p. 28)

These considerations would apply equally to nineteenth century Germany or the United States, to Meiji Japan or prerevolutionary Russia as well as to the postcolonial societies of the twentieth century.

3. **Takeoff:** For the move into the takeoff stage, economic growth has to outpace population growth or the economy, in effect, simply stagnates. But, for this to happen, there have to be crucial changes in attitudes toward risk-taking, toward the application of science and the adoption of new methods of production and working practices. It needs to become established that capital investment can be undertaken according to approximately rational considerations and is a worthwhile proposition (ibid., pp. 20 and 50).

Different economic sectors, at different times and in different societies, may play the key role in the accumulation of capital for investment. This function operates partly through the profits made and invested elsewhere but mainly by attracting capital which is then spent on capital goods, so stimulating the rest of the economy into sustained growth. The cotton industry played this role in England before 1830, railway development in Canada, USA, France, Germany and Russia had the same effect, while expenditure on the armed forces in Russia, Japan and Germany in the nineteenth century and local consumer goods in Australia and Argentina during the depression of the 1930s and the Second World War were key sectors. Rostow mentions the timber industry in Sweden and dairy production in Denmark. We could extend the series with steel and shipbuilding, motor vehicles and consumer microelectronics in the growth of East Asian economies since the 1970s. Besides the contribution of these growth sectors to compound capital accumulation they also alter the character of economic management and managers.

4. **The drive to maturity:** This stage tends to be reached, Rostow estimates on the basis of European experience, about sixty years after the Economic takeoff has begun. It may be argued that in the case of Korea, Hong Kong, Singapore and Taiwan, this timescale has been considerably foreshortened. In the Drive to Maturity we again see an interplay of structural and cultural changes as economic growth becomes self-sustaining. The economic transition gathers strength with the continuing redeployment of the population, from over 75 per cent in agriculture to the majority of jobs in industry and trade, communications and the services sectors.

Economic activity, like political and intellectual activity, broadens its horizons from the local self-sufficient regional level to the national and, increasingly, the international setting. Domestically family circumstances change with continuing economic development. Instead of children being regarded as both a blessing in themselves and an insurance against the hardships of their parents' old-age, new considerations tend to bring about a decline in birthrates. Falling fertility rates contribute to a rise in average living standards, but in the Drive to Maturity this needs to be contained to maintain a high level of investment. In traditional societies spending power much above the needs of minimum consumption was largely confined to the land-owning class. In sustaining economic growth this surplus, 'must be shifted into the hands of those who will spend it on roads and railroads, schools and factories, rather than on country houses and servants, personal ornaments and temples' (ibid., p. 19). This far through the transition, class and lineage are no longer the exclusive determinants of personal standing. More and more what matters is an individual's ability to perform a specific, and increasingly specialized, task.

The fifth and final stage of Rostow's model of economic growth is:

5. **The age of high mass consumption:** At this point economic growth has become an institutionalized expectation with the parallel assumption of continued full employment. Concern switches from production to consumption and the maintenance of demand levels in the economy as a whole and consumer satisfaction at the individual level. But, with the mature development of economic potential, there are choices that remain to be made about the further direction of social development.

With economic maturity the choice of national objectives remains to be made. Rostow argues that societies might opt for:

- Foreign influence – including military influence, which may involve diplomatic belligerence and war.
- The development of Welfare State measures and the redistribution of income, which may erode the accumulation of investment capital with damaging consequences for future growth; or

- High mass consumption of consumer durables and services.
  Different countries have made different choices, but Rostow
  concludes that only the last of these encourages capital investment
  in productive capacity, and therefore makes for vigorous and
  continuing economic growth.

Economic growth is only one of the possible choices that may be
made. Cultural, social and political factors all have independent
effects upon what those choices, deliberately calculated or
unthinking and uninformed, might be: '... it follows', says Rostow,
'that the central phenomenon of the world of post-traditional
societies is not the economy – and whether it is capitalist or not –
it is the total procedure by which choices are made' (ibid., p. 150).
    Here then, finally, we have an action theory of social evolution,
not as an escalator you cannot get off till you get to the top; but
the outcome of the choices people make in the light of their cultural
background, political circumstances and the opportunities available
to them.

4

Theories of Revolutionary Change: Marx and Contradiction

Marx's legacy

There have been other revolutionary theorists and other theorists of revolution, but none have had anything like the impact of Marx (1818–1883) on the great stage of history or in the more sheltered groves of the academic world. For the theory which developed from the work of Marx and his collaborator, patron and friend, Engels, is aimed not just at understanding the world but at changing it. The political influence of their ideas either in directly inspiring, or through being abused and distorted by the likes of Lenin, Stalin, Mao and innumerable Marxist political activists in many countries during the course of the twentieth century, gives them an extra dimension of significance, out of the common scope of sociological theorists.

Even academically, through the work of Marxist writers and teachers, and of those who have critically or sceptically engaged with them, Marxist ideas have dominated the growth of social theory for the past 40 years and, in Europe at least, for probably twice that length of time. However, in this chapter, I want to concentrate on the work of Marx himself, rather than attempt to deal with the many branching paths of subsequent Marxist scholarship and polemic. The theoretical perspective he and Engels developed deserves attention in its own right, though any account of it is sure to be inadequate in the eyes of at least some of those who think of themselves as Marxists. The original work is extensive, immensely rich in ideas and rhetoric. Some major texts were not published in his lifetime, some only rediscovered in the twentieth century. As a result, it has given rise to many different interpretations. There are those who stress, and those who deny, the importance of his early ideas. There are those who believe his late writing, from the 1850s onward, represents a summation of everything important that went before, and others who argue that it indicates a new, less-humanist departure in his thinking. There are, or have been, structural Marxists, neo-Hegelian Marxists, Stalinists, critical theorists, even vulgar Marxists, Maoists and Trotskyites, existentialist Marxists, Marxist feminists and, no doubt, many, many more sects and deviants. Apart from them all agreeing that Marx was right, there is very little else that they all agree on, including what it was he was right about. However, there is little profit in reviewing the spectrum of post-Marxian controversy. In looking at Marx and Engels' work itself, I hope we can discern what is distinctive about the ontology and epistemology of Marxist theory and how it represents an approach, or perhaps a range of approaches, to social change which is different from all the others.

The intellectual background

Marx was a highly charismatic genius whose profound intellectual impact derives not so much from the sheer originality of his ideas as from the intoxicating synthesis he created of historical analysis, metaphysical certainty, moral critique, political commitment and rhetoric. His political economy, the stress on the productive process, the analysis of the conflict of interests in market-orientated relationships, together with the exploitation and alienation which it entailed, he took from Saint-Simon, for whom Comte had worked, and, particularly, from Adam Smith. It is true he was not above misrepresenting Smith's argument in his own commentaries upon it (see *Grundrisse*, 1973, pp. 100–111, and cf. Chapter 2, above; The *Grundrisse* was written in 1857–8 but not published until 1953), but one of the stimulating features of Marx's writing is his use of scathing, and sometimes misleading, criticism as a method for developing his own point of view. Following Smith's description of the merchants' and manufacturers' rapacious pursuit of profits, Marx argued that the conflicting interests of economic classes was the factor responsible for bringing about change. For Marx, however, this would lead to revolutionary change as the class struggle ended in the overthrow of the previously ruling and exploiting class, so dramatically illustrated in the 1789 French Revolution. This certainty Marx derived from the philosophy of Hegel, who claimed that there is a dialectical law of historical development which explains not only the past, but reveals the future inherent in the dynamics of the present. Adapting this dialectic to the materialism of political economy, this theory complemented the socialism Marx mainly learned in France, where its passionate concern for the propertyless and exploited masses already inspired an important group of radical theorists and revolutionaries.

This mixture of a materialist analysis of economic relations which unmasks the real interests of competing groups, plus the moral force of socialist idealism and a theory of history which offers a key to an inevitable future is an immensely seductive intellectual cocktail. The ultimate incompatibility of the component parts, as with all cocktails, has been of relatively minor importance in comparison with the excitement of what it seems to promise. The promise of Marxism was a better explanation for the social, political and economic realities than anything offered by the established authorities, a just cause for action and the philosophically guaranteed certainty of eventual triumph.

In order to appreciate the roots of Marx's theory, it is worth examining in a bit more detail the work of Hegel. In the early years of the nineteenth century, G. W. F. Hegel (1770–1831), a professor at the University of Jena, had produced a series of studies in which he developed an Idealist theory of history. That is to say, he argued not as an idealist in the sense of a high-principled or utopian optimist, but from the philosophical point of view that the world about us is a particular manifestation of abstract ideas. Any given trooper, dragoon or grenadier is a particular representation of the general idea of a soldier, the ideal soldier. To recognize what they have in common, we need to relate them to that idea of a soldier. So too for material objects and for abstractions like beauty, truth and reason. What we meet are specific examples, but the beauty which is in a flower, a sunlit riverbank or a person is an ideal abstract principle which animates them all. Through them we can come to appreciate what beauty itself is. The reality behind human history too is the abstract ideas, truth, freedom, power and so forth, which have shaped it. From an earlier writer, the founder of German nationalism, F. Herder, Hegel took the notion that each society is the objectification of the spirit of its people (the Volksgeist). Thus what makes a German a German is his Germanness, and that spirit, manifested in each individual, is not simply the sum of the personal characters of all the individual Germans, but is a <u>pervading spirit or culture</u> <u>which persists through time and gives the individuals</u>, and all their artistic and other creations, its own <u>recognisable</u> character. For Hegel, the divisions among all the self-interested individuals, and between the different social ranks, are transcended in the nation state.

The nation state represents a higher level of reason than that attained by any individual member of society. In the development of reason, and therefore of the freedom of the human spirit, the spirit of the time (zeitgeist) represents the stage which has been reached in the progress toward Reason's final fulfilment. That will be achieved with the realization of the essential spirit of humanity (the Weltgeist), through the ultimate triumph of Reason. This <u>progressive rationalization of the world</u> is brought <u>about by the workings of Reason itself</u> and not by the intellectual activities of mere individuals. <u>Reason is working itself</u> out through history <u>in a dialectual confrontation</u> of ever more profound and rational ways of understanding. The process is akin to the development of a formal debate, where the presentation of an argument (thesis) raises the objections of a contradictory point of view (antithesis or negation) based on opposing assumptions. The confrontation of these, testing the strengths and weaknesses, the plausible and implausible elements in each, provides for the development of a new, more satisfactory position (synthesis or the negation of the negation) omitting the mistakes, but incorporating the sound parts of both. As a description of an intellectual disputation that may sound plausible, and its extension to a process whereby historical change is a matter of the evolution of abstract, organizing principles is not inconceivable. Thus mankind's earliest responses to experience of the world were poetic or artistic. Homer was not just telling a story, but giving an account of the world, offering a way of understanding it. This aesthetic response was superseded by a more moral and theological grasp of the truth given by the ideas of religion. The religious spirit, in its turn, has been displaced by the progress of Reason with the advent of rational philosophy – the application of reason itself in the philosophy of G. W. F. Hegel. Expanding nations and cultures like Germany (Hegel was German) embody this advance of the world spirit. This achieves its fullest expression, above the contentious trivialities of civil society, in the form of the state.

Though the reactionary implications of Hegel's views about the state are readily apparent, his dialectical analysis of history, with its emphasis on the progress of Reason and the growth of positive freedom, had a great attraction for young German radicals in the 1830s. Rejecting both his philosophical idealism and his political idealization of the state, writers like Bruno Bauer (1809–1882) and Ludwig Feuerbach (1804–1872) developed radical and materialist critiques of the state and the religion that upheld it.

Marx's links with these young Hegelians while a student probably prevented him from getting an academic post after completing his doctorate in Berlin University, since their views were seen as politically dangerous by the deeply reactionary European political regimes in the unstable years following the Revolution in France and the defeat of Napoleon in 1815. Marx met Engels in 1843, during his first stay in Paris after the paper he edited in Cologne had been closed down by the authorities. Engels, who ran his family's cotton mill in Manchester, had already written his study of working-class poverty there (1845). Over the next few years they wrote a great deal together, much of which was not published until after their deaths but, nevertheless, helped to develop their ideas. They began that collaboration almost immediately by criticizing the radical work of Marx's former associates, mainly on the grounds that though they rejected Hegel's Idealist philosophy, they had failed to recognize the fundamental economic interests that underlay the processes of political and moral domination. From his reading in political economy while in exile in Paris and his increasing interest in revolutionary socialism – principally from Adam Smith, on the one hand, and from Henri Saint-Simon, on the other – Marx came to regard the central dialectical conflict of history as not a matter of the clash of the essential ideas of the age, but as a much more immediate and bitter struggle over

Maslow's needs

the necessities of daily life. As he and Engels put the matter in characteristically down-to-earth terms: '... life involves before everything eating, drinking, a habitation, clothing and many other things. The first act is thus the production of the means to satisfy these needs, the production of material life itself' (1846). Thus the dialectical opposition in each era is between those who have at their disposal the material resources whereby society may provide for its physical subsistence, and those, for whose very lack of such means, they are able to coerce into bearing the whole burden of productive work. The dialectic, in other words, is a material one between classes divided by their struggle to control the means of production.

Hegel's explanation of historical change was unsatisfactory because it made people into nothing but the manifestations of impersonal ideal absolutes. The 'materialist conception of history' as Engels termed it, was, in contrast, especially significant when linked to the third element in Marx's concerns, the struggle for socialism. As Marx and Engels put it in their critique of the young Hegelians, '... the philosophers have only sought to understand the world, the problem is, rather, to change it' (ibid.).

Socialism did not begin with Marx. Equality and common ownership had been a theme in the Peasants' Revolt in England in 1385 ('when Adam delved and Eve span, who was then the gentleman' was the slogan) and, during the seventeenth century English Civil War and Commonwealth, of the Diggers, the Levellers and others too. The immediate socialist forebears in Europe were the revolutionary August Blanqui (1805–1881), who had led an unsuccessful insurrection in France in 1839, and Henri Saint-Simon. Saint-Simon had already emphasized that before all intellectual or other considerations, people had to eat. The most important factor was the production of the means of subsistence. In his view, power should be transferred to the productive classes, the inheritance of property should be abolished and rational administration would remove the sources of social conflict and make the state unnecessary. Saint-Simon's ideas were probably the most influential among the radicals in Paris in the early 1840s when Marx was in exile there. Other socialist influences, however, include the Belgian revolutionary activist Pierre Joseph Proudhon (1809–1865), whose phrase 'property is theft' (1840, Ch. 1) summarizes his belief in the communism of ownership, who wrote the *The Système des Contradictions Economiques* in 1846 and whose book on poverty Marx severely attacked. While in exile in Brussels, Marx and Engels were invited by the existing Communist League to write for them *The Communist Manifesto*, which they produced in 1848. Marx, then, did not originate socialism or communism, but learned from them and, in return, gave them a powerful armoury of argument and analysis in the shape of Marxist theory.

After visiting Paris again in 1848, during the revolution of that year, and attempting to relaunch his newspaper in Cologne, where it was again suppressed by the authorities, Marx went into exile in London in 1849, where he stayed until his death in 1883. Engels, who also lived in London till his death in 1895, maintained the interest of the family textile business, as well as his more theoretical studies. Marx was a revolutionary and a poor man all his adult life, and in exile lived in Hampstead on occasional journalism and an annuity derived from Engels's capitalist enterprise in Manchester and Germany.

From these three tributary streams of influences flow three currents in the Marxist theory of social change. These are:

1. Change as the unfolding of historical inevitability.
2. Change as a revolutionary process generated by the structural characteristics of the social system.
3. Change as an emancipatory goal and aspiration to which we are asked to give a moral commitment.

The three currents flow together and give added impetus one to another. But there are some rocks and shoals in the confluent tide of theory and we will need to look briefly at some of those too in the course of our exploration.

The materialist conception of history

Like most other nineteenth-century social theorists, including, as we saw in the previous chapter, Comte and Spencer, Marx thought of human history as a succession of stages or epochs. In his version, each epoch was differentiated from the others by the *mode of production* which determined its characteristic pattern of economic and social relationships. Each mode of production involves:

a. the available *means or forces of production*, that is, the raw materials and equipment, plant, machinery, foundries and furnaces or the land and livestock, which can be used in the production process; and
b. *the relations of production*, which is to say, the current pattern of organization, management and exploitation by those who own the means of production of those whose work creates the product.

All the people in a given society who share the same position in the relations of production comprise a *class*. Those who are able to control the means of production, because they own them, are, as a result, *the ruling class*. Engels claimed that,

> It was Marx who first discovered the great law of motion of history, the law according to which all historical struggles, whether they proceed in the political, religious, philosophical or some other ideological domain, are in fact only the more or less clear expression of struggles of social classes.
>
> (1852, Preface)

Marx, then, believed that the history of society could best be understood as a dialectical process, but a material dialectic. Instead of the opposition and negation of abstract principles, dialectical materialism consists in the confrontation of conflicting class interests. As Marx and Engels put it very simply in the opening words of *The Communist Manifesto* (1848): 'The history of all hitherto existing societies is the history of class struggle.' And in this dialectic of class against class, the negation of their negation is the emergence of a new social order. So the ancient society of the Graeco-Roman world ended with the collapse of the Roman Empire, out of which arose feudal society which lasted in Europe until the new bourgeois order of capitalist society was born out of its ruins. The conflict of classes and the inherent contradictions of the capitalist system will lead to its overthrow in the revolution, which will usher in the socialist era.

Put another way, the <u>successive stages</u> in the development of history are 'just so <u>many different forms of ownership</u>' (Marx and Engels, 1846). Firstly, in *Tribal societies* without private property, because no class exploited another by exclusive ownership of the simple means of production, there was a primitive communism. In the *Ancient* or *Slave Mode of Production*, which existed in the city states of ancient Greece and throughout the Roman world, with the establishment of private property rights, handicraft manufacturing and a settled agriculture had emerged. The owners of the estates whose crops fed the city worked their land with slave labour. The slaves had no property and no rights over their own persons. The owners lived in the city and their internal political power struggles were expressed in rivalries with neighbouring cities. The resulting wars led in the end to the imperial dominance of Macedonia and then of Rome, till the system became overextended and incapable of coping with the barbarian incursions of the fourth century.

The Feudal Mode of Production which arose out of the fragments of the Roman empire was dominated by a military class, who divided the land amongst themselves. The largest part of the population, the serfs, belonged to the land they worked and were allowed no freedom of residence or travel. In exchange for service in peaceful times on the land of their lord, and payment to him of a proportion of what they grew for themselves and armed·support in times of war, they were allowed to work holdings which he granted to them. On this arrangement, the feudal lord was able to keep himself and maintain his military strength, his armour, his castle and his armed retinue. In contrast with slavery, the traditional rights of serfdom gave the peasants a degree of control over the means of production and over their own labour power so that, for a part of the year, they were free to work on their own plots of land. Feudalism was destroyed by the growing power of the bourgeoisie, a class of town-dwelling merchants who traded with, and lent money to, the spendthrift landowning aristocracy. The latter weakened their own following, while at the same time providing the labour supply exploited for their own profit by the bourgeoisie, in creating a growing class of landless labourers driven off their feudal holdings by landlords eager to enlarge their own lands or lease them out for money rentals.

The dominance of the merchants and manufacturers, who comprised the bourgeoisie, brought about the dominance of *The Capitalist Mode of Production*. In capitalist society the workers are nominally free to work for any employer as they please, but are compelled by need to work for the owners of the means of production. Though the labour market is formally free, the owners of the indispensable means of production are able to force an exploitative bargain upon those with the need to eat, but no means of providing for themselves except by seeking employment. The owners pay their workers just enough to provide for their needs in return for work which not only covers that cost, but produces a surplus value in the shape of goods and commodities which are sold for the owners' profit. Marx regarded this expropriation of surplus value created by the workers as the source of the capital accumulated in the hands of the bourgeois employing class. This accumulating capital becomes the new forces of production in the continuing competition within the bourgeois class for more profit. Already, in the first half of the nineteenth century, the process had brought about astounding changes. In the *Communist Manifesto* (1849), Marx and Engels commented on the growth in the forces of production under capitalism.

> The bourgeoisie, during its rule of scarce one hundred years, has created more massive and more colossal productive forces than have all the preceding generations together. Subjection of nature's forces to man, machinery, application of chemistry to industry and agriculture, steam navigation, railways, electric telegraphs, clearing of whole continents for cultivation, canalization of rivers, whole populations conjured out of the ground – what earlier century had even the presentiment that such productive forces slumbered in the lap of social labour?

This exploitation of the potential of natural resources, and the titanic enlargement of the means of production, changed the character of the relations of production and of the whole social order. As they noted earlier in *The German Ideology* (1846):

> In big industry and competition the whole mass of conditions of existence, limitations, biases of individuals, are fused

together into the two simplest forms in private property and labour.

The confrontation of these classes with their opposed interests generated an explosive power, which would eventually explode in social revolution. As Marx wrote in *The Poverty of Philosophy* (1847): 'An oppressed class is the vital condition for every society founded on the antagonism of classes. The emancipation of the oppressed class thus implies necessarily the creation of a new society.' The creation of the new society that will replace capitalism will be the last product of the bourgeois mode of production.

In broad outline, the Asiatic, ancient, feudal and modern bourgeois modes of production may be designated as epochs marking progress in the economic development of society. The bourgeois mode of production is the last antagonistic form of the social process of production – antagonistic not only in the sense of individual antagonism but of an antagonism that emanates from the individual's social conditions of existence – but the productive forces developing within bourgeois society create also the material conditions for a solution of this antagonism.

(Marx, 1859)

In passing, we should note Marx's reference to the Asiatic mode of production – a stage in parallel to slave societies in the dialectical sequence outlined so far, to accommodate the great river valley civilizations of Mesopotamia, Egypt and Imperial China. These long-enduring cultures present a major problem for the universality of Marx's dialectical materialism. As John Hall points out, they failed over several thousand years to demonstrate any sign of class conflict bringing about change. Either they were not critically divided by class or the repressive state set above the class struggle was capable of overwhelming the dialectical process (see John Hall, 1986, pp. 12–13; and Karl Wittfogel, 1957).

Within the main dialectical sequence of modes of production, it is clear that the bourgeois is the last because it alone can create the conditions for the ending of all class antagonism. The abundance of material wealth created by capitalism means

[handwritten notes: Inevitable, unlimited wants, limited resources]

that the <u>conflict between classes over scarce resources is no longer inevitable</u>. However to bring it to an end requires that class divisions must (and will) be abolished in the revolutionary transition to socialism. But, as Marx argues in this passage, socialism will be achieved only when the full productive potential of bourgeois capitalism has been realized. One further condition needs to be met before that realization can be brought about. The dialectic of class conflict means that the workers must come to identify the origin of their oppression in their position as the exploited class. They need to become a class in their own eyes, a class for itself, in order to strike at the very source of class division, the capitalist mode of production. When they can do that, with a consciousness of their own class identity, their own class position and their own class potential, they will be on the threshold of a socialist society.

> Economic conditions had first transformed the mass of people of the country into workers. The combination of capital has created for this mass a common situation, common interests. This mass is thus already a class against capital, but not yet for itself. In the struggle, of which we have noted only a few phases, this mass becomes united, and constitutes itself as a class for itself. The interests it defines become class interests.   (1847)

In the coming *Socialist Society*, the <u>common ownership of property</u> will mean that no class will exploit the labour of another. The succession of modes of production will therefore come to an end (Marx and Engels, 1846).

> Does this mean that after the fall of the old society there will be a new class domination culminating in a new political power?

Marx answers firmly:

> No. The condition for the emancipation of the working class is the abolition of every class, just as the condition for the liberation of the third estate of the bourgeois order was the abolition of all estates. The working class, in the course of its development, will substitute for the old civil

society an association which will exclude classes and their antagonism, and there will be no political power since political power is precisely the official expression of antagonism in civil society.   .   (1847)

This is an appealing promise but a doubtful one, doubtful on two scores. Firstly, Marx's analogy between the future abolition of *classes* and the abolition of *estates* (feudal ranks), which liberated the bourgeoisie to become the ruling capitalist class, is incongruent with the argument in *The Communist Manifesto*, for example that all hitherto existing societies have been *class* societies anyway. So what exactly was abolished? And whatever it was, how is it relevant for the next transformation of the mode of production? In short, the small print of this part of the guarantee is far from clear. Secondly, the wary potential revolutionary should note that politics and political power will oppress no-one under socialism because, in the passage quoted, politics and political power have been *defined* out of socialism. Whatever we might want to call it, it won't be political oppression. This is an argument that, in the course of the past century, has often been made use of by the repressive states that have called themselves socialist.

Base and superstructure

Let us now look more closely at the determining role of economic factors in Marx's dialectical theory. Although it is men who make history in Marxist theory, who labour, suffer, oppress and exploit, their actions are entirely conditioned by society. Their consciousness and identity itself is determined by their social being. Man is '... an animal which can individuate itself only in the midst of society' (Marx, 1857). The society which thus moulds the psychology of its individual members is itself wholly structured by the mode of production upon which it is based. The clearest statement of Marx's view on these matters is to be found in his relatively late work, the Preface to his *Contribution to the Critique of Political Economy*, written in London in 1859.

In the social production of their life, men enter into definite relations that are indispensable and independent of their will, relations of production which correspond to a definite stage of development of their material productive forces. The sum total of these relations of production constitutes the economic structure of society, the real foundation on which rises a legal and political superstructure and to which correspond definite forms of social consciousness. The mode of production of material life conditions the social, political and intellectual life process in general. It is not the consciousness of men that determines their being, but, on the contrary, their social being that determines their consciousness.   (1859)

One could scarcely have a clearer or more unambiguous statement of sociological realism than that. Relations of production, he says, are independent of the will of individuals, that is to say, they have no choice but to pursue their class interests. The suggestion that these correspond to the development of the material productive forces almost amounts to a technological determinism. But whether the technology or the exploitation by those who own it of the labour power of those they employ is the crucial factor, all the complex legal and political structures, the social and intellectual life of society is founded upon that economic base. Consciousness itself is socially determined.

Nevertheless, the nature of the relationship between economic base and social, political and intellectual superstructure, however intimate the bond, is not wholly clear. When Marx says the mode of production conditions the social, political and intellectual life of society and that men's social being 'determines their consciousness', it is not altogether obvious how strictly we are meant to interpret the terms. That is to say, at first reading it looks as though he has in mind a simple *causal* relationship of the kind 'a virus causes mumps'. Alternatively, G. A. Cohen has argued that these are *functional* relationships, in that the legal, political and intellectual systems which emerge in society are those which support and sustain the existing relations of production, but are not, as it were, mechanically caused by them (1978). Even in the latter case, the primary role of the economic basis of conflicting class interests founded in the relations of production is clear. It is responsible not just for the institutional structures of the social order, but also the ideas about art, politics, religion, and so on, which have currency in the culture of the age.

> The ideas of the ruling class are in every epoch the ruling ideas: that is, the class which is the ruling *material* force of society is at the same time its ruling *intellectual* force. The class which has the means of material production at its disposal, consequently also controls the means of mental production, so that the ideas of those who lack the means of mental production are on the whole subject to it. The ruling ideas are nothing more than the ideal expression of the dominant material relations ... the relations which make the one class the ruling one ... the individuals composing the ruling class ... among other things rule also as thinkers, as producers of ideas, and regulate the production and distribution of the ideas of their age ... their ideas are the ruling ideas of the epoch.   (Marx and Engels, 1846–7)

Marx and Engels's general position, from these quotations, seems to be fairly unambiguous. The values, attitudes, opinions, concepts and theories that predominate in any era are those that rationalize the rule of the class that dominates within the prevailing relations of production. Except when the contradictions of the mode of production have become sufficiently acute to make their rule precarious, no other class is likely to have the means to disseminate, or even perhaps to conceive of any alternative. In the feudal period the ruling ideas were the values of chivalry, duty, the belief in divinely ordered tradition and social rank that justified the honour (and power) of the aristocratic order. In bourgeois society the values of the market, of individualism and opportunity legitimize the competitive relations of capital and the exploitation of the propertyless.

In some of his more specific analyses, however, such as the study of the 1851 *coup* in which Louis Napoleon seized power eventually to establish the French Second Empire, Marx appears to go outside the dialectical model of the opposition of ruling and exploited classes. Thus he discusses the role of a wide range of social and political factors, the state bureaucracy, the military, the Paris rabble (lumpen proletariat) and the opinions of the peasantry, over and above the specific class relations of production in France at the time. This has led some later Marxist or neo-Marxist theorists to argue that political or cultural factors can have an autonomous role in maintaining class power. Gramsci, for instance, argued that the ruling class maintained its hegemony over the society by its control of the ideological apparatus of the state, the educational institutions, the press, and so on (Gramsci, 1970). The critical theorists of the Frankfurt School were particularly preoccupied with cultural factors in the alienation of the masses in modern urban industrial society. The French sociologist Bourdieu, indeed, evolved the concept of cultural capital in order to account for continuing inequalities in children's educational attainments between those from apparently equally propertyless families, in terms of ownership of the material means of production, in the professional and the manual worker strata (Bourdieu and Passeron). They may, of course, all have been quite right. But these developments are hard to reconcile with either Marx's own general statements about the determining role of the relations of production or with his devastating criticisms of earlier theorists. Who now reads Bruno Bauer or Ludwig Feuerbach except as objects of his scorn? Yet Marx rejected their materialist critiques of religion as a delusion serving the interests of the powers that be, precisely on the grounds that they neglected the fundamental economic dimension of the relationship between ideology and its basis in class conflict (Marx, 1843, 1845). The idea that, through a repressive state apparatus or by the manipulation of the ideological media, the powers can maintain their domination by *political* means is, in essence, what the radical Young Hegelians had maintained. If the later theorists are right, then it would imply that Marx's attacks on them were mistaken. That would also mean the abandonment of the central element in his work that distinguishes it from other materialist and evolutionist theory. The economic conflict over the forces of production is the engine that drives the materialist dialectic. That is why it constitutes the foundation upon which all the rest of the imposing social superstructure is based.

There are two versions of economic determinism in Marxist writing: a strong version and a weak. In the strong version, culture, politics, and so forth, are economically determined and that is that. They are simply ideological expressions of economic class interests. That may seem a bit simplified but at least it is clear. The weak version is that politics, culture, and so on, have a logic of their own and are determined by economic class interests only 'in the last instance' or 'in the last analysis'. Thus there is some degree of freedom, a looseness of connection between them and the relations of production. So we might argue, for instance, that the popularity of rock 'n' roll in the 1950s and 1960s was a mainly cultural development; that Fascism collapsed in Spain for primarily political reasons; that Ireland changed the constitution to allow divorce mainly as a result of changes in moral and religious beliefs, and only 'in the last analysis' as a result of shifting class interests. But when do we come to the last instance? When is an explanation enough? In other words, we may find explanations reasonably plausible, but *a priori* they will never be seen as the last instance unless we stop the chain of reasoning at some economic point, thus the analysis will *by definition* remain incomplete. Surely that is too incoherent an argument to be altogether persuasive. Though there may be a degree of ambiguity in Marx's economic determinism when we consider it more closely, the foundation of his diagnosis of the ills of capitalism is his analysis of what he saw as its inherent contradictions as an economic system.

Contradictions of the capitalist mode of production

The bourgeoisie have called into being the unprecedented productive powers of modern industrialism, ever seeking improvements in existing methods or wholly new ways to make a better profit from their invested capital. They thrive on technological innovation, the continuous transformation of the means of production. In *Capital* Marx made the consequences for capitalism quite clear: 'Its technical basis is therefore revolutionary, whereas all earlier modes of production were essentially conservative' (Vol. I, 1867). No past society ever had the economic potential of capitalism. But the purpose to which these powers are dedicated is not some human end. There is no question of simply making things that will be useful, instead the system is one developed for turning out commodities for sale. The end product of the workers' labour is valued in terms of the price it will fetch in the market, and the same goes for the efforts of the workers themselves. It is a system where all human ties are simplified to market relations – in Marxist terminology, to the cash nexus. It is a society in which every thing has a price and other values, <u>compassion and tradition count for nothing</u>.

Rather than a <u>self-equilibrating system</u> where supply adjusts to demand through the price mechanism, Marx regarded the market as an essentially unstable competitive arena of winners and losers. And losers do not survive. Thus, as the successful prosper and grow while the unsuccessful are forced out, the market tends in the long run to be <u>self-extinguishing</u>. The throng of market competitors is replaced by unchallengeable monopoly. But while the bourgeoisie destroy one another in the competition for markets, they foster the growth of the class that will in the end ruin them all, the labouring class.

The landless peasants and the dispossessed, who have only their labour to sell in order to find a meagre subsistence as wage workers, are formed into a class by the bourgeoisie who employ them. By organizing that labour so as effectively to deploy the means of production, by exploiting their efforts so as to create surplus for the profit of the owners of capital, the industrial workers are given a common grievance in the struggle for their day-to-day subsistence and, in the longer term, a common cause in seeking their final emancipation from the alienating consequences of serving the interests of capital instead of their own human fulfilment. As a <u>class-conscious</u> class, they will become the agents of their own liberation, but they are formed into a class in the first place by capital.

> What the bourgeoisie produces above all, therefore, is its own gravediggers. Its fall and the victory of the proletariat are equally inevitable.   (Marx and Engels, 1848)

Capitalism then is a self-destroying system. The contradictions of the capitalist mode of production are properties of the system itself. As in any mode of production, <u>change is endogenous</u> rather than a consequence of external intrusion. As Marx describes it, the system cannot survive.

Thus, to summarize:

1. The accumulation of profit involves competition between capitalists, and market competition creates a tendency toward monopoly as economies of scale help larger producers undercut their smaller competitors.

2. To maintain their competitive position, producers must increase their investment in the latest equipment and up-to-date products, with a proportional growth of fixed capital (in Marx's terms, the organic composition of capital increases), but, as commodity prices are constrained by the market, this leads to a falling rate of profit on the invested capital. $L_e \uparrow K \rightarrow \uparrow L$

+ diminishing returns

3. The economic crises which the falling rate of profit brings about intensify the pressures on the weaker capitalists so that, as they fail, competition is further reduced. Remaining investors withhold investment because there are fewer profitable outlets. Aggregate demand, for producer goods especially, falls and brings about a crisis of overproduction, with consequent rising levels of unemployment and a fall in demand for consumer goods too.

ρ mechanism $\downarrow \rho \rightarrow \uparrow Q_\rho$

4. Technological innovation, before the crisis of overproduction, uses the accumulated profits of the bourgeoisie to exploit labour more effectively – a necessary step in the evolution of the forces of production towards the socialist era of abundance. However, in the labour process, machines come to run people rather than vice versa. Work ceases to be an outlet for creativity and becomes increasingly dehumanizing – merely a means to make the money to buy commodities. Consumerism (Marx's commodity fetishism) may reconcile the workers to the system for a while, but makes the reaction to rising unemployment all the more powerful. The concentration of workers in large-scale productive units – the better to exploit their labour – furthermore, makes their mass organization and mobilization in the revolutionary struggle easier.

5. Each crisis in the system is necessarily more severe than the last as the organic composition of capital is higher each time. The exploitation of the workforce therefore intensifies with the increasing 'immiseration' of the proletariat.

> The greater the social wealth, the functioning capital, the extent and energy of its growth, and therefore also the greater the absolute mass of the proletariat and the productivity of labour, the greater is the industrial reserve army, ... the more extensive ... the pauperized sections of the working class and the industrial reserve army, the greater is official pauperism. This is the absolute general

law of capitalist accumulation.   (Marx, Vol. I, 1867)

So capitalism inevitably increases unemployment and brings down the living standards of even the employed workers to bare subsistence.

> ... the general tendency of capitalist production is not to raise but to sink the average standard of wages, or to push the value of labour more or less to its minimum limit.
> (Marx, 1865)

or as he put it in vivid terms in *Capital* two years later:

> Accumulation of wealth at one pole ... is at the same time accumulation of misery, the torment of labour, slavery, ignorance, brutalization and moral degradation ... on the side of the class that produces its own product as capital.
> (Marx, Vol. I, 1867)

6. The bourgeoisie was the revolutionary class in feudal society and so, as a class-for-itself, became the dominant class in capitalism. Their ideas became the ruling ideas of the new epoch (Marx and Engels, 1846). But their own revolutionary ideals of equality, liberty and democracy, when adopted by the subordinate class, serve to undermine their own rule.

7. The deepening crises of capitalism and the growing impoverish-ment of the proletariat (those without property) encourage class consciousness. The increasing concentration of capital encourages class mobilization against an increasingly focused target for the revolutionary displacement of the bourgeois class in favour of the workers.

> Along with the constantly diminishing number of the magnates of capital ... grows the mass of misery, oppression, slavery, degradation, exploitation; but with this too grows the revolt of the working class, a class always increasing in numbers, and disciplined, united, organized by the very mechanism of the process of capitalist production itself. The monopoly of capital becomes a fetter

upon the mode of production, which has sprung up along
with, and under it ... the knell of capitalist private
property sounds. The expropriators are expropriated.

(Marx, Vol. I, 1867)

With a revolutionary scenario like that, how could they lose?

Contradictions of Marxist theory

This is a <u>rationalist theory of social change</u> where, given the
known laws of capital accumulation, the <u>inevitability</u> of the
<u>transformation seems logically compelling</u>. The certainty that
Marx seeks to convey derives from the internal contradictions
within the capitalist mode of production which must, in the
end, destroy it. To draw a comparison with twentieth-century
social theory (cf. G. A. Cohen), we might describe this view as
Marx's structural dysfunctionalism. Because of the way the
system works, the revolution *must* follow. It seems almost naive
to observe that it hasn't so far, and that after a 150 years or so
of expecting it quite soon. To consider briefly some of the
<u>reasons why it has not happened</u> yet may help us appreciate
better the structure of Marx's theoretical argument relating to
social change.

Unfulfilled prophecies

Perhaps least theoretically consequential, though of course the
most important in practice, are the prophecies that did not
come true. We can designate them prophecies rather than
forecasts because they do not take the conditional: 'if x then
y' form, but boldly state the inevitable working out of the laws
of capitalist accumulation, a specific instance of the laws of
the materialist historical dialectic.

Firstly, it is clear that the final crisis and overthrow of
capitalism has not yet occurred. The revolutions that have taken
place in the name of socialism have not occurred in the most
advanced capitalist societies but in some of the least capitalist,
where industrialization had but a precarious foothold, the urban
proletariat was vastly outnumbered by a revolutionary

peasantry and a capitalist bourgeoisie was notably absent (see, e.g., Frank Parkin, 1978). Socialist revolutionary consciousness is notably subdued in the working-class politics of the most advanced capitalist societies like the USA or Japan or Switzerland. Ostensibly socialist revolutions have happened in then newly industrializing countries, like Russia early in the twentieth century or in predominantly peasant societies like China in the 1940s. Nineteenth-century revolutionary insurrections, like the 1848 revolution in France or the Chartist unrest during the 1840s in England, took place in societies going through the early stages of industrialization rather than when they had reached full maturity. Some later Marxist writers, Althusser and Poulantzas for example, have proposed a theory of the state, dismissing the precondition of a mature capitalism as a narrow economism and aiming to give a theoretical justification for the capture of the state by what Lenin called the Vanguard party, that is, a party not of the masses, but claiming to represent their 'true' interests (see L. Althusser, 1969; N. Poulantzas, 1973).

Part of the explanation for this theoretically premature revolutionary ardour or subsequently misplaced apathy is, of course, that the immiseration of the poor has never been greatest in the most advanced capitalist economies either. The mesh fences along the Rio Grande are there to keep out the poor trying to get into the United States rather than the reverse, where even the poor are better off. Third-world poverty is notoriously worst in the least capitalistic countries such as Ethiopia or Bangladesh. In the more developed economies, instead of greater polarization, the expansion of the professional and managerial classes has generated rising absolute rates of upward social mobility and an increase in the proportion of the population in the middle-income bands. Already, in mid-nineteenth-century England, the Factories Acts, the Ten-Hour Act restricting worker's hours, and the extension of the vote, first in 1832 and then 1867, to the majority of men in the working class, together with rising real wages, cast doubt on the polarization thesis, on the inevitability of wages being forced down to subsistence level, and, for that matter in the minds of many, on the inescapability of class conflict.

This awkward evidence, and especially after reflecting on the Bolshevik revolution in Russia, led some western Marxist and former-Marxist writers into various attempts to revise Marx's clear prediction of the overthrow of capitalism in the most advanced capitalist societies.

James Burnham argued that, with the changing structure of capitalist enterprise, the dwindling importance of sole-ownership and the growth of massive joint-stock corporations with thousands or tens of thousands of shareholders, the organic composition of capital was being dissolved into its separate component functions of ownership and control. The spread of ownership amongst large numbers of otherwise uninvolved shareholders left the control of capital in the hands of a new managerial class. The class of managers exercised the power of vast concentrations of capital without necessarily owning any of it. However, whether in privately owned capitalist companies or in state-owned socialist bureaucracies, these widely recruited expert managers had become a class in (and perhaps already for) themselves, with distinctive class interests of their own (Burnham, 1945). In other, past revolutionary transitions from one mode of production to another, the dominant class was always replaced by a new class, and not by the oppressed masses. Thus the slave-owning Roman senators were not succeeded by their former slaves, but by a feudal aristocracy of one-time free-booting warriors. The feudal aristocrats were not swept away in a peasant revolt by their serfs, but were outsmarted by the merchant bourgeoisie. In Marx's historical scenario, only in the revolutionary overthrow of capitalism will the exploited class displace the formerly ruling class; and as no others will survive the polarized cataclysm of capitalism's demise, class itself will no longer divide people from one another. This must follow, in Marx's view, since classes can only exist in relations of exploitation. The former Yugoslav Party leader Milovan Djilas was expelled from membership and imprisoned for many years when, on the basis of his observations in the Soviet Union and at home, he argued, in his book *The New Class*, that the ruling Communist Party had itself become a new class of officials and bureaucrats controlling the means of production, distribution and exchange, as well as everything else, and exploiting the labouring masses in the communist world much as the capitalist class did in the West (Djilas, 1957).

In the capitalist West Marx's argument that property relations must become 'the fetter of the forces of production', creating the crises that would lead to the era of social revolution (see Marx, 1859), has also been undermined by later developments. Shareholding in joint stock companies and corporations has largely divorced ownership from management, providing for a vast access of capital investment and consequent growth without seriously inhibiting the entrepreneurial freedom of initiative or the development of new forces of production. Indeed, with the growth of the great corporations with their massive Research and Development (R&D) budgets, the speed of technological innovation has increased and the forces of production have continued to expand. Furthermore, with the increasing significance of institutional ownership through pension funds, insurance companies, investment trusts, and so forth, new forms of property have continued to evolve.

Problems with the past

Most of these developments lay far in the future and, if Marx had not insisted so firmly that he knew the shape the future would take, one might regard them as unforeseeable at the time and therefore not a fair test of his argument. But there are also problems with his view of the past which need to be addressed. Though for most of us the past is settled and done with once and for all, our ideas about what really went on then don't stay that way if the historians have anything to do with it. We regularly have to revise our understanding of history as new facts emerge and critical scholarship prods at, and often deflates, what seemed like well-established views. It is not that anyone has argued that the Battle of Hastings happened in 1067 or that Harold won, but ideas have changed over the years about whether the outcome was on the whole a good thing or a bad thing, or whether or not that might be an unhelpful way of looking at it anyway. And if the prophetic Marx is the most politically stimulating, his historical interpretations are the more theoretically significant since if they should turn out to be problematic, then the foundations of the whole confident dialectical programme are shaken.

To begin with, Marx and Engels were too strongly influenced by the English experience. England was the first country to industrialize (see Deane, 1979; Matthias, 1983, Rostow, 1960) and therefore is a unique and, in many respects, a misleading case. All subsequent industrializations were examples of deliberate emulation by states seeking to catch up and overtake the economic strength already developed elsewhere. In every other instance, industrial development has been instigated, or at least carefully fostered, as *state policy* and not just in the Soviet Union, but in Tsarist Russia, as well as in Imperial Germany and Meiji Japan, right up to the NIEs (newly industrializing economies) of the Pacific rim in the 1980s and 1990s. This pattern was pointed out by the German theorist Friedrich List in the nineteenth century, though seemingly forgotten again until the ebbing of Marxist intellectual orthodoxy in the 1990s (F. List, 1885). The bourgeoisie, then, did not typically create the industrial capitalist state but, in every case except the first, was created along with it by the politico-absolutist state as an instrument of economic development (see Perry Anderson, 1974).

Even with regard to the first industrial revolution there is a problem with Marx's analysis. His focus on the emerging forces of production led him to identify capitalism with industrialism. But capitalistic enterprise not only had its roots, but was firmly established in the towns of mediaeval Europe long before the industrial revolution (see H. Pirenne, 1925). As Braudel has pointed out, even in mid-nineteenth-century England, the major form of capital was agricultural capital, though it coexisted with very old patterns of commercial capital and finance capital, which long predated the industrial capital that began to be significant in the mid-eighteenth century (Braudel, Vol. 2, 1984, p. 604).

> The whole panoply of forms of capitalism – commercial, industrial, banking – was already deployed in thirteenth-century Florence, in seventeenth-century Amsterdam, in London in the eighteenth century. It is undoubtedly the case that in the early nineteenth century, the coming of machines made industrial production a high profit sector and capitalism went over to it on a massive scale. But it was by no means confined to this sector.   (ibid., p. 621)

Thus the transition from feudalism to capitalism was neither

dialectical nor sudden, but was geographically dispersed and
long drawn out.

System inconsistencies

A logical rather than a historical difficulty arises in respect of
the seeming contradiction between two of Marx's contradictions of the capitalist mode of production. In their study
Monopoly Capital, Baran and Sweezy point out that the trend
towards the concentration of capital ending in the monopolistic
domination of markets is inconsistent with Marx's 'law' of the
declining rate of profit, since monopolies are not vulnerable
to the market pressures which bring it about (Baran and Sweezy,
1968). Either might be seriously damaging to the future of the
capitalist system, but they cannot both damage it at the same
time.

A slightly different kind of problem, a problem of rhetoric, I
suppose, rather than one of logic but similarly likely to
misdirect an argument, concerns the idea of capitalistic
exploitation. Marx's use of the term 'exploitation' to describe
the value of production above what would be enough to pay
the producers' wages, which is retained as profit by the
employer, raises a different kind of problem. He plays upon
the moral ambiguity of the term. On the one hand, exploitation
of the weakness or gullibility of others is an obnoxious practice
and deserves our condemnation. But 'exploitation' also has a
neutral meaning, as when we talk about exploiting resources
of natural gas, meaning only to make the most of existing
potential. Marx uses the term to suggest the latter is as wicked
as the former. All economic development requires investment
– therefore the accumulation of capital is a prerequisite of
development. Even under socialism, unless technological
innovation is to cease with the revolution, all economic
resources including labour will need to be fully exploited. This
is particularly so according to the labour theory of value since
that implies that, strictly speaking, labour is all that can be
exploited. Exploitation of economic resources is necessary:

a. to maintain the nonproductive part of the population, that
   is, the old, the sick, children, 'each according to his needs';

b. to provide for the replacement of worn out plant and machinery and new investment. New investment will be required to cope with changes in the environment, for example the depletion of natural resources, changes in the population, new technological possibilities for the more efficient use of raw materials, new medical or communications potential, and so on.

The capital for all that must be saved and concentrated from ongoing economic activity. If all was returned directly and immediately to the direct producers, nothing could be developed. The concentration and management of accumulated capital resources may be directed by those who claim ownership rights or by state bureaucrats. Which pattern is adopted in a society is a matter of (somebody's) political preference and technical effectiveness. But the process of exploitation is unavoidable in any economy beyond the bare and precarious subsistence of primitive hunting and gathering. The problem of alienation, which arises whenever the worker produces the surplus value for which he is exploited by the owner-employer, it follows, is of doubtful salience in distinguishing stages of development in the relations of production after primitive communism.

Marx's early and, in his lifetime, unpublished work on the alienation of the workers under capitalism (Marx, 1844), expressed a general distaste for the impact of early industrialization, which, as we have seen, was there in the writings of Adam Smith 70 years earlier, and was common amongst those who deplored the long hours, low wages, the dangerous work and squalid living conditions endured by workers and their families in the rapidly expanding early industrial towns (see Engels, 1845; Braudel, Vol. 3, Ch. 6). Marx held that as, in the capitalist market economy, work was reduced from a creative activity engaged in for the subsistence of the worker and his dependants and became a commodity, something he sold in return for a wage; he 'alienated' not only the product of his labours, but also part of his life, part of himself. Work divided men from their fellows, competitors for profits, competitors for a job; from their families and from their community at work in the mills and foundries, during all the hours of daylight. Indeed, they were alienated from themselves as their lives were spent in supervised and regimented activities

drive for gains thru collaboration?

organized by their employer for his own commercial purposes, without consideration for the aspirations, the needs or even the comprehension of the workers themselves. Reduced to mere appendages to the machine, cogs in the productive process, the workers under the capitalist mode of production are alienated from their 'species being'.

The problem with all this is not that it exaggerates the deprivations, poverty and exploitation, in the worst sense, of the early phase of industrialization, for it does not greatly, if at all. The problem is the theoretical one concerning whether 'man' has some kind of 'species being' to be alienated from. The simple empirical difficulty of deciding whether the miserable, frustrated worker or the cheerful and contented worker is the alienated one is not a frivolous objection. The first may be regarded as unalienated because conscious of his exploited class position, or alternatively, alienated because of the distress his exploitation has induced. The second one may be regarded as adjusted to his social position and fulfilled as a human being by the creative opportunities and rewards it brings him, or alternatively, as more truly alienated than the other because apparently oblivious to his exploitation.

The very notion of alienation presumes an authentic individual character or spirit antecedent to the social conditions and class relations within which the worker evolves his consciousness of himself. That is to say, it is essentially an idealist notion, fundamentally at odds with Marx's general position that consciousness and human identity itself is a social product. Very sensibly, in his later work after 1850 or so, he abandoned the notion of alienation and it does not feature in the analysis of capitalism he was still working on at his death in 1883 (see L. Althusser, 1969). The rediscovery and publication of the Paris manuscripts, after almost a hundred years in 1932, appealed to a generation of intellectuals in the industrial capitalist countries responding to the failure of the proletarian revolution to materialize, and seeking to rationalize in Marxist terms the lack of support for revolutionary politics in the most developed economies (see, for example, Herbert Marcuse, 1964). It represents, however, not so much one of the contradictions of capitalism as one of the contradictions of Marxism.

This problem derives from the practical impossibility of

reconciling the Hegelian structure of Marx's theory and its materialist content. The same goes for the difficulty of fitting the complexity of economic and political change into a dialectical framework, and attributing the causes of all major social change, in the last analysis, to class-exploitative relations of production. The apparent rationality of the dialectic may usefully dramatize the confrontation of intellectual or moral paradigms, but only makes an unconvincing melodrama in five acts out of the uneven and uncertain processes of historical change.

Marxist ideology

The basic unit of Marx's historical analysis is the mode of production. His theoretical position, therefore, is sociologically realist and materialist. It is also, obviously, conflict orientated: change is generated endogenously by the dialectic of class struggle. It is historicist since he believed history to be governed by known laws whose ultimate outcome can be known in advance. It is rationalist since – in principle if not, it seems, always in practice – all specific explanations can be derived from these basic axioms. It is also ideological. Marxist analysis is part of Marxist praxis. This last consideration means we have to deal with his ideas and arguments as manoeuvres in the war against the bourgeoisie. The prophecy of socialist revolution aims to be self-fulfilling. It is concerned to bring about that particular result. That makes it hard, in its own terms, to refute it on merely factual grounds, either with respect to predictions unrealized or to past situations represented in an excessively theory-friendly light. From a Marxist point of view, the arbitration of independent evidence is an irrelevant delusion: there is no such thing as *independent* evidence. It is, therefore, perhaps the internal coherence, or contradictions, of the Marxist perspective that is most critical.

Interpreters and followers of Marx have read quite different things into and out of his voluminous work. In the nineteenth and the early twentieth century, when a good deal of it was still unpublished, those describing themselves as Marxist on the whole took the view that economic factors determined everything else. In social theory today, Marxism is hardly a single point of view any more. Though the same sort of terminology is used: people speak of class struggle, modes of production, alienation, surplus value, dialectical relationships, and so forth; there are many different styles of argument and often quite different conclusions reached. One thing they all have in common, despite their substantial disagreements, is that Marx was always correct in anticipating any development in the social order of any new conceptualization with which they are concerned. They may vigorously attack other Marxists' interpretations, but will very rarely admit any observation critical of Marx's own views. It is as though, for many describing themselves as Marxists, the label has assumed the religious significance of revealed, if necessarily interpreted, ultimate truth. In this respect, Marx achieved what Comte set out to do, the establishment of a sociology as a source of meaning and value, a moral binding force in a society where other loyalties of belief and community have withered away.

If, for Marx and his followers, like the earlier evolutionists, the sweep of historical change has been essentially progressive in the movement towards the liberation of mankind, other theorists have foreseen no such enlargement of the human spirit; either because, in their view, change has generally been for the worse or because, in its essentials, the harsh realities of social life have not changed at all. In the next chapter we shall look at two examples of these more pessimistic views which have anticipated, in one way or another, a good deal of the subsequent discussion of social and cultural change.

5

Reactionary Theories: The Loss of Community: The Persistence of Elites

The bodies of theory that we have discussed in the preceding two chapters are, on the whole, optimistic. Revolutionary theorists, it is true, tend to argue that things may first have to get a good deal worse before they get better. But, like evolutionists, they seem to believe in progress. Evolutionary theories point out that things are becoming more advanced, more liberal, democratic or more rational than they were, and may be better yet in times to come. But, to some, social change does seem more a cause for regret, or alarm, rather than for hope.

The emergence of industrial capitalism in the nineteenth century was not only criticized from a radical point of view. To the socialists, however, it was at least a painful, but necessary, step towards a better society in the future. Those conservatives who deplored the threat to the traditional social order, and the traditional values they associated with it, on the other hand, saw the industrial revolution as entailing irreparable loss. The shriek of the locomotives would destroy the peace of the countryside forever. The horses would be frightened, and city ways and city ideas would despoil the innocence of village life and immemorial custom. The horror of the manufacturing towns, of the factories and the railways, associated with the romantic writers of the early nineteenth century, show that concern with the invasion of the traditional rural landscape and way of life, and the loss of natural environmental amenity, is as old as industrialization itself. Much of this response was deeply reactionary, against all change, regardless – as much of it still is today.

Much of the conservative reaction to social change was romantic and aesthetic. A nostalgia for the presumed religious, and other, purities of the Middle Ages is evident in the arts and architecture. In comparison with the advocates of progress, the conservatives showed little sign of theorizing about their concerns and produced little in the way of sociological analysis. However, their views were influential and two important late contributions are briefly examined here. Though neither inspired a school of followers of their own, both have had an extensive influence either directly or indirectly on the development of later sociological thinking, and no discussion of the ways in which social change has been theorized would be complete without their critique.

The first of the two writers to be considered, Tönnies, represents the philosophically idealist and romantic perspective. The second, Pareto, illustrates the less nostalgic position of an aloof materialist. He is equally sceptical about the achievements of progress, but pictures no past era as a preferred golden age.

Tönnies: *gemeinschaft* and *gesellschaft*

Ferdinand Tönnies (1855–1936) was a good man who, at the end of a long life, was deprived of his long-held professorial post at the University of Kiel because of his vocal opposition to anti-Semitism and the Nazis. The outrageous developments in Germany, which he attacked in his late years, must have confirmed, and far exceeded, his worst thoughts about the moral emptiness of modern society. His scepticism about modern society, however, developed early. In his doctoral dissertation, he developed the idealist argument that social phenomena are the products of human thought. Social groups express the collective will of their members through the norms and rules, which regulate actions in line with the shared values of the group. In his great book, *Gemeinschaft und Gesellschaft*, first published in 1887, (published as *Community and Association*, 1955) the same year his doctorate was awarded, he explored the disturbing implications of the change in the character of the collective will which had come about in the course of the transition from feudalism to industrial capitalism.

The title of the work encapsulates the contrast which is the heart of its argument.

The contrast between *gemeinschaft* or community, on the one hand, and *gesellschaft* or association, on the other, is one of different types of social order and different types of human relationships. The English terms, 'community' and 'association', each have so many connotations and different overtones that it is difficult to use them with any precision in sociological discourse. In discussing Tönnies's ideas, therefore, it is usual to keep to the German terms to avoid probable confusion. At the same time, the terms also have a wide range of reference in German, and it will be noticed that *'gesellschaft'* is used to designate a commercial firm which is much more specific than Tönnies appears to have had in mind by his application of the word to a very general concept. Using terms from another language can sometimes be useful in eliminating most of these associations and ambiguities, at least as far as the less polyglot of us are concerned.

Tönnies's contrast is a contrast of ideal-types. That is to say, the argument does not depend upon any particular example of a *gemeinschaft* (community) or *gesellschaft* (association), or of an average of such specific examples. Max Weber, who we shall discuss in the next chapter, was to propose the use of ideal-types as an essential methodology for sociological theorizing. But, as Tönnies illustrates, as a way of thinking about society, the method goes back much further than Weber and, to a certain extent, indeed, may be characteristic of all social theorizing. In devising any typology or categorization, it would seem almost impossible to begin without some such approach, even if the final outcome is something more empirically watertight. But ideal-typical cases are indispensable to thinking about what is distinctive about the members of any general category; about communities or associations, about capitalism or feudalism, social classes, firms, families, and so forth. An ideal-type should be free of the idiosyncrasies and historical peculiarities of particular cases.

The ideal-typical case may be seen as a kind of thought experiment, something with which we can compare reality. It is 'ideal' not because it is desirable or admirable, but because it is only an idea, not a description of any real instance. It is typical because it is composed of all the essential characteristics and no others. What is it we mean when we describe a group or a locality – a village, say – as a community? If we leave out all the particular personalities, the accidental relationships, all the confusing elements, what are the remaining defining features it shares with other communities? The defining features comprise an ideal-typical case. Perhaps no real community exactly corresponds in every respect to this pattern, but it is the extent to which they do that leads us to regard them as communities. As contrasting ideal-types, the *gemeinschaft* and *gesellschaft* are defined as having opposite defining characteristics and as sharing none. A *gemeinschaft* or *gesellschaft*, Tönnies argued, expresses the general will of its members. That is to say, it is the individuals who belong to a group who make it the kind of group that it is. Their beliefs and intentions determine whether it will be one kind of group or another. The ideal-typical cases he contrasted were, therefore, the product of two contrasting kinds of general will: on the one hand, (a) *Natural Will*; and on the other, (b) *Rational Will*. *Natural Will* springs from our common, shared experience. Drawing on a common past, the natural will expresses itself in the consensual, traditional relations of the gemeinschaft. *Rational Will* is orientated towards the future and the effective achievement of specific goals. Where natural will is an expression of shared being, rational will is focused on doing. The rational will is instrumental and is expressed in the contrivance of new means, new organizations, new procedures and relationships which would maximize efficiency rather than intrinsic qualities. It finds no satisfaction in action and relationships valued for their own sake. In the modern world, dominated by commercial, calculative and instrumental values, the *gesellschaft* organizations and the relationships they contain express this rational will:

> In the conception of *gesellschaft* the original or natural relations of human beings to each other must be excluded. (1955, p. 77)

In the ideal-typical *gemeinschaft* community, relationships are valued for their own sake. People encounter one another as whole persons. Economic relations may be a matter of barter or the reciprocal exchange of services. The culture is stable and homogeneous. People share the same, often religious, values with a strong sense of common identity. They will talk of what 'we believe', or what 'we all do' where they live. In their close-knit relationships they play their ascribed roles according to traditionally prescribed expectations. Family, neighbourhood or friendship groups may still have something of this sort of character. In the feudal past, perhaps most people lived out their lives within *gemeinschaftlich* relationships. Industrialization, however, has shifted the emphasis to the *gesellschaft*:

> ... here everybody is by himself and isolated, and there exists a condition of tension against all the others. (1955, p. 64)

In the *gesellschaft*, relationships are segmentary, that is, individuals for the most part know one another only in a particular setting, and not in the other roles they play in life. Relationships are transitory. As we move from place to place, from school to work, from job to job, we lose touch with those we once knew. Above all, *gesellschaft* relationships are instrumental:

> In *gesellschaft* every person strives for that which is to his own advantage and affirms the actions of others only in so far as and as long as they can further his interest. (1955, p. 78)

We associate with other individuals in a particular setting for a particular purpose. When that is accomplished, we go our separate ways. Relationships, as a consequence, tend to be impersonal and impoverished. Intimate personal contact is replaced by relations between strangers. The structural basis for shared norms scarcely exists. With only formal and contractual obligations regulating behaviour, traditional and religious structures break down. *Gemeinschaft* relationships are the fruit of organic growth. They are the unselfconscious and uncontrived expressions of inherited and shared identities. A *gesellschaft* is more like the product of social engineering:

> *Gemeinschaft* should be understood as a living organism, *Gesellschaft* as a mechanical aggregate and artefact. (1955, p. 34)

It is the *gesellschaft* structures deliberately created by the rational will, however, that are the dominant institutions of the modern world.

This polarization of traditional, close-knit, diffuse and particularistic relationships in the *gemeinschaft* and the instrumental, segmentary and impersonal relationships identified with the *gesellschaft*-dominated modern society, was clearly the major source, many years later, of Talcott Parsons's pattern variables, which we will discuss in Chapter 8. A possibly more important theoretical consequence was the influence Tönnies's pessimism had on Max Weber's discussion of the progressive rationalization of the world. We will look at that later in Chapter 6. But the contrast is a powerful and stimulating one which sharply focuses a great deal of diverse human experience. It is one of those sociological formulations that crystallize a lot of things that people encounter in the real world. To give one instance, W. F. Whyte's widely read 1950s study of *The Organization Man* describes the attempts of personnel psychologists and various human resource management experts to create the impression that the identity and feelings of those on the payrolls of the large corporations really matter to their employers. The strategy often favoured is the creation of a sort of pseudo-*gemeinschaft*, the image of the company as just one big, happy family.

Conservative romanticism

Tönnies's description of the dominant values of preindustrial and industrial societies is vivid and persuasive. We can recognize in the rural communities of the past, and sometimes in our own family history, the *gemeinschaftlich* values and relations he identified. And in the commercial and governmental organizations and corporations engaged in industrial production or providing administrative, social welfare or even leisure and entertainment services, we can observe the specialist, calculative values and relationships of our modern, urban, impersonal society. What is lacking is an explanation of why this has come about. Tönnies suggests the cause is the predominance of rational will over natural will in the modern world, but – cause or consequence – we are given no explanation of why it happened. If the description is persuasive, a theory explaining the change is absent.

The contrast between 'natural' and 'rational' here is essentially romantic. Rationality, what men deliberately contrive for themselves, for the improvement of their condition, in other words purposive change, it is suggested, is implicitly unnatural and humanly impoverished. But if we look at the communal solidarity of the morally traditional, emotionally supportive, close-knit and religious *gemeinschaft* community, we should also consider the costs. If we observe the individualistic, segmentary, transitory, emotionally impoverished instrumental relations of the *gesellschaft* type, we should also notice the worldwide preference for modernization, the migration and urbanization of populations, the industrialization of economies, the general preference for at least nominal liberalization and democratization of states. The feudal *gemeinschaft* of lord and peasant, each knowing and respecting their respective traditional rights and privileges, secure in their mutual concern, their time-honoured and hallowed customs and mores, was not merely a community with a low standard of living even for the most privileged. It was a community of entrenched inequality of rank. It was also a community of rigidly intolerant custom, where choice of belief or behaviour was almost inconceivable or harshly discouraged. Social mobility was extremely rare and only to be achieved by exile from friends and family. It was a community ignorant of other customs, of other possibilities, of other communities. The price of unquestioned tradition is intolerance, ignorance and stagnation. Tönnies contrasts the rewards of community, of the natural will, only with the costs of the rational will. These are genuine and high, but the rewards of liberty of thought, or opportunity to pursue one's own inclination, even though the risks of failure are great, may be high too. Then the adaptability of society itself – in the face of a changing environment, population growth, current poverty or the enlargement of human understanding – is possible only within the organizational framework of *gesellschaftlich* relations. To advocate only these benefits and dismiss the human cost is the moral fallacy of liberalism and its still more radical derivatives. To draw attention only to the costs of progress and the virtues of a romanticized *gemutlich* past is the moral fallacy of ideological conservatism. The conservative critique of social change exemplified by Tönnies, and those who share his views, is illuminating in alerting us to the price that has to be paid for modernization, the risks and dangers of the present and future, and of what we stand to lose from the past. But it is necessary to recognize that the virtues of the past were paid for then, and that the price we have to pay today is the cost of benefits we enjoy, which were denied to earlier generations. They are the heads and tails of the same coin, we cannot have one without the other. Tönnies suggests misleadingly that the past and present are one-sided coins.

Pareto: rational and non-rational action

After he gave up business and, in middle age, devoted himself to the social sciences, Vilfredo Pareto (1848–1923) made important contributions to sociology and, especially, to mathematical economics. Outside the economic rationality of models of market behaviour, however, Pareto recognized that much social behaviour was in fact non-rational. The rational calculation of means/end efficiency and optimal utility do not figure much in most of social life. It is not really that people are generally irrational in the sense of being stupid or mad, but rather that what they do isn't always logical given what they say their intentions are. Pareto believed that it was necessary to preserve some degree of scepticism about what people say they are up to.

He argued that the sciences, including the social sciences, should define their concepts in terms of observable realities. Thus, on the basis of 'historical knowledge and careful observation of what people actually do, sociology too can develop a far more perceptive understanding of society than any purely hypothetical speculation about a metaphysical ideal state. As a science, however, sociology cannot claim to offer us solutions to the problems of society. Policies must be determined by goals and should be guided by principles. But these can only reflect the values and the sentiments of policy makers. Scientific sociology will naturally be concerned to understand how values are in practice linked to actions, but has no warrant to say either how they ought to be, nor to prescribe what those values themselves should be. The values, moral principles, concepts and beliefs that people use to justify or to make sense of their actions to other people, or sometimes even to themselves, often have little logical connection with what really motivates them. Pareto argued that people wish to act, or wish to appear to act, rationally and they are therefore ready to offer all sorts of reasons, arguments and explanations for their behaviour: 'Human beings have a very conspicuous tendency to paint a varnish of logic over their conduct' ((1916) 1963, § 154). One of the tasks of sociology is to show how these rationalizations relate to the fundamental states of mind they often serve to mask:

> Logical actions are at least in large part the results of processes of reasoning. Non-logical actions originate chiefly in definite psychic states, sentiments, subconscious feelings, and the like. It is the province of psychology to investigate such psychic states. Here we start with them as data of fact, without going beyond that. (*Mind and Society*, § 161)

When all the theories and justifications are stripped away, Pareto concluded that a residue of basic instincts remained. These he described as *Residues*. The window-dressing of ostensible beliefs and rationalizations, he called *Derivations*.

There are, of course an infinite number of Derivations. They equal, that is to say, they equate to the limitless range of beliefs that people have used to explain their behaviour. There are, however, only six basic kinds of residues:

1. the instinct for combinations;
2. the instinct for the persistence of aggregates;
3. the need to express sentiments by external acts;
4. residues connected with sociability;
5. the instinct to preserve the identity of the individual;
6. sexual residues.

(*Mind and Society*, Book II)

Psychologically the instinct for combinations (class (i) residues) is concerned with seeing relationships and associating things together. We cannot help ordering and structuring our experience of the external world. Like tracing the shapes of constellations in what at first appears to be the random scatter of stars in the night sky, the human mind is naturally given to finding patterns, correspondences, relationships and meanings in the stream of events and sense impressions it encounters. Human beings therefore do not merely react to circumstances. They are instinctively inclined to scheme and plan and coordinate their actions so as to impose some sense upon their world, in other words, to discover or construct associations of ideas and actions. This instinct for combinations is the underlying basis of our means/ends purposive behaviour and of social organization in general. Equally basic, in Pareto's view, is the instinct for what he termed the persistence of aggregates (Class (ii) residues). We are constitutionally inclined, he held, to cling to our first impressions, to maintain established structures of ideas and action, to continue with familiar routines. It is how we cope with the inherent unpredictability of life. Our instinct is to make the world seem familiar and therefore more manageable. Sociologically, this instinct is the basis of cultures and tradition, of social control and social order. The other residues are more or less self-explanatory: the need to express ourselves; the need for social contact with other people; self-protection; the sexual instinct. All motivate people's actions at one time or another, singly or in combination, with different degrees of urgency and priority. It may be noted in passing that, in contrast with Freudian theory, Pareto believed that sexual drives (class (vi) residues) were only one sort of basic motivation among others. In general, however, the explanations people give for doing what they are doing, no matter how seemingly rational, whether religious, moral, metaphysical, apparently scientific, or just commonsensical, are derivations. If we want to know what really motivates them, what we must look for are the underlying residues.

This argument has some affinity with Marx's notion of ideology, but Pareto was critical of Marxist theory as too narrowly economic. Class struggles, he argued, have not always been about conflicts over the means of production. Conflicts between classes, between the magnates and the lesser gentry, court and country interests, merchants and landowners, even between financial and manufacturing capital, have often been more obviously about the exercise of military force, or more directly over the control of the state. Marxism itself he believed to be the ideology of a new elite seeking to rise to power on the backs of the proletariat. The derivations are expressed in the political slogans, the residues (mainly residues (i) and (ii)) are those concerned with the pursuit of power.

The circulation of elites

The most important aspect of society, for Pareto, is the power structure. What distinguishes one society from another is what sort of people rule. In all societies there is a fundamental division between the ruling *elite* and the masses:

> So we get two strata in a population: (1) a lower stratum, the *non-elite* with whose possible influence on government we are not just here concerned; then (2) a higher stratum, the *elite*, which is divided into two: (a) a governing *elite*; (b) a non-governing *elite*.' (*Mind and Society*, § 2034)

The non-elite masses may be either content or miserable, creative or downtrodden, peasants or artisans, but everything they do is influenced by the actions of the elite who rule them. Ousting a ruling elite merely replaces it with another from the non-governing elite. After the revolution to overthrow capitalism, Pareto argued, the result would only be the creation of a new privileged elite claiming to represent the proletariat. As things turned out in Russia, he was, of course, right. Ruling elites in time, however, become decadent. The abilities and ruthlessness, which gave them the capacity to seize and hold on to power, relax or become diluted over the generations. They become civilized or complacent and their grip weakens:

> They decay not in numbers only. They decay also in quality, in the sense that they lose their vigour, that there is a decline in the proportion of the residues which enabled them to win their power and hold it. The governing class is restored not only in numbers, but – and that is the more important thing – in quality, by families rising from the lower classes and bringing with them the vigour and the proportions of residues necessary for keeping themselves in power. It is also restored by the loss of its more degenerate members
> (*Mind and Society*, § 2054)

The dominance of an elite may be strengthened by the loss of the more feeble from their ranks as the dim and incompetent descendants of some of the founding robber barons decline into mediocrity. More directly, the absorption of the ambitious and vigorous elements from the masses can help to shore up and prolong the life of the *ancien régime*. But these inward and outward movements tend to be resisted as respect for an admired name is extended to its later, less admirable bearers, and the resentment of upstarts discourages the acceptance of new blood. Elite renewal perpetuates the existing order, but social conflict arises from the accumulation of superior elements in the lower classes and of inferior elements in the governing class:

> Revolutions come about through accumulations in the higher strata of society – either because of a slowing down in class circulation or from other causes – of decadent elements no longer possessing the residues suitable for keeping them in power, and shrinking from the use of force; while meantime in the lower strata of society elements of superior quality are coming to the fore, possessing residues suitable for exercising the functions of government and willing enough to use force.   (*Mind and Society*, § 2057)

Ruling groups cling to power, but with the elapse of time, sooner or later, power slips through their fingers, or is torn from their grasp, by more determined successors: 'History,' Pareto commented, 'is the graveyard of aristocracies'(*Mind and Society*, § 2053).

Pareto's account of society is focused almost entirely on power and who holds it. The crucial factor here is the psychology of those who comprise the elite and of those prepared to displace them. The potential for conflict is a perennial feature of social order, but does not have to destroy society itself. An equilibrium is maintained by the renewal, or replacement, of the dominant elite and with it the continuity of power. In this cyclical process Pareto identified two recurring and alternating types of elite, which he labelled Lions and Foxes. These, he argued, represented the different kinds of residues that predominate among ruling groups.

The rule of Lions is based on the use of force or the threat of force. Lions are elite groups that take power, even when it is by invitation or election, because they are known to be prepared, if necessary, to resort to violence. They appeal to the revulsion against the devious and self-serving politicians. They proclaim themselves to be the upholders of incorruptible standards and traditional values. They display a motivational and behavioural pattern strong in class (ii) residues – the persistence of aggregates.

The Foxes, on the other hand, rule by guile and cunning. They are innovators and political manipulators, who find the workable compromise when situations reach deadlock. They get things working again after the inflexibility of the Lions has brought the give and take of ordinary political management to a standstill. Their actions reveal their predominantly class (i) residues – the instinct for combinations. An elite with a balance of class (i) and class (ii) residues is likely to be the most effective (1963, Book IV) but the balance is hard to maintain. The other residues they share with the rest of humanity may give a distinctive character to one elite or another, for example. the evidently low level of class (iii) residues among the classical Chinese mandarin class, the high level of class (iv) residues in the ruling families of the city states of Renaissance Italy, or the comparative strength of class (vi) residues at the Restoration court of Charles the Second. But these are very rarely of any significance in terms of the tenacity of their hold on power.

Pareto argued that, historically, there has been a tendency for the two types of elite, Lions and Foxes, to alternate in a cycle of political change. The history of military *coups* in developing societies, when the colonels decide that the corrupt politicians can no longer be tolerated and take over in the belief that order and military discipline can restore society, is the continuation of an ancient pattern. Cromwell and the major-generals' takeover of the Commonwealth parliament, Caesar's march on Rome are examples of a very numerous kind. But if the regime they establish is to last and not to ossify, the Lions need to bring in the political talents and administrative adroitness of Foxes willing to serve. But the Foxes in due course become indispensable and gradually assume commanding influence over all the key elite positions. The old revolution-aries may still appear on the balconies in their medals on state occasions, but the *éminences grise*, the bureaucrats and committee men, wield the real power. And, eventually, the uniforms and the conservative facade are abandoned in favour of innovation and progress. The ruling class has become an elite of Foxes. The liberalism and scepticism of the era of Fox rule are vulnerable to external and internal threat. Lions thrive on real, or imagined, threat and will engage in external adventures if their hold on political affairs at home seems to be slipping, so as to demonstrate the need their nation has of them. The brinkmanship of the Cold War may be seen in this light, while the 1983 Argentinian military junta's invasion of the Falklands was an ultimately unsuccessful example of this tactic. Foxes, however, seek to avoid direct confrontrations and overt conflict. So even a small minority willing to make use of violence may capture the state, as the Bolshevik October *coup* against the democratic Duma under Kerensky in Russia in 1917 illustrated. To protect themselves the Foxes may recruit their own Lions. Generals or workers' leaders may be brought into governments of career politicians. But Lions do not cope well with wheeler-dealer politics and are likely to reject compromises to seek the simple, decisive solution. As allies of the Foxes, they become impatient with trimming political solutions, abandon their untrustworthy allies, and make a direct appeal for faith in the nation, religion or the revolution. So the cycle continues.

It will be noted that democracy, nationalism, religious belief, socialism, freedom, brotherhood, reason, tradition and so forth, in this analysis, are all treated as derivations. The political doctrines based on them, Pareto regarded as rationalizations used to win the support of the gullible in the endless struggle for rule:

> ... an individual who has inherited a sizeable patrimony can easily be named Senator in certain countries, or can get himself elected to parliament by buying votes, or, on occasion, by wheedling voters with assurances that he is a democrat of democrats, a socialist, an anarchist ...
> (*Mind and Society*, § 2036)

The alternating balance of the residues, the instincts that govern non-rational action, are however what drives the continuing circulation of elites.

Conservative cynicism

In economic terms, the Lions, defending tradition, tend to be associated with, or drawn from, the landowning classes. The Foxes are speculators, innovators, bargainers and are more likely to be drawn from a merchant or professional background (1963, Book IV). Pareto's psychologically based theory rather neglects the significance of these social background factors and the possible structural determination of motivation. To give social determinants greater weight would also entail a less dismissive attitude toward the actual content and meaning of what he dismisses as derivations. The persuasiveness of Pareto's argument, after all, lies very much in his capacity to reveal the truth hidden behind all the pious sentiments and stirring rhetoric. And the apparent truth he reveals depends upon the disparagement of all the surface arguments so as to expose the underlying political motivations at the level of the instinctive, non-rational residues.

Without denying the technological changes and economic growth, and the social developments that obsessed the sociological theorists of the nineteenth and early twentieth centuries, Pareto chose to emphasize the essential continuities of social experience: in particular, (i) the predominance of non-rational, non-logical thought and action; and (ii) the enduring fact of the domination of the mass of the population by a ruling elite. The character of the ruling group may change from time to time. Elites decay as the ambition and abilities, the vigour and ruthlessness of their founders fade. They are then liable to be deposed and replaced by some emergent counter-elite. But regardless of the ideological rationale offered (the derivations), the group is always primarily concerned with its own self-perpetuation and the maintenance of its own privileges and, above all, with its own continuity in power. As Pareto observed: 'All governments use force and all assert that they are founded upon reason' (1963, § 2183).

In his book, *The Ruling Class* (1896), Gaetano Mosca had already argued that there is always a ruling class, which was strengthened by the recruitment of the able and the ambitious, on the one hand, and the elimination from it of the feeble and the feckless, on the other. However, Mosca's identification of the ruling class was in terms of a set of ruling positions in a structure of unequal relationships. Pareto's analysis deals with persons rather than positions. His elites come and go. He believed there would always be groups or individuals who intimidated or inveigled their fellow citizens into subordination, but that, nevertheless, these ruling groups might be replaced. His is a theory of change, of ineffective change it is true, but of change through the cycle of the circulation of elites. For Mosca, on the other hand, a change of personnel is of no significance. The positions which comprise the ruling class are part of the social system and are not subject to change except from exogenous intervention. The circulation of Pareto's elites changes the outward character of society, the age of reason gives way to the era of faith. This cyclical movement may bring about, or at least facilitate, real long-term changes in the culture or the economy as innovations are retained and built on or, alternatively, progress gives way to stagnation. But the political inequality of elite domination of the mass is unchanged by the circulation of elites. There may be more liberalism with the Foxes in power, more risk of intolerance under the Lions, but human society, from the ancient kingdoms and the vanished empires to the present day, remains essentially similar in this respect. Elites rule.

Thus where, for Tönnies, modern society represented a major change and a change for the worse; for Pareto, though modernization was real enough economically or technologically, because mankind is essentially non-rational, these processes are not fundamentally important and change nothing that already is. Elite rule of the masses continues, inevitably, as before.

Tönnies's idealist argument that the normative structures of social relations and social groups are expressions of human will is obviously consensus rather than conflict orientated. His descriptive analysis contrasting ideal-typical sociocultural patterns, however, is sociologically realist. Ideal-typical analysis, taken by itself, is a rationalist procedure and his, very general, assumption that the essential tendency of modernity is toward the predominance of the rational will would seem to be, on the whole, an historicist position. The one-sidedness of Tönnies's evaluation of the social costs of modernization is, furthermore, in effect strongly ideological.

Pareto's position can be sharply contrasted with Tönnies's in most respects. He, however, can also be designated a sort of historicist, though his overall view of history is cyclical rather than linear. Nevertheless, although, in contrast with Marxist or evolutionist teleology, no end-state is posited, the future is, in essentials, known. In contrast with Tönnies's approach, the circulation of elites, a conflict model of history, is explained in methodological individualist terms and is rooted in a materialist psychology of non-rational residues rather than in the expression of the ideas, which merely serve to rationalize them as derivations. In the discussion of non-rational action, the identification of concepts on the basis of observed behaviour rather than arbitrarily appears to be broadly empiricist in approach, and the description of the circulation of elites is based in extensive historical case material. Pareto's use of historical evidence to substantiate his argument and the analysis of residues and derivations also appears to be scientific in intent. His views sustain little admiration for any party or interest group and, on that score, might not be adjudged ideological. They are, however, cynical and, in focusing on the unchanging fact of elite domination, rule out of account all potentially significant change *a priori*. Pareto tells us that nothing really important ever changes, and backs up his case by saying that anything that changes isn't really important. That may not be non-logical thinking, but it looks as though it is a conclusion that has been settled before the argument was ever begun, and that is what finally makes it ideological too, since the present order of things would appear to be as good as anything we might swap it for.

The writers discussed in this chapter reacted negatively to social change, but in different ways. The one, Tönnies, responded with dismay at the social and cultural costs of modernization. The other, Pareto, with apparent indifference to the price to be paid, argued that, because rule by one elite or another is unavoidable, change leads us nowhere but in circles. In the next chapter, we turn to a writer – Weber – who, rather like the former, saw the emergence of modern industrial capitalism as a tragic moral paradox and, rather like the latter, believed that the structure of power was the central organizing principle which determined the character of society. He argued, however, that historical social change could only be understood in terms of the purposive activity of people guided by authentic values in the pursuit of human freedom and reason.

6

Social Action Theory: Weber

Weber's methodological individualism

The key to understanding the work of Max Weber (1846–1920) and the value of his approach to sociology both lie in his methodological individualism, the conviction that, in the end, any account of society must be grounded in the intelligible activity of individuals. Weber was the greatest exponent of methodological individualism within the framework of a scientific method and had a most profound influence upon subsequent developments in sociological thought. All his more concrete or substantive interests were not merely influenced by this point of view, but are expressions of its implications in the real world. It is a perspective which embodies the values to which Weber was most deeply committed and which not only inspired his thinking, but also determined its limits. It is therefore worthwhile looking at this aspect of his thought in some detail, before we move on to examine how it shaped Weber's ideas about social change.

In Weber's view, the social sciences differ from natural science because they are about people. The molecules in a chemical reaction do not care about one another, do not choose whether to bond or not. The molecular code is automatic. But the objects social scientists study involve people's conscious or unconscious feelings and ideas. The people themselves, the cultural objects they produce and the cultural practices they follow are meaningful to the actors involved. The way they act and interact makes some kind of sense to them. The social sciences therefore confront a different sort of problem from the natural sciences. They have to acknowledge, Weber argued, the meaningful character of their subject matter. Social scientific explanations cannot be solely in terms of *causes* and effects, they have to take into account the *reasons* people have for acting the way they do. To be convincing, that is, they have also to be adequate at the level of meaning.

For Weber, then, <u>sociology is the science of social action</u>. It is the *science* of social action because, although each of us has his or her own preferences and prejudices, and our interests are guided by what is of cultural and biographical significance to us, it is nevertheless possible to strive for some detachment about the assumptions and values to which our social being commits us. These values, religious, cultural, moral, political, and so forth, direct our interest in, or away from, social and sociological questions in the first place. After all, many people prefer to devote themselves to gardening, music or shopping. At the same time, though it is far from easy, we should be wary of our values not only drawing our attention towards certain questions, but also prescribing what answers we are likely to find acceptable or, indeed, are capable of recognizing. The issue, as Weber saw it, was the evident need to remain constantly on guard against blurring the distinction between empirical findings and one's own feelings or evaluative judgements about them. (See 'Science as a Vocation', in Gerth and Wright Mills (eds), 1967.) The sciences are necessarily *value-relevant*, at least to the scientists themselves, or else nobody would bother, but they must at the same time be *value-free*, or else they would amount to nothing more than <u>elaborate ways of confirming existing prejudices</u>. Sociology is scientific precisely to the extent that, in the search for explanations, sociologists are committed to objectivity, to the belief that they should acknowledge valid and reliable evidence, however personally inconvenient or distasteful it might be. Otherwise, the account which is produced is merely fiction or propaganda but not science, and not sociology, at least as Weber understood it.

But sociology is the science of *social action*. Being concerned with *action* rather than with behaviour in general, it addresses not just anything that people might do, but what they <u>do purposively</u>. Being concerned with *social* action it focuses on <u>how they act in relation to one another</u>. In this formula we have two of the central assumptions of Weber's sociology. First, his approach seeks to root any account of social situations firmly in the actions of individuals, not in the general operation of some abstract collectivity. Secondly, this interactive, purposive activity is essentially *meaningful* to the individuals themselves.

Weber also distinguished between rational action and non-rational action. *Non-rational Actions* may be simply: (a) *traditional*, following custom or meeting everyday expectations; or (b) *emotionally* driven, acting upon impulse or the expression of a person's feelings. The relative lack of conscious purpose in non-rational actions sometimes robs them of the meaningful character of deliberate action and they may verge upon mere behaviour. The two types of *Rational Action* he distinguished are more clearly consistent with Weber's own definition of social action:

a. **Instrumentally rational action** (*zweckrational* in Weber's terminology) is the kind of action directed towards attaining some specific objective. We work together to decorate the hall for the Welcome Home Party on Saturday. That would be social, purposive and rational because it would be an efficient way to achieve our common objective.

b. **Value rational action** is the expression of a value, religious or political or whatever, because that is the right thing to do, regardless of the consequences. So one may join a demonstration, write to the papers, make a stand. This, on the one hand, may sometimes seem hard to tell from emotional or affective action, on the other, the difference from instrumental rationality isn't entirely clear-cut either. So one might also argue that this type of action actually has a communicative purpose, to let the bureaucrats know we disapprove, to show there are still some honest people around, and so forth.

The line is also hard to draw between subjectively meaningful action and other behaviour. Customary action may be hard to distinguish from habit. The line between emotional impulse and emotionally motivated action is easily crossed. However, as far as Weber was concerned, social action is behaviour directed towards a goal (therefore *action*, not mere reaction), which is guided by the actions and anticipated actions of other people (that is what makes it social). Because it and the reciprocal actions it takes into account are goal directed, social action is meaningful and can be *understood* (in German *verstehen*) as well as explained. That is to say, one can discover reasons for social action in addition to seeking causes. This *verstehen*, empathy with the subjects of historical inquiry, is a vital element in a truly insightful reconstruction of the past. However, historiography differs from historical romance, or other fiction, because it does not stop at getting a feeling for the situation. That is only the beginning of scholarship. The social sciences might be different from the other sciences in subject and method, but not in the essentials of objectivity:

> ... the situation is absolutely identical in such fields of knowledge as mathematics and the natural sciences ... They all begin as hypotheses, flashes of imaginative 'intuition', and are then 'verified' against the facts – that is, their 'validity' is tested by means of the empirical knowledge which has already been acquired and they are 'formulated' in a logically correct form. The same is true of history.
> (Weber (1906), in Runciman (ed.), 1978, p. 121)

Thus the concern with meaning and the subjective experience of people in history is not instead of an interest in causes, but in addition to such a quest. Furthermore, Weber's insistence on the reality of meaning, and therefore for a sociology concerned with people's reasons for action, is not a call for a literal-minded empiricism of motive. In *Economy and Society* ((1920) 1968, pp. 21–2), he puts the matter in methodological perspective:

> The theoretical concepts of sociology are ideal types not only from the objective point of view, but also in their application to subjective processes. In the great majority of cases actual action goes on in a state of inarticulate half-consciousness or actual unconsciousness of its subjective meaning. The actor is more likely to 'be aware' of it in a vague sense than he is to 'know' what he is doing or be explicitly self-conscious about it. In most cases his action is governed by impulse or habit. Only occasionally and, in the uniform action of large numbers, often only in the case of a few individuals, is the subjective meaning of the action, whether rational or irrational, brought clearly into consciousness.

Thus *verstehen* should not be taken too literally. Weber was interested in the ideal-typical understandings of the ideal-typical individual in a given situation, not in the unarticulated, half-unconscious, vague ideas of the real protagonists. Weber's point is that action may be rational, and intelligible because it is inherently rational, even though the actor does not articulate –

neither for other people, nor even perhaps for himself – the essential rationality of his actions. He may feel he is 'just getting on with things' without conscious thought, but still be acting rationally in terms of his real interests or goals.

Weber's Puritans or bureaucrats are not discovered as a result of attitude surveys, they are not averages of the views and actions of real individuals, but intellectual constructs purporting to show what such a person in that setting and acting rationally would do or think, regardless of whether anyone was ever in that position and did in fact act that way. They are not historical descriptions, but explanatory theoretical hypotheses (ideal-types) against which we can examine the actual historical outcomes.

Runciman argues that what is distinctive in Weber's views about the social and natural sciences is his reluctance to accept, on the one hand, that there is no difference at all or, on the other hand, that they are so different that they cannot adhere to the same scientific principles: 'This compromise view does not itself escape some serious objections. But it has the overriding merit of taking seriously the most persuasive of the arguments of both sides' (1978, p. 65).

Ideas and social change

Weber started out as an economic historian, making large-scale studies of rural labour in East Prussia, the agrarian economy of ancient Rome and of mediaeval trading companies. These interests were not as remote as they may seem from his concern with the late industrialization of his own country. They helped to clarify the issues of large-scale social change. Social change was rapid in late-nineteenth-century Germany. Weber's commitment to the civilized values he identified with German culture meant that he thought the country needed to be united and strong if they were to be upheld. This demanded the industrialization of the predominantly rural economy so as both to stand on at least equal terms with her western neighbours France and England, but, at the same time, to resist the encroachments of growing Slav nationalism, all too evident in the nineteenth-century expansionist policy of Tsarist Russia in the east. His loyalty was to the values of the Enlightenment, of Goethe and Kant: individualism and the rule of reason, expressed in a commitment to German culture, which he believed enshrined those values.

Like the other great sociologists of nineteenth-century Europe, Weber was stirred by the transformation of society brought about by the emergence of industrial capitalism. Weber's studies in economic history focused his attention on the historical uniqueness of this process. Capitalism, in one form or another, has existed in many societies. *Financial Capitalism* is very ancient. Moneylenders in medieval Europe and in traditional rural India lived on the interest earned from the loans they made. *Adventure Capitalism* also existed in earlier societies, where merchant adventurers lived well off their high-risk, high-profit trading ventures, retiring if successful to set themselves up as landowners and gentlemen. Almost legendary examples include Ralegh's expeditions to the Americas and Sir Richard (Dick) Whittington's perhaps apocryphal feline investments. *Mercantilist Capitalism* has generally been the practice of courts, where monarchs granted trading monopolies in some commodity or for some market, patents and exclusive state contracts to those they favoured. The difference between these and modern *Industrial Capitalism* is that none of them altered the basic structure of the societies they operated within. Unlike them, industrial capitalism is, in present-day terms, a non-zero sum system. It isn't a closed share-out of a fixed amount of wealth, it is a system of continuous trans-formational growth.

It was in modern western Europe that industrial capitalism became the dominant social form, displacing other modes of exploiting the resources of the economy, and increasingly involving all sectors of society, all aspects of social relations and spreading outward to dominate the whole world. In Germany, France and elsewhere among the later industrial capitalist states, in Russia and Japan for instance, this was at least initiated by direct state intervention and direction. That was largely a political reaction to the economic power of the earliest industrial societies, especially Britain, which came to dominate the world in industrial manufacturing in the 1840s and 1850s. That was easy enough to understand given the existence of industrial capitalism already. Weber, however, believed the really difficult problem for the social sciences was to account for that initial beginning, primarily in England, from which all the rest followed. For those who have been concerned with subsequent development in newly industrializing countries, however, focus upon Weber's argument has thus been a largely misleading distraction.

In his *General Economic History*, Weber reviewed a variety of possible explanations for the emergence of modern capitalism. Macfarlane has neatly summarized his argument:

> He rejected the crudely technological and materialistic ones: colonial trade, population growth, the inflow of precious metals. He then isolated some of the necessary but not sufficient 'external conditions', the particular geography of Europe with its cheap transportation by water, the favourable military requirements of the small states, the large luxury demand from an unusually prosperous population. Ultimately, it was not these external factors, but something more mysterious that was important. It was the ethic, the justification of the pursuit of profit.   (1987, p. 172)

Weber's social action approach required that the emergence of capitalism should be intelligible. The explanation, that is to say, should be adequate at the level of understanding, in terms of the social action of individuals. Weber stated:

> In the last resort, the factor which produced capitalism is the rational permanent enterprise, rational accounting, rational technology and rational law, but, again, not these alone. Necessary complementary factors were the rational spirit, the rationalization of the conduct of life in general and a rationalist economic ethic.   (1920) p. 354

Rationality is what is distinctive about capitalism not mere acquisitiveness or greed. Weber wrote:

> 'Acquisitiveness', or the 'pursuit of profit, of monetary gain', has in itself nothing to do with capitalism. It is and has been found among waiters, doctors, coachmen, artists, tarts, venal officials, soldiers, brigands, crusaders, frequenters of gambling dens, beggars – one might say 'among all sorts and conditions of men', in all ages and in all countries of the world, wherever the objective possibility for it has existed or still exists in any form. Such a naive definition ought to have been given up once and for all at the nursery stage of cultural history. Unbridled avarice has no resemblance whatsoever to capitalism, still less its 'spirit'. Capitalism may actually amount to the taming, or

at least the rational moderation, of this irrational impulse. At all events, capitalism is the same as the pursuit of profit by means of continuing rational capitalistic enterprise: that is, for the constant *renewal* of profit, or *profitability*.

((1920) quoted in Runciman (ed.), 1978, p. 333)

This rational calculation of profit and loss, and the margin of return on capital risked, is an attitude of mind that is rarely encountered in the history of human cultures. This is no slavish following of tradition – never mind if we have always done things that way, will it still pay? Affective behaviour, spontaneous emotional reaction, is contrary to its calculating spirit. Equally alien is the *wertrational* action of those who want to bear witness to the values they believe in, regardless of the cost or the outcome. Thrift, investment and profitability are the keys to capitalist accumulation. But how did such attitudes come to overshadow hedonism, enjoyment, extravagance, fecklessness, benevolence and indulgence? What was the source of that rational pursuit of profit which ensured that these human weaknesses (and strengths) should not waste whatever luck and hard work might gather. Weber pointed to what was already apparent to contemporary observers in the seventeenth century:

This has already been emphasized by Petty in his *Political Arithmetick*; all the contemporary sources without exception speak especially about the members of the Puritan sects (Baptists, Quakers, Mennonites) as belonging to a stratum of society which was partly without resources and partly consisted of small capitalists, contrasting them both with the aristocracy of great merchants and with financial adventurers. It was precisely this stratum of small capitalists, however, not the great financiers, the monopolists, state contractors, state moneylenders, colonial entrepreneurs, promoters and so forth, which was responsible for the characteristic feature of western capitalism – the bourgeois private enterprise organization of industrial labour.

(quoted in Runciman (ed.), 1978, p. 164)

The identification of industrial capitalism not just with a class but in a distinctive religiously sectarian movement gave Weber the heart of his argument. The emergence of that rational ethic, indispensable

to the development of industrial capitalism, was closely associated
with the rational religious ethic of the Puritans. They not only
appeared on the stage of history at about the same time, but often
were themselves directly active in setting up the commercial and
industrial enterprises of early capitalism. For the Puritan:

> The working life of man is to be a consistent ascetic exercise
> in virtue, a proof of one's state of grace in the conscientious-
> ness which is apparent in the careful and methodical way in
> which one follows one's calling. Not work as such, but
> rational work in a calling, is what God requires. In the
> Puritan idea of the 'calling' the emphasis is always on this
> methodical asceticism in the practice of one's calling, not,
> as in Luther, on contentment with the lot once and for all
> assigned to one by God. Hence, not only will the question
> whether anyone can combine several callings be answered
> with an unconditional 'yes', provided it is beneficial either
> for the general good or for one's own and not injurious to
> anyone else, and provided that it does not lead to
> unconscientiousness or 'unfaithfulness' in one of the callings
> so combined. But also it will not be regarded as in any way
> in itself objectionable to change one's calling, provided it is
> not done frivolously but in order to take up a calling which
> will be more pleasing to God, that is, in accordance with
> the general principle, a more useful one.   (Weber, 1905)

This distinctive religious ethic, Weber argued, was to be found
only in the Protestant countries of north-west Europe. In order to
understand its affinity with the rational conduct of capitalist
business, in some of his later work Weber made a close examination
of the other-worldly orientation of Indian religions and the
traditional religions of ancient China which, in both cases,
appeared, by contrast, to have inhibited economic development.
The Confucianism of Imperial China was a worldly religion,
concerned with good conduct and our duties in the world. Unlike
Puritanism, however, it was deeply traditionalist rather than
innovative. The acquisition of wealth was approved, but trade and
commerce were considered ungentlemanly and too sordid for the
spiritual life. The Confucian family ethic too was very strong, with
emphasis on one's ancestors and kinsmen and a consequent distrust
of strangers, again in sharp contrast with the Puritans' emphasis

on the community of all the faithful (Weber, 1957.) The other-worldly religions of India, Hinduism and Buddhism, tend to emphasize withdrawal from the practical matters of everyday life. Holiness is achieved by transcendence, by detachment from this false and transitory world of mere appearances. This-worldliness is a snare and a corruption of true spirituality, and should be avoided as far as possible by the sincere believer. While the mundane concerns of everyday life are unavoidable for the majority of people, the other, spiritual world is still a major influence for the devout Hindu or Buddhist. Prayer, sacrificial offerings, magical charms or fortune-telling may all be resorted to in order to bring about a desired result in one's daily life. So to ensure the birth of a son, success in love or business, a pass in an important examination, or to win a court-case, the intervention of the spiritual world is invoked (Weber, 1958). In traditional Indian belief systems, Weber argued, there was an absence of the opposition between 'the divine' and 'the world' which, in the west, made the rationalization of conduct in *this* world entirely a *human* responsibility (but see W. Davis, 1987).

In contrast with eastern transcendentalism, in the Christian west one's conduct in this world matters much more. The very notion of God in the world is central to the Christian message. But the traditional Catholic view of conduct governed by grace, by the forgiveness of sin through penance and the intercession of priests and saints, Weber held, was not conducive to the rationalization of conduct either. Sin and indulgence which can be retrieved by confession and penance focuses attention away from our conduct here to sacred intercession and the divine.

Some may ask how the religion of God's love, of that Christ who cast out the money-changers from the Temple, who said it was easier for a camel to pass through the eye of a needle than for a rich man to enter the Kingdom of Heaven, could possibly justify capitalist accumulation. Catholicism and even some of the Lutheran Protestant sects encouraged a pious, but essentially passive acceptance of the Will of God. In His disposition of worldly positions, we are born high or lowly and should accept His Will and His Mercy. In contrast, the Puritan sects encouraged a quite different orientation to the world. Influenced particularly by the teachings of John Calvin (1509–1564) on predestination, Puritans believed it was their duty to glorify God by striving to make the most of the 'calling' in which they found themselves in this world that they might be sure of their salvation in the next. We can find the ethic of self-denial, of this-worldly asceticism, in the doctrine of duty to labour in the Lord's vineyard or in St Matthew's parable of the good servant, who used his talents to the Lord's greater glory while the less gifted servant, who did nothing with his talent, was cast into outer darkness:

> For unto every one that hath shall be given, and he shall have abundance: but from him that hath not shall be taken away even that which he hath. (St Matthew, 25, vv. 14–30)

We can see how the Puritan doctrine of self-denial, of this-worldly asceticism, plain living and the dignity, indeed the sanctity, of work produces not only a productive and conscientious worker and trader, but is also conducive to the accumulation and reinvestment of income instead of its present enjoyment. Wealth too must be made to work, to glorify the works of God by putting them to the most diligent use.

Yet what we have here is not an account of how any one individual Puritan felt, or what he believed, but an abstraction, an account of an ideal-typical Puritan, a serious, sober, industrious man. From careful consideration of how he would have acted, it becomes possible to observe the extent to which the actual historical events, as they have unfolded, manifest a rational, though obscured, pattern rather than a mere chapter of accident and fortuitous circumstances.

In his account of the role of religious ideas in the emergence of industrial capitalism amongst the Puritans of seventeenth-century England, it is, of course, a crude misrepresentation to represent Weber as opposing an idealist account of social change to the materialism of Marxist theories. On the one hand, modern Marxist writers reject as mere vulgar-Marxism the economic determinism which most late-nineteenth- and early-twentieth-century Marxists, perhaps following Engels's interpretation of his friend's work, emphasized. It is probably fair to say that it was this 'materialist conception of history' that Weber was trying to criticize in his own work. On the other hand, his emphasis on the importance of beliefs was not intended as a denial of the importance of material factors in historical explanation,

We have no intention whatever of maintaining such a foolish

and doctrinaire thesis as that the spirit of capitalism ... could only have arisen as a result of certain effects of the Reformation, or even that capitalism as an economic formation is the creation of the Reformation. (Weber, 1905)

Material economic conditions were of course crucial causal factors in the development of industrial capitalism. It is just that ideas and values, including religious beliefs, play an important role too, especially in relation to the reasons for men and women beginning to act in a new way so as to bring about a new social order.

It is interesting to contrast Weber's treatment of religious belief with that of Marx and Durkheim. For Marx and Engels, religion was the expression of material interests. They termed religion 'the opiate of the masses', and argued that it served directly ideological purposes. For Durkheim, religion was the expression and projection of collective identity, not simply of economic collectivities or their justification, but of any moral community. For Weber, religious ideas had a degree of autonomy, not mere reflections of material or ideal interests, though selected in terms of some elective affinity with them. But ideas also have an independent role in guiding action if not necessarily determining it and, above all, are necessary for an *understanding* of how action may align with interests, of what sense people make of their motivations. In this, Weber's position resembles Pareto's interpretation of derivations (which we discussed in Chapter 5), except that, for Weber, the actual rational content of belief plays a much more significant part.

Weber's theory of the role of the Protestant Ethic, really the Puritan ethic, has been enormously influential both in historical analysis and as applied, retroactively as it were, to the present. Weiner's powerful indictment of British economic decline, from its apogee as 'the workshop of the world' in the 1850s to the status of a second- or third-rate industrial power, is based on his assumption that the Protestant work ethic had given way before the public-school ethos of gentlemanly ineffectuality. (Wiener, 1981).

It is perhaps unfortunate, given the persuasive power of the Weber thesis, that it has turned out to be wrong in almost every respect. MacKinnon's argument that Weber's account of Calvinist theology is wrong (MacKinnon, 1988) may in itself not be too damaging a criticism if what the Puritans believed in practice was

what mattered. However, that is also very doubtful, for Macfarlane
has shown that, at least in England, the characteristics of
individualism long predate either the industrial revolution or the
Protestant Reformation with which, according to Weber, they are
supposed to be associated. 'A world of individual private property,
of contract, of high social and geographical mobility, of decisions
made by the individual rather than the family, of constant choice
and weighing of advantages', was clearly evident in mediaeval times
(Macfarlane, 1978 and 1987). It is also clear that both Calvinist
countries like Scotland, where the Kirk obstructed commercial
development, and Catholic centres of capitalist trade and industry,
like Flanders and Lombardy, do not fit the thesis at all. G. R. Elton
concluded that:

> There is no good reason for linking Protestantism and
> capitalism in significant relationship ... Looked at with an
> open mind, the whole idea of a meaningful correlation, even
> geographical coincidence, of these historical phenomena
> simply disappears.
>   (Elton, 1963, p. 318; see also Trevor-Roper, 1972)

Weber's argument then, according to more recent and more
thorough historical scholarship, was wrong. But, as with Marx, the
nature of the argument may be more significant than the accuracy
of its conclusions. The importance of Weber lies in his methodological starting point. First explorers do not leave the best maps.
Weber's work remains interesting, and even controversial, because
of the questions he raises about the role of ideas and the
rationalization of the world. This is most evident in his analysis of
the role of structures of power and authority in fostering or resisting
social change. This is not confined to the first emergence of industrial
capitalism, but has a continuing relevance for the present day, both
at the level of large-scale social processes and in terms of the ordinary
experience of individuals in their encounters with a changing world.

Power and authority

In late-nineteenth-century Germany, under the empire established
by the Prussian monarchy, state policy was directed toward the
rapid growth of economic power. At the same time, however,

business and industrial interests had relatively little political influence and the growing working class less still. The state and state policy was controlled by the court and the East Prussian *Junker* aristocracy, still feudal in origin and militaristic in inclination. The policy followed by Wilhelm I's chancellor, Bismark, and his successors was to bribe the more conservative middle classes with official positions and ineffectual representation in parliament, the Reichstag, and, through a paternalistic mixture of welfare provision and political disenfranchisement, emasculate the political potential of the growing working class.

Weber was no admirer of this policy. His family background was one of political liberalism, his father and uncle having participated in the unsuccessful revolution of 1848. His father, after becoming reconciled to the political *status quo*, served as a member of the Berlin parliament. Weber, however, believed the political alienation of the working class and the exclusion of the business class from real influence, while the militarism and economic incompetence of the ruling class continued unchecked, served to undermine the integrity of the nation, generating needless hostilities and antagonisms, which threatened to become unmanageable. In the event, it led to ruinous war, revolution and, eventually, after the virtual collapse of the postwar republic, the rise of Nazism – though that was long after Weber's death. In identifying the potentially revolutionary contradiction between the growing importance of new economic interests and their practical exclusion from decisive political power by a proud and socially exclusive ruling class – whose own material basis in the feudal agriculture of the east was, meanwhile, being eroded by the loss of labour to the industrializing west – Weber had much in common with Marx (see Giddens, 1972).

Weber's view differed from a possible Marxist interpretation, however, in several important respects. Firstly, he discerned that the undiminished power of the *Junker* class (at least up to the First World War) was not grounded on the mere possession of economic resources. Further, it was this class, through the state apparatus it created and controlled, which had been responsible in Germany for the industrialization that had engendered those bourgeois and proletarian groups which they then sought, at that time still successfully, to control. In his later years, during the War, Weber opposed the government and afterwards, after the fall of the monarchy, participated in the creation of the postwar republican constitution. But while Weber was politically active all his life, except when incapacitated (from his breakdown in 1897 to about 1904), and moved steadily leftward from mildly conservative nationalism in the 1880s to a socialist sympathizing position at the end of the 1914–18 War, his committed interest in the politics of his day was combined with a possibly still stronger commitment to value-free academic analysis. He thus never made a good party man, but perhaps contributed a more penetrating account of the political situation as a consequence. The wider significance of his views on the politics of change in nineteenth-century Germany results from the perception it gave him of its structural basis in different kinds of power, on the one hand, and his conviction, on the other, that it must be seen in terms of what it meant for those involved in the process.

We can summarize his political analysis as distinguishing two complementary questions about the pattern of domination in society. Firstly, there is the issue of the social resources upon which domination is founded, and secondly, how can we understand the practice of domination as a process of meaningful social action? From his own contemporary experience, as well as his wide range of historical researches, it was clear that political rule cannot everywhere be reduced to economic power. Often, religious, political or military groups come to command economic resources too, but their material means are not the primary determinant of their power.

Weber defined power in the most general terms as follows:

> The term *power* will be used to refer to every possibility within a social relationship of imposing one's own will, even against opposition, without regard to the basis for this possibility.   (in Runciman (ed.), 1978, p. 38)

Power is the relational or active aspect of social inequality. Inequality is a descriptive, static or quantitative concept: translated into action, inequality becomes the distribution of power. Power in society is not, of course, an all or nothing attribute. Different individuals or groups are powerful to different degrees, and in different ways, because the resources upon which their power rests may differ both quantitatively and qualitatively.

Weber distinguished three basic types of inequality and these divide societies into classes, status groups and parties. Weber's concept of *class* is similar to, but not identical with, that of Marx and is defined in terms of the distribution of economic power in the market. *Status* is cultural property and is a matter of social respect and deference, founded upon the relative prestige accorded to the way of life of some groups in comparison with others less respectable. Though the possibility of being able to afford a particular life-style is usually limited by one's economic circumstances, members of the same class defined in economic terms may not, in all instances, belong to the same status group. The difference between (respectable) old wealth and (vulgar) *nouveau riches* amongst the well-to-do, or between the rough and the respectable working class, are examples of how money may not always be regarded as a leveller. In the same way, people of similar status may also have disparate market situations as, for example, where one Brahmin may be a civil service mandarin, but another from the same caste a poor village teacher. Members of the same economic class share the same market position, but may have very little else in common in the way of a common outlook or life-style. Status groups, by contrast, necessarily involve some sense of belonging, of being, or not being, 'our sort of people'. Weber put the difference in this way:

> 'Classes' are stratified according to their relation to the production and acquisition of goods; whereas 'status groups' are stratified according to the principles of their *consumption* of goods as represented by special 'styles of life'.
> (Weber, in Gerth and Mills (eds), 1948)

When the rate of social change is slow, he argued, the social status associated with different ways of life is likely to have greater influence upon people. In times of rapid technological innovation, social upheaval and uncertainty these social assumptions are more likely to be challenged, and economically defined class position will have greater prominence. In Weber's three types of inequality, the term *Party* refers to a more widespread phenomenon than the national or parliamentary political parties, the Christian Democrats, the Republican Party, or the ANC, for example. In any group or organization, the competition to have one programme adopted rather than some other divides the members into parties. Sometimes, such divisions may coincide with class or status divisions, but equally often parties draw support from people with

different social backgrounds who happen to agree on the issues
the party is concerned about. It may be the pro- and anti-field
sports groups within the RSPCA, pro- and anti-European Union
groups in the Tory Party or the pro- and anti-Gilbert and Sullivan
factions in a local amateur operatic society. Weber wrote:

> In any individual case parties may represent interests
> determined through 'class situation' or 'status situation' and
> they may recruit their following respectively from one or
> the other. But they need be neither purely 'class' nor purely
> 'status' parties. In most cases they are partly class parties
> and partly status parties, but sometimes they are neither.
> They may represent ephemeral or enduring structures. Their
> means of attaining power may be quite varied, ranging from
> naked violence of any sort to canvassing for votes with coarse
> or subtle means: money, social influence, the force of speech,
> suggestion, clumsy hoax, and so on to the rougher or more
> artful tactics of obstruction in parliamentary bodies.   (ibid.)

The power of classes lies in their economic resources and that of
status groups lies in the respect and deference with which they are
treated by others. Parties are divided by their policies and their
power lies in their ability to carry them through to adoption in
the decision-making processes of the larger grouping to which they
belong.

Whatever the kind of resources upon which power may be based,
the processes of domination also need to be understood at the
level of meaning. Thus there are two sides to domination,
inseparable in practice but analytically distinguishable. The pattern
of power is the structure within which domination occurs. The
other side of domination is its justification, the meaning it has in
the eyes of the powerful themselves and, crucially, for those they
dominate. The reason why power can be accepted is because it is
generally felt to be right. In other words, it is invested with
Authority. Authority is the meaningful aspect of domination which
accounts for the actions of the ruler and ruled.
Weber distinguished three types of authority:

a. Traditional Authority
b. Charismatic Authority

c. Rational-legal Authority

The distinction is based upon the kinds of answer we find in different societies or within different contexts within modern industrial society to the question: <u>Why do people obey</u>?

Traditional authority justifies obedience on the grounds that it has always been so. Most societies in the past, including almost all the ancient kingdoms (but not the modern constitutional monarchies), have been ruled by traditional right. The authority conferred by tradition is not a personal thing, no training or personal achievement validates it. Position, as lord or vassal, is inherited and the only possible grounds for redress against the abuse of traditional authority must be in its own terms, with reference to immemorial custom and established practice. An interesting modern example of the appeal to traditional authority, in what is usually a bureaucratic context, is the case of those trade unions which sometimes invoke custom and practice as establishing workers' rights to time off or various 'perks' of the job that have not been secured as part of a formally negotiated agreement with the employers. Invoking traditional authority in such a case, as well as in the more obvious examples of feudal monarchy or clan chieftainship, affirms the <u>acceptance of</u>, and a <u>sense of duty to, the tradition</u> that is upheld. In this the traditional lord, king or <u>chief symbolizes the unity</u> of himself and his followers as one, hierarchically integrated, people. Traditional authority makes sense, it is intelligible to ruler and ruled. It is not irrational, but is non-rational in terms of Weber's classification of action. It is not goal directed nor the expression of a value, though it may become a value in itself.

Charismatic authority is similarly non-rational, but in a quite different way from traditional authority. Indeed, it is its antithesis. Charisma has the appearance of an attribute of the leader, a personal magnetism, a magical aura, a psychic fascination or power of command which, as followers, we accept as an, as it were, God-given right. So when He says follow me, we feel we must follow. The potency of charisma is perhaps most obvious in religious leaders and prophets like Jesus and St Paul, or the Bhagwan and Jim Jones. There have been political leaders, especially revolutionaries, with charisma, such as Lenin and

Trotsky or Hitler and Perón, but more conventionally democratic politicians like Churchill or Kennedy would be examples too. Other instances of charismatic leadership would include inspiring military leaders like Lord Nelson or Moishe Dayan. As the political examples indicate, charisma may not work equally well on everyone. The magnetism is as much an attribution of the followers as an attribute of the leader. Charisma, then, works where a leader emerges, who appeals to the emotional state and political, religious or other yearnings of a group and offers them what they seem to need, a new direction, a sense of purpose or meaning. In times of social upheaval and political or economic uncertainty, this may take the form of a revolt against what have come to seem antiquated and irrelevant established beliefs and practices. Charismatic leadership necessarily arises in contrast with the existing social, cultural, political or religious order, to challenge and overthrow it. It is the expression of a response to an intolerable situation, intolerable at least for some, and it is short-lived. For the moment of revolutionary breakthrough cannot be sustained indefinitely. The inspired authority of the prophet has to be constantly renewed, and the charisma which might, just, be sustained for his lifetime will need to be given a different character if the new order he has founded is to be handed on to his followers. This seems easiest to manage when he dies young, preferably at the hands of his enemies. Otherwise, the prophecy must become traditional or else routinized. The redeemer has to be followed by the Archbishop of Canterbury: the revolutionary by the bureaucrat.

Rational-legal authority is the political institutionalization of instrumentally rational (*zweckrational*) action. In this case, we obey not an individual but a rule. It is rational to do so since the rules have been properly laid down by the proper constitutional process and serve to maintain a social order we accept as valid. Administration through the systematic application of rules is called bureaucracy. In everyday speech, both today and long before Weber, bureaucracy has been identified with red-tape, mindless form-filling, with Kafka's dreadful and inhuman administrative machinery serving nothing but its own self-perpetuation. Weber, however, begins from a quite different set of presuppositions.

In Weber's view, bureaucracy is the embodiment of rational

administration. It may not always be the most expedient form, in the sense that cutting corners, informal 'fixing' or other *ad hoc* procedures may, in the short term, be more directly effective. But these favours or 'arrangements' are not rational, and do not follow the standard application of acknowledged rules. In a number of places in *Economy and Society* (1922), Weber sets out the characteristics of the ideal-typical bureaucracy. David Beetham (1987, p. 12) has summarized the essential characteristics of Weber's ideal-typical bureaucracy as follows:

1. **hierarchy**: each official has a clearly defined competence within a hierarchical division of labour, and is responsible for performance to a superior;
2. **continuity**: the office constitutes a full-time salaried occupation, with a career structure that offers the prospect of continued advancement;
3. **impersonality**: the work is conducted according to prescribed rules, without arbitrariness or favouritism, and a written record is kept of each transaction;
4. **expertise**: officials are selected according to merit, are trained for their function and control access to the knowledge stored in the files.

The aim and effect of all this is that the bureaucratic official should operate with maximal functional rationality. In his official capacity he operates impersonally within a fixed set of rules, and therefore with complete predictability and fairness. The ideal-typical bureaucracy is consistent, thorough and reliable. Its trained officials can be replaced by any similarly trained and qualified experts. They do not depend upon the support of their clients or the personal favour of their superiors for either their income or tenure of office. They are equally obliged to be impersonal and dispassionate in the performance of their duties. The distinctive character of bureaucratic administration, Weber said, is to eliminate from official business 'love, hatred and all purely personal, irrational and emotional elements which escape calculation. This is the specific nature of bureaucracy and it is appraised as its special virtue' (Weber, 1922). Bureaucracy is technically superior, he argued, to any other form of organization:

> The fully developed bureaucratic mechanism compares with other organizations exactly as does the machine with the non-mechanical modes of production.   (ibid.)

It is clear that in the large-scale organizations of the modern industrial state, bureaucratic administration is inescapable and indispensable. The administrative machine will work equally well for whoever controls it from the top. Revolution cannot sweep it away, however, without the utter destruction of modern society. Where the bureaucracy is once established, the possibility of revolution is reduced to a mere change of leadership while the system remains the same. The greater risk, Weber seemed to think, was that no-one could control the state bureaucracy so that the machine takes over. Bureaucratization, then, is inevitable and irresistible but, once established, makes all further structural change impossible, indeed, almost inconceivable.

Rationalization and the modern world

The defining characteristic of modern industrial capitalism is the rational pursuit of profitability. In Weber's view, as we have already noted, capitalist development depends on the spread of rational administration, rational accounting, law, technology and the rational attitudes and values which underpin them. These provide the basic structure of values and institutions in which business can be confidently conducted with a fair expectation of a beneficial outcome. The decline of Puritan asceticism, the growth of self-indulgence and enjoyment of the riches originally gathered for the glory of the Lord, did not retard the processes of rationalization once they became well established. They continued, once well under way. The technical superiority of the rational organization is such that whatever the ethical commitments or value orientations of the entrepreneurs, bureaucrats or policy makers, any alternative way of operating would be self-defeating. The embodiment of rational administration is bureaucracy, and bureaucratic rationality is a matter of efficiently meeting organizational goals. These, however, may not always be clear to all the bureaucracy's individual clients, or even to some of its lower level functionaries. In Weber's eyes this represented a paradox of tragic dimensions.

According to the Enlightenment principles he believed in, reason and freedom are much the same thing. Rational thought, and the action that flows from it, is free from the coercion of caprice, random accident, overmastering emotion or uncontrollable desires. Freedom consists precisely in the ability to follow the path indicated by one's own reason, without being helplessly driven by impulse in this way. The irrational man is not free at all, but is at the mercy of his own psychological condition and of arbitrary external circumstances. But, though reason is the source of human freedom and rationalization is the consequence of systematically applied reason, in a society heading inexorably toward greater rationalization, the future of human freedom looked highly problematic (Stuart-Hughes, 1958, pp. 331–2).

Weber's tragic vision was that the increasing application of rational thought to the world, instead of enlarging the individual dignity of people, seemed only to lead to an increasing depersonalization, reducing individuals to mere cogs in a bureaucratic machine. This was the future for the modern world as Weber saw it: 'The disenchantment of the world,' in the poet Schiller's phrase, seemed to him a dehumanizing of the world too. 'The Puritan wanted to work in a calling; we are forced to do so,' he wrote at the end of *The Protestant Ethic and the Spirit of Capitalism* ((1905) 1958, p. 181),

> for when asceticism was carried out of monastic cells into everyday life, and began to dominate worldly morality, it did its part in building the tremendous cosmos of the modern economic order. This order is now bound to the technical and economic conditions of machine production which today determine the lives of all the individuals who are born into this mechanism, not only those directly concerned with economic acquisition, with irresistible force. Perhaps it will so determine them until the last ton of fossilized coal is burnt. In Baxter's view the care for external goods should only lie on the shoulders of the 'saint' like a light cloak, which can be thrown aside at any moment. But fate decreed that the cloak should become an iron cage.

The care for external goods, that is to say acquisitiveness, and the economic and social order which produces them, are the two jaws of the trap. And individual reason is displaced by the impersonal functional rationality of the bureaucratic organization. The exercise of our highest faculty, of true freedom in the pursuit of rational thought, leads only to this. There is no room for the humane values in the calculative world of rational resource planning and efficient administration. They have been confined to the inward-looking world of purely personal private life. 'The ultimate and most sublime values have retreated from public life,' Weber wrote, '... it is not accidental that our greatest art is intimate and not monumental.' Even in the private sphere, the penetration of pressures for personal efficiency and rational conduct offers a bleak prospect. 'Not summer's bloom lies ahead of us,' he concluded, 'but rather a polar night of icy darkness and hardness' ('Politics as a Vocation', in Gerth and Mills (eds), 1948, p. 128).

There appears to be no way out. Socialist centralized planning of production and the distribution of resources would only create even more bureaucracy than current capitalist market systems do. Giddens summarized these desperate conclusions:

> ... western society can be said to be founded upon an intrinsic antinomy between formal and substantive rationality which, according to Weber's analysis of modern capitalism, cannot be resolved.   (Giddens, 1971, p. 184.)

That is to say, there is a basic incompatibility between modern organizations which are designed to carry out their functions in the most efficient way and any sense of rational purpose for most of us who have to operate within their structures. All that society has to offer is a livelihood in exchange for a lifetime of personally meaningless effort. The only prospect for escape from the system that Weber anticipated was the emergence of a charismatic leadership which would reinvest the soulless machine with human values. Weber's views were ahead of the times by a few years, for in the later 1920s and 1930s charismatic leaders of mass populist parties, who would no doubt have horrified him, did emerge, opposed to the values of the rational-legal bourgeois state. But the yearning for charismatic leadership seems to have died with the defeat of fascism in the Second World War.

It can be argued, however, that it was Weber's own rationalism which brought him to this despairing position. Yet the stark alternative of soulless rational-legal authority or the irrationalism of charismatic leadership is a misleading dilemma. That was not, and is not, the only choice. The ideal-typical method is a rational hypothetical construct based on a critical analysis of traits and tendencies. It is not an empirical summary or extrapolation of those traits and tendencies themselves. It is, therefore, not so apparently vulnerable to empirical falsification. But if taken for the reality it rationalizes, it can lead to conclusions which not only happen to be wrong as things turn out, but are inevitably false. This is because any ideal-type is purposely a systematic simplification and not a description of any concrete situation.

The formal characteristics of Weber's model bureaucracy may sometimes resemble the organizational chart hanging on the director's office wall, but do not correspond to the realities of day-to-day administration. The employees of large organizations remain stubbornly human. To take one example from a large literature, Kohn found that, contrary to the cogs-in-the-machine image, bureaucrats placed more rather than less value on self-direction, were more open-minded and receptive to change than people working in less-bureaucratic settings. Bureaucracy, he concluded, does not produce placid conformists, but can be personally liberating in providing more scope for the individual than they might find in a small firm (1971, pp. 461–74). Empirical research into large-scale organizations without exception shows that they do not correspond to the ideal-typical bureaucratic pattern Weber set out (see, e.g., Blau and Meyer, 1971.) Rules are bent, people ring up Harry to fix things, the rulebook is referred to *post hoc* to legitimate disciplinary action or in self-justification when things go wrong. Weber overlooks the persistent micro-politics, the informal networking, and the humanity of those who devise and implement organizational procedures. Even functional rationality is a hard-won, and fragile, social achievement in the exigencies of day-to-day administration. Weber's error was the result of rational deduction from what he believed were the principles of bureaucratic organization, which he applied to the world of real organizations.

There is no single universal system of management which is more rational than all others for achieving all administrative objectives (see Albrow, 1970, Chs 5 and 6). Organizations are diverse and, whether they are manufacturing firms, banks, government departments, or educational institutions, they never have just one single unambiguous purpose. The goals they encompass will, of course, include their own smooth running and continuity, but also their obligations to customers or clients, investors or funding agencies, the public at large, legal obligations and many more. Even if service to the customer or meeting the expectations of investors have high priority, there will usually be many reasonable ways of doing so. In other words, organizational rationality cannot be functionally defined with reference to just one specific objective, but must be a negotiated condition 'satisficing' an apparently optimal balance among a range of different and sometimes conflicting goals (see, e.g., Simon, 1952; Cyert and March, 1963; March and Olsen, 1976.) Thus it is not just the human failings of bureaucrats, but the specification of rationality itself which presents a problem when we confront Weber's ideal-type with real-life organizations. Burns and Stalker pointed out that it is not just that every organization pursues a multiplicity of goals, but that they also operate in very different environments. Weber's ideal hierarchical bureaucracy might work well in the fairly routine administration of an unchanging system. But in an environment where the organization has consistently to deal with new and different problems, what is needed is adaptability and the capacity to innovate. Burns and Stalker distinguished organizations with a *mechanistic* structure, broadly those with the sort of characteristics Weber identified with rational administration, adapted to operations within a stable environment, and those with an *organic* structure with a flatter managerial hierarchy, much more lateral cooperation and com-munication, which were generally more fluid and were adapted to coping with the uncertainties of more competitive or more changeable circumstances (Burns and Stalker, 1961; see also Mintzberg, 1983.)

In brief then, in modern industrial societies: (a) bureaucracies are not, in fact, like Weber's ideal-typical pattern; (b) bureaucracies are not the only type of rational organization; (c) even bureaucracies have the problem of meeting a plurality of goals; and (d) the rationalization process, as a consequence, is consistent with a much greater organizational and therefore greater personal diversity than he seemed to believe. If we are all cogs, then we are all different sorts of cogs, in widely different sorts of machine. Weber confused his ideal typification with reality. His dispiriting view of the future was like making shadows of long-leggedy beasties on the bedroom wall and frightening ourselves so much we are afraid to go to sleep. If it exists at all, the iron cage of modernity looks much more like an open prison than he led us to believe.

To summarize then:

1. Weber argued that change originates endogenously from the rationalization of society. His concern with the structures and processes of domination is clearly within a conflict model of interests.

2. Weber's view of history in general is open ended. The development of industrial capitalism centred on western Europe has been in distinct contrast with the unchanging centuries of traditional cultures in ancient China or India. There is no overall pattern to human history. In western capitalism, it is true, the trend of rationalization appeared to Weber to be irresistible and irreversible. But that does not make the future known or the argument teleological. The logic of rationalization is of determinism by antecedent causes. Given the circumstances, this is the way things are going.

3. Weber was a methodological individualist, but was primarily interested in large-scale historical processes. He never addressed the particularities, or even the regularities, of face-to-face interaction. He was concerned, above all, to make these social processes rationally intelligible in terms of social action, that is to say, as the outcome of comprehensible rational thought rather than the product of impersonal forces operating at a structural level, or of psychological dynamics below the threshold of rational reflection. In this sense he was not only pre-Freudian in his thinking, but also, perhaps, pre-Hegelian too. For him the progressive rationalization of the modern world *was* the result of the actions of individuals not of the mysterious workings of the zeitgeist. On the other hand, Scott is misleading in suggesting that Weber's conception of rationalization is a matter of individual subjective meanings (Scott, 1995, p. 22). As Weber describes it, it is a general institutional process and involves the spread of *functional* rationalization, at the expense of substantive rationality at the level of individual men and women. That is why, according to Weber, there is an iron cage.

4. The role of ideas is merely complementary to the causal influence of material factors. His critique of materialist theory

was not an argument seeking to contradict the importance of economic or political factors, but to demonstrate that values and beliefs also have an independent influence of their own. Nevertheless, the ideal-type analysis of the rationalization process, both in capitalist enterprise and the rise of industrial society, leaves little for material factors to do in the dominant processes of social change in the modern world. As an account of social change, Weber's analysis is primarily idealist.

5. Methodologically, Weber was deeply committed to the scientific approach, but within a rationalist perspective. It seems likely that a more empiricist analysis would not have led him into the blind alley with only the iron cage or the charismatic hero at the end of it. The tragic appeal would have been absent, and we should probably have lost a striking illustration of the potency of social action theory in the analysis of social and cultural change on the grand scale. It is, after all, in the challenge of his arguments that the enduring value of Weber's work remains rather than in the accuracy of his conclusions. We must still confront the questions he identified. In that we can still learn from him, we remain in his debt.

7

Sociological Realism: Durkheim

Emile Durkheim (1858–1917) is one of the major figures in the foundation of sociology as an academic discipline. Much in structuralist and functionalist theorizing, in the methodology of sociological research, and the empirical study of social deviance and law, suicide, education, the sociology of religion and the sociology of knowledge has been built upon his pioneering work, though sometimes in ways which he would probably have regarded as one-sided or distorted. His dedication to the establishment of sociology as a value-neutral and objective science grew out of his profound moral concern with the value of individualism, and the critical dilemmas it created and was threatened by in modern society. He believed that only through the achievement of an objective understanding could sociology enable us to begin to cope with these problems. In relation to social change, Durkheim's primary importance is in his <u>explanation of some of the consequences of structural change</u> rather than in offering any very original ideas about its causes.

Social change and the emergence of individualism

critical mass of right movements

The main lines of Durkheim's sociology are clear in his first major book, originally his doctoral thesis, *The Division of Labour in Society*, published in 1893. He says relatively little about what drives the differentiation process. He mainly attributes its origins to an <u>increase in the *moral density*</u> of society, by which he seems to mean not just the physical or geographical concentration of people, but the <u>extent to which they interact with one another.</u> This may be the result of demographic growth and the formation of cities (ibid., 1956, pp. 258–66), but he did not

145

examine which might have come first, or which caused the other, in any great depth. He tells us less about how it might have come about, and what factors sustain it in the present, than Adam Smith had done long before.

For Durkheim, the division of labour in society is essentially a 'given', a starting point for his analysis. His originality appears in his discussion of the social consequences of the division of labour. For this purpose he offers two ideal-typical social patterns, the first with a low level of specialization, and the second where the division of labour has progressed to a high degree of social differentiation. These are presented in a sort of 'before and after' contrast from which we can, he indicates, infer the pattern and direction of change. In Durkheim's view, the increasing specialization of function under the growing division of labour not only meant an increase in productivity, but, much more important, a change in the social relations within society, a change in the nature of social solidarity. He described this crucial transformation as a change from *mechanical solidarity* towards what he called *organic solidarity*. Social solidarity is hard to define very precisely, but means the way in which a society holds together. It has to do with the extent to which the constituent parts of a society cohere into a single, unified, bounded system. A society whose members had no great sense of common identity with one another, whose component institutions functioned with little reference to one another, might be thought of as having little solidarity. 'A high level of social solidarity' would describe the opposite case.

Simple societies have what Durkheim described as mechanical solidarity. That is to say, in such cases, the segments of society, its constituent parts, the tribes, clans, settlements, communities, and so forth, hang together precisely because each is virtually identical with the next. Each peasant farm is just like another. They work and live in the same way. Each stem family household, each clan, is just like every other. They have the same sort of beliefs and expectations. The coherence of the society is a composite of almost indistinguishable units, mechanically related like the stones in a dry-stone wall. Each element plays its part in the overall unity of the whole and it is the same part that all the others play.

With the increase in the social division of labour, the specialization of functions into priests and merchants, craftsmen and healers, farmers and fishermen, miners and soldiers, clerks and teachers and so forth, the nature of social solidarity cannot be the same. Durkheim was inclined to discuss the social order in terms of the organic analogy. That is to say, the components of society, the political institutions, the economic system, family life, the arts, religious practices, and so on, can be thought of as like the organs of the body, each contributing in its own way, to overall viability. They are mutually interdependent through the effective functioning of the complete system. Some may be more indispensable than others but none can survive in isolation from the organism as a whole. Durkheim argued that the progressive division of labour, intensifying with the industrialization of the nineteenth century, accelerated this move towards an organic solidarity in society and away from the mechanical solidarity of the past. This transformation of the type of social solidarity brings about changes in people's sense of belonging, in their general social awareness, in what Durkheim refers to as '*la conscience collective*'. This term is especially hard to translate. It does not mean collective consciousness in the sense of a 'group mind' distinct from the thought processes of ordinary individuals, nor yet a general conscience in the sense of an external moral censor upon our behaviour, though it implies a little of both of these. It includes all the beliefs, language, moral values and common-sense assumptions that we share with other members of our society. It refers to our sense of belonging together and therefore to our sense of social, collective and individual identity, which also has a moral component within it. Feelings, ideas and values that are included within the conscience collective have a sense of 'rightness' about them. Anything that challenges the conscience collective must be disturbing, hard to accept, perhaps threatening.

In the societies characterized by *mechanical solidarity*, the lack of differentiation produces a strong *conscience collective*, a sense of belonging within a community of similar people. The members of such a society share the same beliefs and attitudes, the same ways of doing things and the same moral values. They identify with their community and are likely to speak of 'what we think', 'what we always say' or 'how we do things'. Their sense of themselves as individuals, with opinions that might differ from what everyone else thinks, is undeveloped or is, indeed, resisted.

Moral norms are strong, deviants are a threat to social solidarity
and are not much tolerated. The conscience collective dictates a
homogeneity of culture, resistant to change and prescribing a
clear path for all to follow. In a society of organic solidarity,
with a highly developed division of labour, the conscience
collective will be quite different too. The sense of individual
difference, Durkheim argued, will be much more developed, the
uniqueness and value of individual experience, individual self-
expression and individual liberty becomes much more prized as
an element in the good of society.

Durkheim believed this could be shown in the development
of law from the punitive, or as he described them, *retributive*
penal codes of simpler societies, with their harsh penalties for
every crime against collective values, to the greater emphasis
on civil codes and contract law in modern societies. With
organic solidarity, the law is increasingly concerned with the
rights of individuals rather than exclusively with the good of
the social order as a whole. In societies with a complex division
of labour, legal systems have to cope with the more complex
pattern of interrelationships, and the emphasis shifts from the
punishment of offenders to *restitutive* sanctions against
breaches of contract, and we observe the growth of business
law and the pursuit of settlements through civil proceedings,
or administrative tribunals. In our own time, the development
of family and divorce law, or of employment law, might
illustrate this sort of change.

On the other hand, the argument is historically rather
doubtful. In many feudal and pre-feudal societies, killing, for
instance, could be compensated for by payment of an
appropriate 'wergeld' – the sum that the life of the dead man
was thought to be worth – by the family of the killer to the
next of kin of the corpse. This, in Durkheim's terms, was a
restitutive sanction (see, e.g., Whitelock, 1952), only later
replaced by the repressive mandatory death penalty for
homicide. But then, there are grounds for doubting whether
the Anglo-Saxons, who followed this practice, ever felt all that
much mechanical solidarity anyway (see Macfarlane, op. cit.).
The possible bluntness of this criticism of Durkheim's
argument, however, would imply the sharpening of another,
that is, that organic solidarity was not a late development but,
at least amongst the Anglo-Saxons, coexisted with a relatively

simple division of labour. There is a further problem with Durkheim's use of legal evolution to illustrate his argument. In relating the two sets of changes: in the type of social solidarity and in the character of the law; he explains the second change as being attributable to the first. But the main evidence that he cited to show that the first change had occurred was that it is demonstrated by the second, the change in the law. The historical connection might possibly be valid and the argument seems plausible enough but, nevertheless, this verges upon circular reasoning.

Even in the organic division of labour, the conscience collective ordinarily plays an important role in the relationships between people, especially between relative strangers. Durkheim wrote of the 'non-contractual elements in contract' to demonstrate the absurdity of extreme methodological individualism. So, even in business dealings where every clause is apparently spelled out, drawing up a contract implicitly invokes shared assumptions, and a public acknowledgement of the legality of the agreement between the parties who sign it. Furthermore, the wider society is directly involved, in the shape of the civil law, as guarantor that the contract will be honoured and compensation paid if one party or another should fail to meet the agreed terms. In less formal dealings between people, opinion and moral disapproval provide the same sort of 'non-contractual' element in our relationships with one another. When the conscience collective is no longer effective in this way, all social relations are jeopardized.

The rights of the individual were among the most important of Durkheim's values. The seriousness of this commitment was demonstrated by his support for Captain Dreyfus in the celebrated case of 1896. Dreyfus was an army officer convicted of spying, who was held to be doubly in the wrong for challenging the authorities' verdict. His innocence of the crime and wrongful imprisonment seemed to count for less than the fact that, by exposing officialdom's prejudice against him as a Jew and their refusal to amend their errors, he and his supporters would severely damage public respect for the established political order. Durkheim's association with the campaign on behalf of Dreyfus reflects his *moral individualism*, that is, his opposition to collectivist and traditionalist doctrines which put the good of the state or of the community above

individual rights. But to believe in individual moral responsibilities, and to argue that the object of ethical conduct should
be to promote the good of individuals, does not necessarily
mean we can only talk about individual behaviour, or even only
about individual ideas. It is essential to recognize that social
life has its regularities and rules, which sociology studies in
their own right, just as one might study the phonetics or the
syntax of a language. So while Durkheim was opposed to ethical
collectivism, he was equally opposed to *methodological
individualism* in social theory.

He rejected the individualism of Utilitarian theorists such as
Spencer (whose work we discussed in Chapter 3), Bentham and
Mill, and that of the Enlightenment philosophers before them.
They portrayed society as the product of individuals making
rational choices about the situations that confronted them. The
individual, acting primarily in his own self-interest, was the
starting point for their analyses. Durkheim argued that society
could not be a result of either rational or non-rational choice
since everyone is always born into an existing social group. To
start one's analysis from individuals would, in any case, make
sociology no more than a summary of psychological events,
and would therefore obscure what should be obvious, that is,
that social factors exist irreducibly in their own right. For him,
the growth of moral and cognitive individualism was grounded
in the social transition from mechanical solidarity to organic
solidarity. Individualism – both as a positive value and also as
a commonsensical awareness of ourselves as uniquely different
from others, with our own rights and our own attitudes and
ideas – is a social product. With the complex division of
increasingly specialized labour, individuals become more wholly
autonomous than ever before, as they simultaneously become
more totally dependent upon society for their survival (1893,
p. 294).

It is interesting to consider the obvious similarities between
Durkheim's types of social solidarity and Tönnies's earlier
distinction (discussed in Chapter 5) between *gemeinschaft* and
gesellschaft. Tönnies's descriptive contrast is perhaps easier to
grasp, and Durkheim's concept of solidarity is difficult to pin
down satisfactorily. Both draw attention to the qualitative
aspects of change in the process of modernization. Both, in
essence, are ideal-typical portrayals of contrasting principles

of organization. Where Tönnies's discussion, based on the difference of natural and rational will, is psychological and moral in character, Durkheim argues that psychological and moral change are themselves the result of social structural change, the increase in the division of labour.

Pathological forms of the division of labour

There are, in Durkheim's view, several dangers for society in the move towards an increasingly organic solidarity and the progressive division of labour. It is not just that individualism might foster social deviance. All societies experience some deviance from generally accepted social norms, and indeed a certain amount of deviance, Durkheim argued, was normal. By that he meant not only statistically normal but, paradoxically, also normal in the sense that it was healthy too. That is not to say it was good for any likely victim of someone else's deviance or even for the deviants themselves. He was being provocative, but not heartless. But a society without any deviants would not be a normal society in any sense. Durkheim's inclination to see society as like an organism led him to judge things normal or pathological, in the way one might judge one's bodily state of health. In a healthy society the various elements all work effectively to promote the viability of the whole. Any characteristic or condition which threatened the survival of the society would, from that point of view, be categorized as pathological in the sense that a diseased kidney or a tubercular lung is pathological. The healthy society he described as normal, the pathological state as abnormal. Using the word 'normal' in this way, to mean conforming to the norm of good health, is easily confused with the statistical sense of 'normal', meaning ordinary, usual, general, average or occurring frequently. But in an epidemic, only the exceptional may escape sickness. Ill health is normal then, and also, more generally, in that nearly everybody is unwell sometimes, but it should still be avoided if possible.

Durkheim apparently meant that crime is statistically normal because it occurs in all societies, but also that some deviance may be innovative and possibly adaptive in coping with change. Even when this is not the case, as with most crime which is merely destructive, or other deviance from moral or ethical codes, Durkheim suggests that a certain amount of social deviance serves to remind the rest of us, presumably non-deviant citizens, of what the moral norms that have been broken are. The offender, whether identified and punished in one way or another, or not at all, reinforces the *conscience collective* by reminding the rest of us of our commitments to it. Even in modern times, the severity of the penalties for crime is proportional to the gravity of the offence, and not to the likelihood of reform on the part of the convicted criminal or the deterrence of others who might be led into future crime. Imprisonment or financial penalties are not after all for the good of the offender, but an expression of the outrage occasioned by his crime. As Durkheim remarked: '... we can thus say without paradox that punishment is above all designed to act upon upright people ...' (1893, p. 108). Though it is doubtful whether we *can* say so 'without paradox', I think this view would still attract widespread agreement as regards public views on sentencing if not always amongst the judges.

Durkheim was seriously concerned about what he called the abnormal forms of the division of labour, where organic solidarity is itself threatened. That is to say, the division of labour, he believed, could develop in ways which, for the society as a whole, are pathological, and therefore potentially destructive both for the social order and also of the individualistic values which it had generated. Durkheim identified two abnormal forms of the division of labour: *the Forced Division of Labour* and *the Anomic Division of Labour*. However, as with some of the other distinctions he made, it is not always easy in practice entirely to distinguish between them. Their origins are almost contradictory, but, in their pathological consequences, they overlap a great deal.

The Forced Division of Labour was the effect of excessive social inequality. Instead of specialization increasing productivity, raising living standards and easing social tensions in the society as a whole, the movement of individuals into social positions where their talents could best serve can be obstructed by inherited advantage, deprivation and ignorance. Ability is wasted through the denial of opportunity, on the one hand, and by incompetence protected by privileged access to responsible positions, on the other. This forced division of labour not only makes for a lower level of effectiveness over all, but the anger and frustration at the inequality it creates itself fuels class conflict and if allowed to grow, leads in the end to civil war:

> If one class of society is obliged, in order to live, to take any price for its services, while another can abstain from such action thanks to resources at its disposal which, however, are not necessarily due to any social superiority, the second has an unjust advantage over the first at law. In other words there cannot be rich and poor at birth without there being unjust contracts (1893, p. 384)

In a healthy society, Durkheim argued, this kind of inequality would not occur. It is not merely that education and every career should be accessible to anyone with the necessary abilities, but, following Saint-Simon, he advocated abolishing the inheritance of private wealth, which perpetuates social privilege without regard to personal merit. Everyone should at least begin equal if the organic solidarity of modern society is to be sustained:

> It is not merely a matter of increasing the exchanges of goods and services, but of seeing that they are done by rules that are more just; it is not simply that everyone should have access to rich supplies of food and drink. Rather, it is that each one should be treated as he deserves, each be freed from an unjust and humiliating tutelage, and that, in holding to his fellows and his group, a man should not sacrifice his individuality. And the agency upon which this special responsibility lies is the state. (1957, pp. 71–2)

Of course, only the state could bring about these aims, and only through a programme of clearly socialist measures. Other parties might stand for the dignity of the individual, opportunity and general welfare, but only the socialists would seek to achieve these objectives primarily through the state and the abolition of private wealth. Durkheim's sympathies for the concerns and aspirations of socialism are evident in his lifelong friendship with the socialist leader, Jean Jaurés, and in his own extensive studies in socialist theory, including the available works of Marx and the earlier French socialists, among them, especially, the theories of Saint-Simon. His attitude to socialist theories was sympathetic, but he regarded them as unscholarly and utopian:

> The only attitude that science permits in the face of these problems is reservation and circumspection, and socialism can hardly maintain this without lying to itself. And, in fact, socialism has not maintained this attitude. Not even the strongest work – the most systematic, the richest in ideas – that this school has produced: Marx's *Capital*. What statistical data, what historical comparisons, what studies would be indis-pensable to solve any one of the innumer-able problems that are dealt with there! ... Socialism is not a science, a sociology in miniature – it is a cry of grief, sometimes of anger, uttered by men who feel most keenly our collective malaise. Socialism is to the facts which produce it what the groans of a sick man are to the sickness with which he is afflicted, to the needs that torment him
>   (1959, p. 40)

Given these sentiments and, particularly, his views on wealth, it may seem hard to understand how Durkheim could have been regarded as part of a conservative tradition of social thought. Nisbet, for instance (1966), seems to allow for only: (i) Marxist/revolutionary; (ii) liberal/individualist; and (iii) conservative/holist perspectives. Since Durkheim was neither a revolutionary nor a methodological individualist, he must belong with the third strand. There are similarities it is true, but scarcely enough. Nisbet's interpretation of the sociological tradition: (a) misleadingly narrows the range of possibilities; and (b) applies what is really a politically based classification to the possibilities of sociological theory, when political and sociological perspectives are not necessarily related at all.

The other pathological or abnormal form of the division of labour that Durkheim identified was the *Anomic Division of Labour*. In contrast with the excessive rigidity of the Forced Division of Labour, the anomic form occurred where the structural conditions were too fluid and uncertain. Durkheim's concept of *anomie* literally means 'normlessness', that is, the absence of social standards. Social cohesion in every society or group, even in a fight, is only possible to the extent that those involved recognize one another as fellow participants, and regulate their behaviour so as to be intelligible for one another. The absence of commonly shared norms would mean that the behaviour of others would be totally unpredictable, would make no kind of sense. Interaction, relating one's behaviour to the likely responses of others, would be impossible. Durkheim believed that modern economies were especially prone to anomie because growth tends to be greatest where it has been freed of all regulation. For the individual too, the economic system seems especially geared up to encourage an anomic state of mind. Durkheim anticipated the modern consumerist, 'shop till you drop' outlook a hundred years ago. In modern society:

> ... irrespective of any regulatory force, our capacity for social wants becomes insatiable and a bottomless abyss: the more one has, the more one wants, since satisfactions received only stimulate further wants. (1893, pp. 247–8)

As the division of labour progresses further, the increased individualism – not only with its growing sense of the uniqueness of every person, but also with a growing divergence of values and of everyday experience – meant that the conscience collective could be severely eroded. The awareness of our common interdependence could all too easily wither and die. With each individual or group pursuing its own interests, not only regardless of one another but regardless of the destructive consequences for the society as a whole, anomie is a persistent danger for modern societies. Anomie is not just a condition of the individual but of the society to which he or she belongs. The anomic society is one where the decline of the conscience collective, the disappearance of shared moral values and the sense of collective identity which they provide, is clearly a pathological condition. The anomic society is a society that is falling apart.

Durkheim saw symptoms of both these conditions in France at the end of the nineteenth century. As we have seen, he favoured a Saint-Simonian solution for the forced division of labour. The anomic division of labour, however, was a more intractable problem. Durkheim's career, first as a school teacher, then as Professor of Educational Sociology at the University of Bordeaux before he moved to the Sorbonne in

Paris in 1902, must have given him some faith in the power of
social and moral education as a major factor in countering
anomie. In the training of teachers, and as an academic subject
taught in its own right, he believed here sociology had an
important part to play. In his view, an unbiased, factually based,
but theoretically informed sociology could give people a proper
awareness of the complexity of modern society, and thereby
directly contribute to the conscience collective. This was not
to make the subject a mere ideological crutch propping up a
tottering social order. On the contrary, the scientific pursuit
of the truth about society would reveal the pathological effects
of privilege and self-interest, and help to sweep them aside.
Only the truth can give us any hope of effective social action
to deal with the destructive effects of the forced division of
labour or the dissolution of organic solidarity in anomie.

Solutions to pathological social forms would not evolve
simply as the product of impersonal social forces, however.
Their attainment, he believed, would entail deliberate moral
action:

> A state of order or peace among men cannot follow of itself
> from any entirely material causes, from any blind
> mechanism, however scientific it may be. It is a moral task.
>   (1957, p. 12)

Durkheim is clearly making a distinction here between the
world of action, in which we have to make real decisions and
choices, and the less apparent, but no less real, world of
historical social processes. Though his discussion of large-scale
social change and its problems, the division of labour and its
abnormal forms for instance, is carried through in terms of
macrosocial processes, it is also clear that he did not regard
individuals as helpless pawns in a game played over their heads
by impersonal social forces . For the responsible and thoughtful
citizen, and for political action in general, injustice and social
cohesion or breakdown are moral issues requiring an individual
response. It is, however, only as a consequence of the historical
development of a particular kind of social solidarity that a
personal moral response to such questions is possible. Without
a *conscience collective* founded in organic solidarity, such moral

issues would hardly be apparent; indeed, given a very low level of individuation, they could scarcely be meaningful till then. The fact that we are faced with them in this kind of society, at this point in its historical development, is a *social* fact, something generated by social change. The recognition of this social dimension is what sociology is about.

Durkheim's emphasis on the structural determination of consciousness is of critical importance in his theory of how our values and cognitive ordering of experience have evolved. It represents his most important contribution to the exploration of the consequences of social change and it is to this aspect of his work that we now turn.

Social facts as things

After the history of political upheavals in nineteenth-century France, with restorations, second and third empires, second and third republics, foreign invasion and defeat, the Paris Commune and its repression, and numerous revolutions and *coups d'état*, Durkheim was not a believer in revolutionary action. After all the barricades and bombast, the death and destruction, the aspirations of the great 1789 Revolution seemed as far from realization as ever. And yet he was a social critic, a moralist concerned with the achievement of freedom and equality and brotherhood. He wrote:

> Society has no justification if it does not bring a little peace to men – peace in their hearts and peace in their mutual intercourse. If, then, industry can be productive only by disturbing their peace and unleashing warfare, it is not worth the cost. (1957, p. 16)

What form the necessary political action to ensure a little peace in men's hearts should take is, however, for others to decide: the democratic, or liberal, politicians he compared to the 'physician of healthy society' (1895, 1982). It was certainly not for the social scientist, still less the teacher, to abuse his professional position by making propaganda for one political programme or another, whatever his private views might be.

Like Weber, Durkheim believed that sociology should be methodical, objective and scientific. In his book *The Rules of Sociological Method* (1895, 1982), he set out the ways in which this could be achieved. This was not a research methods handbook, but more a sort of 'mission statement' for a scientific sociology. Setting aside the prejudices and wishful thinking often disguised in the arguments of philosophical social theory, Durkheim insisted that what was distinctive about sociology, in relation to the other ways in which human behaviour might be studied, was precisely the concern with the *Social*. His axiomatic assumption of sociological realism made possible analyses inaccessible to a methodological individualism: the principle that, in reality, all social phenomena can be explained in terms of the sentiments of individual people. On the contrary, Durkheim argued, social facts cannot be reduced to psychological events. Sociology, he claimed, was therefore to be the science of social facts, and more precisely the science of social institutions.

We live in a society we did not make. Our very ideas of ourselves are shaped by the society we were born into. What we do, for our diverse and peculiar reasons, has consequences we do not anticipate, and our choices and hopes are influenced by circumstances, of which we are not always aware. Thus a given society might be characterized by persistent rates of fertility, unemployment, inflation or suicide, even though individual reasons for having or refraining from having children, for being out of work, as for killing oneself, display an almost infinite diversity of motivation and circumstance. No-one worked out a blueprint for the Highland clan or planned a job specification for the unusual employment relationships of the Mbuti pygmies, but they are social institutions which have shaped people's lives. These things must be treated as realities in their own right, as he put it, '*comme les choses*'. They cannot be reductively explained away in terms of individual actions. Nobody plans the divorce rate or the birthrate, though they reflect purposive activities. Monetary inflation is not the product of deliberate will, even though it is the consequence of human action. Its causes and consequences need to be traced in other social facts.

Durkheim's interest in the autonomy of social facts led him in his later work to explore two topics where this argument would be particularly severely tested. Firstly, in possibly his best known work, *Suicide* (1897), he attempted to show how trends in suicide rates, even the incidence, that is, of what to most of us seems the most private, most individualistic of actions, can only be fully understood in the context of the general characteristics of the social order. The suicide rate in different societies, he concluded, reflects their degree of social integration. When the rate fluctuates that can be related to changes in, or the impact of, events upon the social structure. Later on he turned to what he described as *collective representations*, those general ideas and beliefs which have common currency, with which the members of society make sense of both the social and the material world in which they live. This was the theme of his major work, which preoccupied him more and more in his later studies of religious and other ideas. Collective representations, too, are social facts and need to be understood in their social context, Durkheim wrote:

> A social fact is every way of acting, fixed or not, capable of exercising on the individual an external constraint; or again, every way of acting which is general throughout a given society while at the same time existing in its own right independent of its individual manifestations.
>
> (1895, p. 13)

Social facts then are:

a. **external**: they confront the individual as objective elements in the world he or she has to deal with;
b. **constraining**: they affect the choices and possibilities open to the individual;
c. **general**: they appear the same way for everyone in the same situation. They do not belong to a private psychological domain;
d. **independent**: they do not depend upon individual instances. The common elements of the teacher with her class constitute a social fact, in spite of all the amazing personal diversity of teachers and the appalling differences in behaviour and attitude there can be between 4A and 4C.

The sociological explanation of social facts in terms of other social facts can be attempted in two different ways. The first strategy is to explain things *causally* by looking for their origins in antecedent circumstances. Alternatively social facts may be related to one another *functionally* by showing their mutual adaptation and the contribution they make to the life of the social organism as a whole. This applies to social facts in the same way that you can learn a lot about the lungs from studying how they function within the respiratory process. Each of these approaches, causal and functional analyses, can complement the other and together provide a fuller understanding than either could on its own. However, one or other of them may be all that is possible in any particular discussion. The abnormal forms of the division of labour could be traced back, at least in theory, to their origins in the shift from mechanical to organic solidarity. Durkheim was arguing here about causal sequences based on a – highly speculative – historical model. The origins of moral and religious thought are more difficult. Durkheim attempted in *The Elementary Forms of Religious Life* (1912) to examine the simplest kind of religious beliefs by identifying what seemed to him to be the most elementary, perhaps therefore the earliest, patterns.

It is obviously true that present-day urban industrial societies have evolved from less structurally complex societies in the past. Durkheim, along with most anthropologists in the nineteenth and early twentieth centuries, believed that their contemporary preliterate, technologically undeveloped, kinship-dominated societies represented the sort of conditions from which European societies must have evolved. The difficulty with this is that these societies have histories equally long, though different, as the industrialized societies. Even so, very few of them have reliable, or perhaps any, records of what they may have been like in the remote past. In other words: (a) we do not know for sure that they were always like what they are today; and (b) we do know that over the same span of time they have *not* developed into urban industrial societies. The only thing we can be certain of, therefore, is that they are different. As a consequence, the sort of cross-sectional comparisons between different societies, favoured in the past by evolutionary theorists, cannot be assumed to portray before-and-after differences in the same society over time.

If such diachronic analysis is impossible, the other method of gaining some insight into the working of social institutions, whose origins are either lost in the unknown past or are not thought particularly relevant, is a functional analysis. Durkheim's discussion of religion is about how such ideas and practices can be functionally related to the evolving structures of society. This is probably the most original and fruitful part of his work. For all the criticisms which have been made of the data he used, and of the methodology of his arguments, the ideas he developed in his late work in this area lead us to horizons where we can glimpse how the evolution of human thought itself has been shaped by the processes of social change.

Religion and the categories of thought

Durkheim was by no means the first to argue that religious beliefs reflect the societies in which they are current. As we have already mentioned, Marx famously described religion as 'the opiate of the people' and, before him, the Young Hegelians, Bauer and Feuerbach, had already argued that religion had an ideological function, serving the interests of the ruling groups in society by justifying the existing pattern of inequalities as divinely ordained. And before them, Tom Paine in *The Age of Reason* (1794) had said much the same. If that were all there was to it, however, you might have thought more people would have seen through the sham sooner. These views do not come to grips with:

a. **the universality** of religious belief, which is to say, in every known society there has existed some general set of religious beliefs and practices;
b. **the power** of religions to inspire faith, to command awe from their adherents and require some respect for these powers even from non-adherents; and
c. **the comprehensiveness** of religious belief as: (i) systematic myth; (ii) moral code; and (iii) a cognitive system of ideas and concepts.

Where the social factors in religious belief and practice had been dealt with before, it was in terms of the rational discussion of the credibility of belief and disbelief. It did not give any adequate sociological account of religious faith and the transcendence of ordinary practical reason. This was what Durkheim thought he could explain by analysing belief and practice as social facts.

Durkheim defined religion as:

> ... a unified system of beliefs and practices relative to sacred things, that is to say, things set apart and forbidden – beliefs and practices which unite into one single moral community called a church, all who adhere to them.
>
> ((1912) 1956, p. 62)

The first point to note is the distinction between the *sacred* and the secular world. Some things are set apart from the familiar everyday practical world. They are charged with symbolic power: they include material objects, particular places, ritual acts, names or verbal formulae. They are to be approached with awe and perhaps only by specially designated individuals or only after certain purifying preparations. These sacred things may be purpose-made artefacts or buildings or carefully composed texts or rites, but they can be apparently ordinary enough – water, a big stone, a hilltop, fire – until endowed with the power of sacredness, which on other occasions, or in other instances, they do not have. The objects may be venerated as sacred in themselves or as merely instrumental in representing the sacred symbolically. Religion consists of a set of beliefs about the sacred and the rituals which give us access to it. Such rituals range from a simple gesture, to a short spoken phrase, to elaborate works of great art with full-time specialist performers thoroughly rehearsed for the special occasion. They all serve to bring together, in a single moral community, those who share in the rite, who share a faith in the mystery it symbolizes (see Bellah, 1970).

All societies have had some kind of religion. Often we may know little else about them apart from the sacred objects or the sites of their ritual they have left behind. Durkheim's analysis of religions and their social setting is fairly straightforward. Religious systems are functionally related to the *conscience collective* and type of social solidarity within which they are current. In the simplest hunting and gathering societies, like the Australian aboriginal peoples, simple totemic beliefs reflect the small-scale kinship-based system. Some object

– an animal, or plant, or a feature of the landscape – is held sacred because it is taken as an emblem of the identity of the clan, the way in which we might recognize a flag or a badge. More complex societies have more complex patterns of beliefs. Traditional kingdoms tend to worship a personalized god who rules the people much like their ruler but immortally. In such societies the god is not a personal god, but the god of the people collectively. His blessings and his wrath are manifested in the fertility of the fields, the bounty of the waters, or the terror of the tempest, and the hunger and thirst of the famine years. These fall upon the people, as a whole, for their faithfulness or their sins. The individual suffers or survives with the rest, not according to his personal deserts. This clearly reflects the mechanical solidarity of these societies. Individuals are not singled out. All worship, and all share the same fate.

More complex societies uniting several communities under a high king or emperor generally have polytheistic religions with gods and goddesses of place, and often with different functions. The division of divine labour reflects the rudimentary division of labour in society. It is with the growth of organic solidarity, with the increasing awareness of individual differences that the elemental gods of harvest and war, fertility and thunder become, firstly, gods of justice and creation, and then personal gods of conscience too; and the morality of individual action displaces the submission to the divine will of an arbitrary god. The conscience collective of the most highly differentiated large-scale societies is reflected in the monotheism of a single, all-powerful, universal god who, nevertheless, speaks through the individual conscience. The monotheistic religions recognize a personal god of infinite power and universal relevance. This, Durkheim believed, parallels the individualism of societies of organic solidarity and the universality of the advanced division of labour. As the increase in individualism in society at the same time entails a greater than ever dependency upon that society, so the supreme being becomes almighty and omnipotent in just those religions which focus upon the spiritual cure of each and every individual soul.

We can broadly trace, then, the transition from mechanical to organic solidarity in the symbolic expression of the conscience collective in religious myth. Durkheim is arguing that it is the transformation of society and its meaning for its members that is represented in the awesome personifications of transcendent power. In fact, the power which is eternal, which transcends personal experience and the will of any individual is precisely the power of society itself. Durkheim makes the point clearly:

> In a general way, it is unquestionable that a society has all that is necessary to arouse the sensation of the divine in minds, merely by the power that it has over them; for to its members it is what a god is to his worshippers. In fact, a god is, first of all, a being whom men think of as superior to themselves, and upon whom they feel that they depend. Whether it be a conscious personality, such as Zeus or Jahweh, or merely abstract forces such as those in play in totemism, the worshipper, in the one case as in the other, believes himself held to certain manners of acting which are imposed upon him by the nature of the sacred principle with which he feels he is in communion. Now society also gives us the sensation of a perpetual dependence ... at every instant we are obliged to submit ourselves to rules of conduct and of thought which we have neither made nor desired, and which are sometimes even contrary to our most fundamental inclinations and instincts. (1912, pp. 236–7)

Religion, in a word, is the representation of society in a symbolic form. The anonymous and impersonal force made incarnate in all sacred things is the power of society itself. The powers of the gods over the lives of men and women hardly exceeds the power of society over its members. It was there before them and will not die when they die. It makes them in its own image. It provides for their survival and protects them from enemies. It is the source of most of their joy and all the peace they know. And it will destroy them if they stray too far from its rules. The power of a deity symbolizes this sometimes capricious, sometimes relentless power writ large, perhaps extended to infinite scope, omnipotent, omniscient and eternal but, nevertheless, given a name, an identity, made at least symbolically tangible.

Of course, *prima facie*, the astonishing variety of religious myths, creeds, faiths, doctrines and beliefs, all proclaimed as true by some preacher, priest or prophet, immediately suggests to some people that all of them, or at any rate all the others except the one which the reader adheres, must be false. Durkheim, however, argued that sociology did not justify this view.

> The most barbarous and the most fantastic rites and the strangest myths translate some human need, some aspect of life, either individual or social. The reasons with which the faithful justify them may be, and generally are, erroneous; but the true reasons do not cease to exist, and it is the duty of science to discover them. In reality, then, there are no religions which are false. All are true in their own fashion; all answer, though in different ways, to the given conditions of human existence.   ((1912) 1956 edn, pp. 14–15)

It is sometimes suggested that Durkheim is being disingenuous in this argument and that, in fact, he set out to explain away religious belief as no more than the symbolic manifestation of the worship of society (e.g. Oliver, 1976; Hamnett, 1984) As he said in *The Elementary Forms of Religious Life*, '... god and society are one' (1912, p. 206.) This might be literally interpreted if the god is false – and it can be argued that since many of them make mutually exclusive claims, all the competing religious beliefs cannot at the same time be true, though that does not exclude the possibility of one or some of them being true. Durkheim, in fact, argued that all are true, and this has interesting parallels in Christian theological humanism (e.g. Robinson, 1963; Cuppitt, 1980) and the long tradition of Socinianism (see McLachlan, 1972). Durkheim's ecumenical view, that all religions contain an aspect of the truth, may not much appeal to fundamentalists, either among believers or nonbelievers. The issue really is a matter of what kind of truth it is that religions convey.

Durkheim's view of religion as rooted in social relations does not, by itself, indicate that any particular religious belief is false. The social origins of our religious discoveries – like those of other, for instance scientific, discoveries – may only be the paths which have led us to a truth. It took the technical resources of twentieth-century science, the organizational structures of university scientific research, and a culture of fundamental empirical curiosity for Crick and Watson to begin to unravel the secrets of DNA. What they discovered was, of course, always true, but was not understood previously because neither science nor society had yet reached a position to make the discovery possible. This is equally the case with philosophical or moral truths. Discoveries are to be made. Each new prophet draws upon the possibilities of his time, not necessarily to tell us something new, but something we were not previously in a position to understand. The sociology of religion can tell us nothing about the validity of the beliefs it studies. No amount of sociological research will tell you whether there really are angels or no such things as the winged Eumenides or Odin and his eight-legged horse. Durkheim believed that the discovery of the transcendent, the sense of a power beyond the powers of ordinary people that shaped our lives and prescribed how we should act, was achieved through the symbolic representation of society and the conscience collective in religious belief and practice. Whether they facilitated an authentic discovery or merely an exaggerated and melodramatic projection of this-worldly relationships is, in the end, a theological question, perhaps a matter of faith, but beyond the scope of sociological determination. It remains for the believer and the sceptic to argue their cases as before.

Durkheim's discussion of the close correspondence of the religious and social structural aspects of a culture was apparently based on a detailed examination, drawing on secondary sources, of the totemic beliefs of some of the Australian aboriginal peoples. He thought totemism was the most elementary form of religious experience and ritual. These people worshipped no gods, but each clan group maintained an annual cycle of ritual gatherings in celebration and reverence for their totem, the spiritual emblem of their collective identity. It is not wholly clear that he was correct in assuming this kind of religion was, in fact, simpler in practice, or more elementary in its beliefs, than animist religions. Animists believe that every rock or tree, indeed potentially everything in the living and material world has its *mana*, its inherent spirit which endows it with a kind of supernatural power, which we must acknowledge and, if necessary, propitiate. However, this might not, perhaps, have illustrated his argument so effectively. And, if he had decided that animism really was the more elementary form, it might still have made no difference to his overall conclusions. After all, he had already summarized the core of his argument 15 years earlier in *Suicide*. Religion, he argued there, '... is the system of symbols by means of which society becomes conscious of itself; it is the characteristic way of thinking of collective existence' (1957, p. 312). But, on the other hand, the less obviously social content of animist beliefs would have made a more convincing test of that position were it treated only as an hypothesis rather than as a starting-point assumption.

Nevertheless, Durkheim considered that – what was so obvious to him in these Australian cultures – such direct correspondences between collective identity and religious ritual were elementary in the other sense too. That is to say, they were not just simple, but were the fundamental units out of which more elaborated forms of liturgy, mythology and dogma can be related to their gestation within the processes of more complex social structures.

At the same time, it is not at all evident that more elaborated belief systems did evolve from totemic origins. Drawing inferences about any other culture from this Australian material would, therefore, again be a doubtful procedure. However, even if totemic beliefs are not, in either sense, so elementary as he thought them to be, the general functional argument remains an important one. It still presents us with ways of thinking about religion and society which raise exciting questions we might never otherwise have thought of pursuing. The social facts Durkheim believed he had established about religion in his study of its elementary forms were:

1. The **universality** of the distinction between the sacred and the secular. This reflects the functional significance of the sacred as the symbol of the transcendent powers of the *conscience collective*.
2. The **power** of the sacred focuses the unlimited force of the organized society over and against the vulnerability of the lone individual.
3. The **comprehensiveness** of religious belief as the earliest and most general way in which the *conscience collective* symbolically represents itself. Religious belief is the seedbed from which all other systems of thought have grown.

Durkheim's earlier work gives us a simplified model of social change which provides for a consideration of the possible positive and negative consequences of the increasing social division of labour. He did not live to discuss the implications for this of his later examination of the social facts relating to religious belief and practice. The connection, however, needs to be made and is of obviously central relevance for the further exploration of the wider cultural repercussions of the continuing trend toward what he called, more organic structures. Occupational specialization and differentiation, and the degree of social and cultural pluralism in urban-industrial societies, have increased a great deal since Durkheim's death in 1917. But we can learn a lot from his ideas about the collective representations of modern societies. It is not that he offers us a blueprint for present day cultures, still less of the future, but that he draws our sociological attention to general issues that we might very easily overlook, or fail to think rationally about, without him. That is what he believed sociology was for and, in his case, it fulfils its mission.

Durkheim's most original contribution to the development of sociological thought was his discussion of the social origins of knowledge. Not just our religious beliefs but all our ideas, he argued, have grown out of our evolving collective social experience. Durkheim's sociology of knowledge can be contrasted: firstly, with the tradition of relativist thought, stemming from Marx and developed, for example, through Lukács ((1923) 1971) and Mannheim ((1936) 1960), which located political and moral, religious and aesthetic ideas as, in essence, legitimizing epiphenomena of class interests; and, secondly, with more recent postmodernist discussion of the prescriptive effects of discourse. Durkheim's perspective is more radical than the first, in that he argued that the very categories we employ in organizing our ideas; time, space, causation, totality and truth are the product or, if you like, the achievement of social life (1912, p. 489). It is more grounded than the second in that these organizing concepts are not treated as the arbitrary axioms of discourse, but are related to the structural conditions of human social relations.

Where the German philosopher Kant (1724–1804) had been forced to conclude that the categories of thought were irreducible 'given' properties of mind, that was an inevitable consequence of his individualistic analysis of rational thought.

But if they are not part of the genetically programmed physiological endowment of the human brain, the concepts of time and space, cause and classification and the like, have to be learnt. The senses, sight and smell, hearing and touch, by themselves only provide the separate images which the categories of perception and thought organize into meaningful experience. Durkheim noted: '... the space which I know by my senses, of which I am the centre, could not be space in general, which contains all extensions and where all these are coordinated by personal guidelines which are common to everybody' (1912, p. 441). He argued instead that sociological realism allows us to see how it is the shared experience of the conscience collective which gives the idea of space a general property we can all acknowledge. Of course, in some sense, space is 'really' out there, but the way we conceive of it reflects our experience of it. So the aboriginal peoples envisaged space as a great circle extending outward from the circle of their encampments, and we, if we are up to it, as part of the curved space-time continuum, and, if we are not, as a three dimensional Euclidean geometry going on endlessly in all directions.

Outback time was envisaged in terms of the recurrent ritual of their tribal life, much as in the west the calendar incorporates the yearly cycle of religious feast days and public holidays. Of course, they recognized the succession of day and night and the process of growing older. Again, time itself is not an invention, but they made sense of it, conceived images which made it possible to think about it that were derived from their shared social experience. Similarly, we may subjectively feel the days drag or the week evaporate before it seems like Tuesday, but our impersonal clockwork and calendar time, which moves at its own remorseless pace, is the same for all and comes from our shared experience as people, in different situations, interacting interdependently.

Because concepts come from shared, not purely subjective experience, they must, initially at least, have reflected the life of the collectivity. As distinct from the motivated actions of one individual in relation to another, causal relationships between events can be conceived of because of the impact of collective activities on individual lives. They are both potent and impersonal. Similarly, our notion of truth as an impersonal standard of objectivity, apart from individual tellings and individual preferences, relates personal experience to the collective character of shared social knowledge. It is also society, not any individual, that impersonally, impartially divides up the world of men and things, events and experiences into sacred and secular, this clan and that clan, stranger and brother, men's work and women's work.

> They not only come from society, but the things which they express are of a social nature. Not only is it society which had founded them, but their contents are the different aspects of social being; the category of class was at first indistinct from the concept of the human group; it is the rhythm of social life which is at the basis of the category of time; the territory occupied by the society furnished the material for the category of space; it was the collective force which was the prototype of the concept of efficient force, an essential element in the category of causality.
>
> (1912, p. 488)

The tendency towards the generalization and greater abstraction of these categorical concepts in the sciences, in philosophy, in education and in daily discourse is an indication of the increasing diversity and complexity of the social experience which they have to contain within a progressively differentiated society. So Durkheim argued that not only the moral values of individualism, but the organizing concepts which enable us to understand the world are themselves products of our social experience and were originally presented in the language of religious imagery.

As a moral individualist, believing that individual freedom and reason were the highest values attained in the course of human history, Durkheim was, at the same time, a sociological realist who believed that these values were arrived at as a result of the evolution of human society. That was not to detract from their value or validity, but to emphasize both their vulnerability to changing circumstance and to point to how precious and precarious was their human achievement. As the processes of change continue, no doubt from the fertile imaginations of creative individuals – after all some*one* must have been the first to think of the wheel – new ways will evolve of thinking about nearness or remoteness, or about time. Thus instead of causal determinism being like the calculable impact of a billiard ball as it strikes another, we begin to think in terms of probabilities. In the postmodern world, as we shall discuss in Chapter 9, truth becomes relativized in terms of ideological perspective or is deconstructed, while the individual is decentred from our discourse and there remains only text, whatever *that* means. Durkheim's sociological realism offers us a way into all this relativism and possibly, in the end, a way out too.

In summary: (1) He has little to say about the origins of change. His focus on the *conscience collective* and on collective representations is consensus orientated, though in his analysis conflict arises, sometimes pathologically, but in normal circumstances too. (2) In spite of the single, simple evolutionary trend that seems to underlie his conception of social change, his perspective is not historicist. The future is open-ended and although social processes have their own distinct dynamics, there is an important moral role to be played by the state and by concerned individuals. Durkheim's sociology is (3) sociologically realist, and (4) neither materialist nor idealist. Social facts are explicable only in relation to other social facts and are not reducible to either a material or an ideal substratum. (5) Though his value commitments are clearly evident, the general character of his analyses is scientific rather than ideological, and he was deeply concerned that sociology should become established as an independent social science. However, (6) though his researches on suicide and religion are based on what was, at the time, the best available empirical data, the structure of his arguments is heavily weighted in terms of general organizing assumptions, in the light of which the evidence is interpreted. His insistence on the non-reducibility of social facts is *aprioristic* and the basic model of change in *The Division of Labour* is a contrast of ideal-typical constructs. This adds up to a rationalist approach to science in the European tradition rather than to an empiricist one. Durkheim's sociology, like his view of society, is more than the sum of its parts. For all the reservations on points of detail that, in retrospect, cloud much of his substantive work, the enduring value of it all is in its imaginative range, which was not only pioneering when it was new, but remains challenging in addressing the limits of human understanding. Any exploration of the more far-reaching cultural consequences of social change must cross intellectual territory he was amongst the first to map.

8

Systems Theories: Functional Integration and Global Convergence

The functional analogy and the interconnectedness of change

As we have seen, the idea that the social sciences were especially concerned with explaining the unintended consequences of human action goes back at least as far as Adam Smith and Adam Ferguson in the eighteenth century. It is based on the view that society has the character of a system. That is to say, its different parts are interrelated, interdependent and interactive. The conflicts and cooperation, the dealings people have with one another, the changes and continuities in their relationships and mutual understandings are not separable, unique or accidental encounters; but can only be properly understood when taken together as a whole. The whole is greater than the sum of its parts, and that is what is unaccounted for when we have merely examined each of the constituent activities, relationships or institutions. What even the most searching scrutiny of the particulars leaves out, that is, is the pattern of relationships between them, the system as such.

To perceive and describe a pattern in the constantly changing kaleidoscope of apparently momentous and fleeting events and encounters of social life, we will need to find some schematic image or analogy with which we can begin to grasp its protean diversity. The discovery of simplified conceptual models is, after all, what explanation is about and, to make sense of very complex questions, looking for analogies in other kinds of experience can often be helpful. At the same time, analogies or similes are never exact. Indeed, they can be very misleading if applied uncritically. In looking for parallels, we need to be clear about just how far they in fact correspond to the situations they are supposed to represent.

Durkheim, as we saw in the last chapter, made extensive use of the organic analogy in discussing the differentiation of the social division of labour. But it would clearly be absurd to pursue every possible implication of the comparison in every respect. There are all sorts of ways in which a society is not at all like a living organism. Poetic references to head or heart apart, it goes without saying there is no matching society's social institutions to the organs of the body. What would correspond to the kidneys or the elbow of society? Functionally and developmentally, there are no real parallels either. When new societies are established, they do not recapitulate the life-cycle of their parents as organic life forms do. The Pilgrim Fathers, having crossed the Atlantic to America, did not have to begin again at the neolithic stage. Nor do societies have a fixed or normal life-span. Some ancient cultures lasted relatively unchanged for millennia, while other societies have disappeared after only a few generations. Comparison of the operational conditions of any society cannot satisfactorily be made with the normal life of an organism either. Durkheim's concept of social pathology, on the analogy of organic health or illness, is quite unhelpful. Physical sickness can be defined in terms of functional impairment, but it is much more difficult to disentangle such notions from ethical or political considerations when we look at societies. Was the Soviet Union a healthier society when the Siberian labour-camps were in full operation and the show-trials went unchallenged, or when perestroika began to shake the totalitarian foundations? Only in the case of the structural parallel, and then only in the most general sense, does the organic analogy offer even the loosest thread to guide our explorations in the social labyrinth. But the idea has, nevertheless, often given social theorists whatever confidence they have had that their endeavours were getting somewhere. From the organic analogy, we derive the idea of a systematic interdependence of social institutions; in plain terms, the notion that if changes occur in one area, there will be all sorts of repercussions elsewhere and ramifying consequences in other institutions, which may not have been foreseen. The highly differentiated and sometimes seemingly independent parts of society are all interconnected, and flourish only in the continuing vitality of the whole system.

The three theories I discuss in this chapter share an emphasis upon the way in which social systems structure the possibilities of change. Though they offer quite different accounts of what societies are like and how they work, they have in common a central focus on the systemic properties of the social world. They are species of systems theory. Of course, all theories assume there is some systematic and therefore intelligible pattern of relationships amongst the component concepts they draw our attention to. But for most theorists, it is these ideas themselves that are important. So, as we have seen, one theorist or another will ask us to think of society as composed of economically determined and competing social classes, or as consisting of ideal-typical rational actors, as differentiated in a division of labour, or as following an evolutionary succession of developmental stages, or perhaps as a process of symbolically negotiated interaction, conflict or synergy, or whatever. The theories I want to discuss here, however, have concentrated on the character of the system as such, its 'systemness'. That is to say, these theories take the view that since the whole is more than the sum of its parts, it is only by studying the character of that whole that we can begin to understand what happens. The originality of the theories considered in this chapter does not lie in their conceptual elements, which for the most part they have taken over from other writers, but in their emphasis on the properties of the system within which they operate.

The first, and most general, of these theories I want to look at is the work of Talcott Parsons and his development of Structural Functionalism. We have already considered his neo-evolutionary theory of change in Chapter 3. But Parsons's attempt to offer an abstract and comprehensive account of all social systems has much more general implications, and has been more widely influential than that. Parsons believed that we should take the idea of society as a social system seriously. That would involve recognizing that the formal, almost mathematical, properties that give coherence to any system must also underlie the processes of human society too. Obviously, if societies can be thought of as social systems in this sense, then the possibilities for change will be governed by the same set of ground rules which order societies in general.

The second example of a systems approach is the formerly influential development of Marxist theory as applied to the economic underdevelopment of the less-industrialized countries. Frank's Dependency Theory sought to show, for example, that the economic backwardness of the poorest countries of the world could not be explained in terms of local factors in those countries themselves, but was the inevitable result of the way the world capitalist system was structured globally. Though deploying very different terminologies and concepts, Dependency Theory and Structural Functionalism both treated existing social systems as essentially self-stabilizing states, in which little change takes place except to restore the existing equilibrium. Major social changes would only be possible as a result of some external intervention upsetting the existing balance of forces.

In contrast with the importance given to exogenous change in Parsonian Structural Functionalism, on the one hand, and in Dependency Theory, on the other, the Convergence Theorists, such as Kerr or Galbraith, argued that as a result of the inherent logic of industrial production, all industrialized or industrializing countries will, in the long run, tend toward a similar pattern of economic, social and political organization. Endogenous change is generated within, and by, the logic of the system itself to bring about a convergence in line with the system needs of industrial society. The apparent contrast with the resistance to change emphasized by Dependency Theorists, however, is misleading. Like Parsons's Structural Functionalism, both these theories are equilibrium models, but differ in terms of the point in the equilibrium process they focus on. Convergence Theorists drew our attention to the emergence of an equilibrium, while Dependency Theorists were primarily concerned with the persistence of an equilibrium which, they argued, had already established itself.

Convergence Theory and Dependency Theory offered specific explanations: in the first case, for the kinds of social change we might expect to observe in industrialized societies; or, in the second case, for why we should not expect to see any very great changes at all in the unindustrialized countries. Structural Functionalism, however, is a much more abstract kind of theory. It represents what, in Parsons's estimation, were the essential and universal properties of any and all social systems, and therefore, by implication, the conditions within which any sort of social change might be possible. In all three perspectives, however, the key idea is that, in order to account for change, or anything else for that matter, we cannot look at just one factor, or set of factors, in isolation, but need to understand the system as a whole.

Parsons and the social system

Talcott Parsons (1902–1979) started out as an action theorist, strongly influenced by the methodological individualism of Max Weber, whose *Protestant Ethic and the Spirit of Capitalism* he was the first to translate into English. He attempted to develop a general account of how social systems are constituted from the actions of individuals which are structured through the patterns of role expectations into which the social actors are socialized. At the most general level of analysis, he concluded that the character of social systems was determined by five basic pattern variables. Parsons proposed, that is to say, that the members of every sociocultural system must make a number of general choices about how they will ordinarily act and interact with one another. These choices, he argued, comprise five dilemmas, pairs of action-alternatives which will dictate how the system as a whole will operate.

We encountered two of these pairs of possible patterns of social action when considering Parsons's discussion of modernization in Chapter 3. Modernization, he argued, could be characterized as a replacement of particularistic ascription in the allocation and definition of social roles, by a general preference for universalistic achievement. In modern societies people achieve social positions on the basis of universalistic criteria such as their competence in handling a task, regardless of their social origins. In traditional societies, by contrast, people are ascribed their positions because of who they are, as members of a particular clan or residents in a particular place, and not on the basis of some impersonal assessment of their ability. The other three pattern variables Parsons identified were: (a) *Affectivity* versus *Affective Neutrality*, that is to say, the importance of emotional considerations versus their conventional exclusion from the culturally prescribed way roles are defined or institutions structured. This might be illustrated, for example, by the contrast between what would usually be expected of the relationship between a mother and her children, on the one hand, as against what we would tend to expect of a capable shoe-shop assistant and her customers, on the other; (b) *Self-orientation* versus *Collectivity orientation* appears to refer to a preference for, and identification with, group loyalties, as against, in the case of self-orientation, a kind of utilitarian preoccupation with individual self-interest. This opposition was dropped from

Parsons's later accounts of the pattern variables, presumably because, in practice, it seems hard to distinguish from the final pair; and (c) *Specificity* versus *Diffuseness*, the remaining pattern variable, refers to the limited character or all-embracingness of relationships and the social institutions they may constitute. Specific relations exist for a single, unambiguous purpose without latent overtones; surgeon and patient, waiter and diner, for example. Diffuse relationships involve unspecified commitments and – along with instrumental, practical cooperation in some job for instance – may also entail emotional support in times of stress, leisure-time companionship, political string-pulling or whatever else friends, relatives or neighbours are good for.

The five pattern variables:

Particularism	—	Universalism
Ascription	—	Achievement
Affectivity	—	Affective Neutrality
Collective Orientation	—	Self-orientation
Diffuseness	—	Specificity

are universal dilemmas which have to be resolved in pursuing any course of action, and in structuring the expectations we have of one another in taking on our various social roles (1951, p. 67). All social action must be located within these, and only these sets of alternatives (Parsons and Shils, p. 76). Everything from the role behaviour of individual social actors to complete social systems, therefore, can be classified in terms of the five pattern variables, though Parsons believed that only about half of the 32 possible combinations of options were actually to be found in real societies. They represent a sort of grid reference, which can be used not only to compare different societies, but in principle can be used to map social or cultural change. As we have already seen, for Parsons, the process of modernization can be described as a move from ascription to achievement, and from particularism to universalism. On the other hand, he also appears to argue that the pattern variables should be regarded as dimensions rather than stark either/ or alternatives. So, according to the Human Relations school of management theory, workers supposedly should not be treated in entirely impersonal or universalistic terms, while even American parents do not relate to their children wholly on a particularistic basis, but mostly come to expect them to conform to some general standards of behaviour. The character of any given culture therefore will not be reducible to a simple checklist among polarized variables, but will instead reflect the relative emphasis on some rather than, but not to the exclusion of, their alternatives.

The pattern variables, however, remain an essentially descriptive framework and do not in themselves offer us any explanation of what choices will be made or why change might or might not occur. What is more, and notwithstanding Parsons's belief in their comprehensiveness, they add up to what can only be regarded as either a wilfully blinkered view of history or a seriously deficient imagination concerning the exigencies of even ordinary everyday social experience. The list of dilemmas is really very remarkable for what it leaves out. It disregards such issues as power-endowed or powerless, legitimate or illegitimate, consensual or conflictual, sincere or playful, or any number of other unavoidable dilemmas for social action, role-taking or institutional coherence. But extending the list would not add to the explanatory power of the pattern variables. We might be able to produce more recognisable descriptions of the social predicaments we encounter, but we would still not know why social systems or individuals' social behaviour ever change.

Parsons's later work, however, developed in an important new direction, away from Action Theory and towards a more sociologically realist concern with the emergent properties of the social system itself. From a sociological point of view, this was not only a radical change of perspective, but, potentially at least, promised to go beyond mere taxonomy of social action, and offer a genuine and general scientific account of social order. Instead of a reductionist reliance on the motivations of actors as the ultimate determinant of social processes which Action Theory entails, Parsons now introduced a truly structural vector into his discussion, and with it began to develop an abstract, universally applicable and explanatory Systems Theory. Beginning with *The Social System* (1951), Parsons developed these ideas in a number of later important collaborations with Robert Bales (1956), Edward Shils (1951) and Neil Smelser (1956). Such a theory of social systems could at last offer us another aspect of what Comte had aspired to, that is, a scientific explanation of the universal processes which have shaped societies in the past and will determine how they develop in the future. This project represents a fully mature structural functionalism. Its achievements and limitations, I believe, can tell us a great deal about the potential for any general and abstract sociological theory.

The simple, but profound question which Parsons's structural functionalism confronts is: 'what are the necessary conditions for any society to survive?' If we think of society as a social system, this can be answered in the following way. To endure at all, any system must meet certain conditions in relation to its external environment and its internal cohesion and reproduction. The social order as a whole, or, in fact, any set of relationships, can persist only if some provision is made to meet these needs. The functions of the system, indeed, can be regarded as necessarily directed toward those ends, and how they are fulfilled determines what the structure of the system will be.

In a late article, published in 1961, Parsons summarized, and slightly revised, his earlier discussions of these conditions:

> I have suggested that it is possible to reduce the essential functional imperatives of any system, to four, which I have called pattern maintenance, integration, goal attainment and adaptation. These are listed in order of significance from the point of view of cybernetic control of action processes in the system type under consideration. (1961, p. 38)

These four functional imperatives, or functional prerequisites, of any social system, then, were that:

a. any system must have the means of adapting to its external environment;
b. any system must have some acknowledged way of attaining its goals;
c. any system must be able to integrate its internal component parts;
d. any system must be capable of mobilizing its resources in order to act for the maintenance of the system as a whole. In Parsons's earlier terminology, that is to say it must have latency, but in his later work he described this as the imperative of pattern maintenance.

These issues prescribe the four 'dimensions of the action space' within which social processes take place. (Parsons, 1954, p. 412), though in his later essay, influenced by the then new ideas of cybernetics, he refers to them as control mechanisms (1961). It isn't wholly clear how far this new metaphor represents a real shift in his thinking, or merely a new rhetoric. However, in the context of our concern with social change, the changing imagery is not merely cosmetic, but represents a greater emphasis on social dynamics than in his earlier work. The structures and processes defined by these imperatives, Parsons believed, at last provided for an analysis of social systems which would have all the universality and precision of the natural sciences:

> The functional reference of all particular conditions and processes to the state of the total system as a going concern ... provides the logical equivalent of simultaneous equations in a fully developed system of analytic theory. (1954, p. 218)

Structurally, within any given social system each of the functional imperatives is catered for by a subsystem. Thus we should be able to identify four subsystems within each larger social system. As an open system 'engaged in processes of interchange with environing systems' there will of necessity be:

> ... the subsystem organized about the adaptive problems of the total system. There should then be a subsystem oriented to system-goal attainment, one to system-integration and one to expression and maintenance (including socialization) of the institutionalized ascriptive-qualitative pattern-complex, that is, a subsystem with primarily 'cultural' functions.
>   (1954, p. 399)

Thus for a whole society or nation state, the economy, which provides for the production and distribution of goods through the application of technology, enables the society to adapt to, and survive, in its physical environment. The political system provides for the achievement of the society's collective goals. The various aspects of community life in the family, neighbourhood, congregation and club provide for the integration of the members of society, while the mobilization of potential is given by the cultural values latent in every social institution throughout the system. Each of these subsystems and their component elements, the firms and corporations, the political parties and national assemblies, the kinship networks and churches, all in turn have the same four functional imperatives of operation and endurance. So we can speak of the politics of the firm (Tivey, 1978), the economy of the household (Schulz, 1974), the values of the sergeant's mess. The same goes for cultural subsystems too. A religious creed, a nationalist tradition, a professional code of conduct also need to adapt to their respective environments, both to carry through their goals and to integrate their component elements, and need to be able to motivate and mobilize action.

Thus the systematic analysis applies at each level of structural organization:

> ... a complex social system consists of a network of interdepend-ent and interpenetrating subsystems, each of which, seen at the appropriate level of reference, is a social system in its own right, subject to all the functional exigencies of any such system relative to its institutionalized culture and situation and possessing all the essential structural components, organized on the appropriate levels of differentiation and specification. (1961, p. 44)

As part of the integrative subsystem of the larger society, the family, in general or in each particular instance, can be regarded as a microsystem with the same functional prerequisites. Adaptation to its economic environment may take the form of providing wage-earners and, in return, receiving income and consumer goods. Goal attainment for the family involves a decision-making system, which in some societies may be predominantly patriarchal or, in others, allow for more joint decision making. Integration will be sustained through the rituals of eating and shared leisure activities, and all motivated – to a greater or lesser extent, at different stages in the family cycle – by the ties of affection and the duty felt by, that is to say the values shared by, family members (Bell and Vogel, 1964).

The functioning of each subsystem has repercussions for the way all the others operate. So, at the level of society as a whole, with the advent of industrialized manufacturing, the adaptive subsystem of society was so extensively restructured that the goal attainment systems, notably the political representation of new economic interests and the social groups they gave rise to, had to be accommodated in parliamentary reform. Within the integrative subsystems of society, industrialization had a profound impact on communities, and family life had to adapt to the new patterns of work and career, with a shift away from extended kinship networks to more geographically mobile nuclear family units better able to respond to the changing circumstances of a changing society (Burgess and Locke, 1953; Harris, 1983). The pattern-maintenance system changed too, with a decline in the value placed on traditional ways and a new emphasis on the individual, and upon individuals' rights and opportunities. So the industrial revolution, far from being merely a series of technological innovations, had ramifications throughout the social system, with every subsystem adapting to the new circumstances (Smelser, 1964).

It is easy to see, then, that the systems model clearly should have implications for our better understanding of change. Changes in one subsystem will bring about changes in each of the other subsystems. They in turn will have further effects elsewhere, including on the subsystems where the initial changes occurred. Unfortunately, it is, however, far from clear what sort of changes we should expect according to the theory, and less clear still how far we should expect them to go.

In dealing with such a formal and abstract theory, we will leave aside, for the present, the historical accuracy of structural functionalist accounts of, for instance, the social and cultural repercussions of the industrial revolution in Russia or the structure of present day Korean family life. Some of the critical findings we referred to in discussing Weber (e.g. Laslett, 1969, 1977; Macfarlane, 1978, 1987; Nimkoff and Middleton, 1960) present equally serious objections here too. But as with other theorists we have considered, the most damaging weaknesses of structural functionalism are to be found in the structure of its arguments rather than in the dubious quality of the historical data which may be supposed to illustrate them.

To begin with, however, the frequently raised objection that functional explanations are unsatisfactory because they are teleological, that is, because they explain things in terms of their goals or consequences, must be dealt with. This is not a valid criticism of systems theories. Of course, they explain why things are the way they are in terms of their purposes or aims. What is wrong with that? Many familiar systems can only be understood in terms of what they are set up to do. Feedback mechanisms like the thermostat in a central-heating system operate so as to bring about and maintain a desired state. A great deal of human, meaningful activity can only be understood in terms of the future it is concerned to bring about. Only the coming harvest can account for the spring sowing. A great deal more only makes sense in the light of a future it cannot avert. The premium you pay for your life assurance is calculated on next year's anticipated deaths, even though it remains uncertain whether you will be numbered among them. There is nothing unscientific about explaining actions with reference to their objectives, or about describing a homeostatic or equilibrium-maintaining system operating so as to maintain a balance between the forces at work upon it. Animate and inanimate systems do it all the time (see Stinchcombe, 1968).

Parsons was, for him, very clear about the variable elements of his theory. He distinguished those internal variables which responded so as to maintain an equilibrium *within* a given social system from those external variables that could produce a change *to* the system itself:

> The concept of equilibrium is a fundamental reference point for analysing the processes by which a system either comes to terms with the exigencies imposed by a changing environment, without essential change in its own structure, or fails to come to terms and undergoes other processes such as structural change, dissolution as a boundary maintaining system (analogous to biological death to the organism) or the consolidation of some impairment leading to the establishment of secondary structures of a 'pathological' character. (1961, p. 37)

This is an important statement for our appreciation of Parsons's developed theory in several respects. Firstly, it distinguishes between short-term or equilibrating changes, on the one hand, and long-term or structural changes, on the other. Secondly, it is clear that Parsons envisaged the termination or collapse of systems as a real possibility resulting from structural change. Thirdly, he makes clear his view that structural changes are the result of external factors. Unlike historicist theories which claim to delineate an already known future, Parsons's structural functionalism describes only the consequences of the imperatives of a social order as it happens to be constituted. Structural change, involving changes to the core values of the system as a whole, cannot be accounted for within the structural functionalist model, though it might accommodate structural change within subsystems. Finally, it is clear from the quotation that the existence of secondary 'pathological' structures incorporates the view that not all the features of the social order always necessarily contribute directly to its effective functioning.

Unlike the Marxist analysis of modes of production, functionalists do not assume *a priori* that social systems must be auto-destructive, but nor do they assume their perpetual survival. While a system survives, in order to maintain the homeostatic balance, each subsystem must continually adjust to changes in the other subsystems, and each functional adjustment feeds back into the functioning of the others. If things turn out unexpectedly, the functionalist will either point to external factors which have intervened to upset the self-equilibrium of the system or, if that should prove to be difficult to show, he would have to admit to having inadequately specified the system he set out to analyse. Even confining our attention to the social system as a going concern and making the 'other things being equal' assumption, however, the apparent precision of the structural functionalist model begins to dissolve when we push the analysis further. Leaving aside what many would regard as the central questions concerning the causes of externally originating change, the promised algebra of mutual subsystem adjustments and compensatory adaptations fails to provide us with either a clear or convincing picture. There are three main reasons for this: they relate to problems of:

a. boundary definition;
b. system integration; and
c. the direction of effects.

a. **Boundary definition**: Each subsystem has to provide for the same four functional imperatives as the larger system of which it is a part. The problem of an analytical infinite regression is obvious where each subsystem necessarily consists of sub-subsystems and so on (Black, 1961). If a system is defined by its maintaining its boundary with other systems, then the boundary-definition and pattern-maintenance imperatives are the same. But the core values of the system as a whole may not be those of the separate subsystems that comprise it, nor may those of one subsystem, the family for instance, be the same as those of another, say the economy. So to discuss the changing pattern of family life, it would seem necessary to decide whether we are to treat it as a system in its own right or only as a subsystem of wider society, but it is not at all clear from the theory which choice we should make. Structural changes in family life, for example, would require us to deal with family life as a subsystem of the wider society, since structural change is always exogenous. But some new development in, for instance, the culturally prescribed pattern of husband and wife relationships could be defined either as a major, that is, structural change, or as only an adaptation of the internal equilibrium of the prevailing family system. But we can only define the boundary for the analysis *after* it has shown us whether the change is structural or internally adaptive. The only thing that is clear about defining system boundaries, therefore, is that the interpretation of events runs a very severe risk of becoming entirely circular. We need to know the answers, that is, before we can begin to ask the questions.

b. **Systems integration:** Parsons argues that social systems are integrated around a core value system, a common culture. It has been argued that real societies are more diverse, more pluralist, than this allows for. Lockwood's distinction between system integration and social integration very usefully illuminates this problem (Lockwood, 1964). We need to distinguish, Lockwood argued, between the extent to which the members of a society are integrated within it and the coherence of the system itself. Thus caste society may be a highly integrated system even though the divisions between Brahmin and Untouchable are so acute that we can hardly describe them as socially integrated. Similarly, the opponents of the capitalist system portray it as a highly integrated mode of production which, nevertheless, alienates the exploited masses so that they can have no interest in its survival. Paradoxically, this criticism offers some possibility of rescuing Parsonian functionalist theory from its evident difficulty in coping with social conflict. Structural functionalism, it could be argued, is a theory of social systems rather than of social relations. Conflict of material or political interest is perfectly possible within a culture of shared core values or where it relates to the problems of mutual adaptation amongst different subsystems (Coser, 1956).

The questions of how integrated the system needs to be and what follows from the apparent looseness or relative disjointedness of some systems still remain. Gouldner pointed out that there may be a degree of functional autonomy for some sections of society. In other words, a deviant culture or regional, class or ethnically based cultural pluralism may evolve within large-scale highly differentiated societies. Such groups might have less investment, less to gain perhaps, from pursuit of the dominant goals and values of society (Gouldner, 1973). To that extent, changes within any one subsystem could have a variable impact on other subsystems. But to acknowledge a degree of functional autonomy for institutions and subsystems within the wider system means that it becomes much less certain how far, and in what ways, changes in one area might bring about consequent changes elsewhere. It could be that a good deal of significant change might occur without any apparent knock-on effects at all.

(c) **Direction of effects**: Finally, there is the question of the direction of secondary changes. Thus, with modernization, the shift toward specificity of relationships and affective neutrality within the adaptive subsystem may well be combined with parallel shifts in the goal-attainment subsystem. Politics, as well as business dealings, becomes less personalized. But should we expect a similar set of changes within the integrative subsystems such as the family or in community life? Or perhaps we may discern a compensatory greater emphasis on emotion so that the nuclear family becomes a haven of feeling in an increasingly impersonal world. Either seems superficially plausible and the theory is of no help in suggesting *a priori* which might be what we should expect. In short, the direction of inter-subsystem adjustments is evidently variable and the conditions for continuous or compensatory (reactive) change cannot be specified within the terms of the theory.

The problem of specifying system boundaries, the issue of subsystem functional autonomy and the impossibility of predicting the direction of adaptive changes all show the structural functionalist systems theory to be a baggier, less coordinated, less decisive creation than it first appears to be. Is structural functionalism, then, incapable of explaining change? The equilibrium model at the heart of Parsons's theory offers us a way of accounting for *consequent* changes within subsystems, but only after the event. This is because we cannot make any general assumptions about the degree of system integration or institutional functional autonomy, and whether the consequences of the original changes will be congruent or reactive only becomes apparent with hindsight. Looking back, *so long as the equilibrium has been maintained*, we can see how subsystems have adapted to changes in other subsystems. Structural changes, however, can only be accounted for by exogenous factors. On the other hand, once structural change has begun and the functional imperatives can no longer be provided for by the existing arrangements, the theory seems to offer a useful basis for tracing out the system's collapse. Of course, the very abstract level at which the theory is pitched is a problem. To apply it to real historical processes involves specifying what changed and how in the kind of detail that the theory does not provide for, and it begins to seem questionable whether it is worth going to the trouble of doing so when a plainer language and a more concrete way of dealing with evidence appear to offer us as much useful insight into the processes of change.

Not all systems theories, however, are either so general or so abstract. We turn next, by way of contrast, to a radical critique of how the international capitalist system has caused the dependency and underdevelopment of the world's poorer countries. In its earliest and clearest form, Dependency Theory was highly specific in identifying the historical processes and exploitative relationships of world capitalism, but although in this it avoided the charges of vagueness laid at the door of Structural Functionalism, it was, as a consequence, all the more vulnerable to the empirical problems of historical validity.

Dependency theory: Frank and Wallerstein

Paul Baran argued that the poverty and underdevelopment of modern India was the legacy of British colonial rule (1957). The chief effect of the empire had been to destroy the potential for autonomous economic growth, stripping local resources for the benefit of the imperial power and reducing the country to little more than a source of cheap raw materials, cheap labour and a market for English mass-produced goods. In his studies of Chile and Brazil in the 1960s, Andre Gunder Frank systematized this extension of the Leninist view of European imperialism (Lenin, (1917) 1966) so as to explain the continuing poverty of former colonial countries, even after more than a century of formal political independence. Frank argued that economic neo-colonialism was responsible for perpetuating the underdevelop-ment of the poorer countries in the interests of the capitalist powers.

Frank focused on the relationship between the advanced, industrially developed countries of Western Europe and North America and the poorer, less-industrialized societies in the rest of the world. He rejected the evolutionists' belief that the latter are simply at earlier stages in their economic development and that they will eventually follow the same path of industrialization, urbanization, demographic change, institutional modernization and growing prosperity of the western economies:

> It is fruitless to expect the underdeveloped countries of today to repeat the stages of economic growth passed through by modern developed societies, whose classical capitalist development arose out of pre-capitalist and feudal society.
> (Frank, 1971, p. 16)

Today's underdeveloped societies are not precapitalist or feudal. Their lack of growth is not the result of internal sociocultural factors, traditionalist ideas, local backwardness and so forth, but is the consequence of their current disadvantaged position within a profoundly unequal capitalist system. They are the victims of the forces of capitalist production. Their continuing exploitation prevents any sociopolitical change or economic development which could threaten the prevailing capitalist order. World poverty is not an inherited condition resulting from outmoded traditions, excessive population growth or backwardness in mobilizing local economic resources. It is the effect of the current capitalist neo-colonialist system:

> It is capitalism, both world and national, which produced under-development in the past and which still generates underdevelop-ment in the present.   (1971, p. 11)

With the possible exception of the socialist economies, Frank argued that all the other countries, willy-nilly, are involved in the world capitalist system. This has

> ... long since incorporated and underdeveloped even the

farthest outpost of 'traditional' society ... .   (1971, p. 16)

The basic structural feature of this system is the <u>division between the economies of the metropolitan core</u> and <u>their satellites at the periphery</u>. At the centre are the advanced industrial countries of Western Europe and North America which politically and economically dominate, and therefore exploit, the periphery of less-developed economies around the world. This pattern of metropole and satellite is repeated within each society, with the metropolitan centres directing and exploiting the satellite regional economies; and again, within each region in turn, local metropoles surrounded by their satellite local economies. Not only internationally, but deriving from the global system of capitalist exploitation:

> ... in chainlike fashion the contradictions of expropriation – appropriation and metropolis – satellite polarization totally penetrate the underdeveloped world creating an internal structure of underdevelopment.   (1971, p. 22)

But the concentration of capital at the core and the process of expropriation of any economic surplus from the producers, and its appropriation by the owners of capital, systematically syphons off resources from the peripheral regions.

The criticism made by some Marxists that Dependency Theory <u>replaces class relations with spatial relations</u> (Laclau, 1977) is misguided. As we can all see, wealth and poverty are visibly spatially distributed, but they are not therefore spatially determined. In the richest countries you will find an exploited underclass: the poorest countries have their local cosmopolitan and parasitically privileged elites. The process of exploitation takes place in identifiable locations as a result of decisions made elsewhere in the metropolitan financial centres. Things have to happen somewhere. But the process involves a relationship between the expropriators and expropriated. It is the defining exploitative relationship at the heart of the capitalist mode of production. But this polarization of world capital and world poverty is replicated within each satellite economy. The economies of the underdeveloped countries are dependent upon the workings of the system dictated by the capitalist core. They have been forced to become underdeveloped by the system. They produce raw materials, minerals and

agricultural primary products for export to the rich capitalist
countries, in return for the expensive manufactured goods they
have to import. The metropolitan countries are able to ensure that
the satellite economies can never seriously challenge the interests
of international capital. The backwardness of satellite economies
and the poverty of satellite populations is therefore both the direct
and indirect result of their dependent position in the system.
Underdevelopment is not a matter of development just not having
happened yet, but is produced and reproduced by the appropriation
of their economic surplus by the capitalist core:

> ... the historical development of the capitalist system ...
> generated underdevelopment in the peripheral satellites
> whose economic surplus was expropriated, while generating
> economic development in the metropolitan centres which
> appropriate that surplus – and ... this process still continues.
> (1971, p. 27)

The direct imperialism of the nineteenth-century colonial empires
proved to be expensive to administer and to police. The interests
of global capital, however, are more profitably served where
national elites can themselves manage the satellite economies
locally. The colonists are freed from the costs and the apparent
responsibility of their domination. The system can in this way
flourish all the more effectively in a postcolonial environment or
in places like Latin America, where political independence was
won in the early years of the nineteenth century before most of
Europe or the USA had industrialized. Each local ruling group or
national bourgeoisie is therefore complicit in the system that
exploits the countries of the periphery. The ties between national
and foreign firms with investments or subsidiaries in the local
economy create a common involvement in the exploitation of the
country, and renders the local bourgeoisie increasingly dependent
on metropolitan economic interests, metropolitan culture and
metropolitan political domination. The incorporation of national
ruling groups further strengthens the system of core domination,
not least because murmurings of discontent or rebellious
movements amongst the poorest and the exploited masses will, in
the first instance, be directed at local targets and, at most, are
likely to lead to the displacement of local elites and only rarely to
even the local overthrow of the system itself. Capital investment

? why challenge IPR!

and the transfer of advanced technology to the poorer economies only increases their dependency. The repayment of interest on loans from metropole bankers, the repatriation of local profits to the metropolitan bases of multinational firms, royalties on patents for new technology to be able to compete in world markets, as well as overseas deposits by local elites providing themselves with escape routes from political uncertainties at home, all ensure that the satellite remains dependent and further than ever from catching up with the core capitalist economies. Indeed, Frank argued, there is no escape from the vicious circle of dependent underdevelopment within the existing system. Only the complete overthrow of world capitalism can liberate the exploited masses in the periphery of the system from their progressive impoverishment and exploitation.

The theory of dependency and its practical revolutionary implications was not, however, accepted by all Marxists. Frank believed that a fully socialist revolution would only be possible if and when the poorer countries were able to disengage themselves from the capitalist system. This is perhaps not quite as circular an argument as it seems if one allows the case of Castro's Cuba as an example of either disengagement or socialism. Warren, on the other hand, argued that the backwardness and poverty of the poor countries was not the result of excessive capitalist exploitation, but of too little (Warren, 1980). Following the logic of Marx's analysis of the conditions for the achievement of socialism, Warren held that only when the development of the capitalist mode of production realized the full potential of the forces of production and generated a class-conscious proletarian class struggle would there be, as Marx had argued, the possibility of a liberating revolution for the people as a whole.

Dependency Theory was, nevertheless, very influential, especially among the radical left and all those opposed to what they saw as American economic and cultural imperialism in the 1970s. It eventually gave way, mostly under the pressure of the obvious. It became increasingly apparent from the 1970s onward that the established capitalist countries were unable to manipulate the world economy in their own interests with the confidence and effectiveness that the theory implies. More dramatically, it became clear that not all the underdeveloped economies, in fact, stayed underdeveloped.

The oil-producing countries threefold increase in the price of oil in 1973–4, and the consequent financial, production and consumer crises that it brought about, showed that Western capitalism did not always have everything its own way in the world economic system. Even more of a problem for Dependency Theory was the spectacular economic growth of a number of newly industrialized countries in East Asia, notably Hong Kong, the Republic of Korea, Singapore and Taiwan, and, of course, before them, the postwar growth of Japan (World Bank, 1993) Their dramatic economic performance with living standards rising to levels comparable with those in many European countries, and the renewal of growth in Latin American countries like Brazil, Argentina, Venezuela and Chile (Nigel Harris, 1986) in spite of various political tribulations, made it very difficult to persist in maintaining that capitalism was able to systematically reproduce dependency in the peripheral economies or that there was no alternative to stagnation except socialist revolution for the less-developed countries.

Modifications to the theory, notably by Wallerstein, sought to relativize analysis of the capitalist system within a wider historical context. We should study, he argued:

> ... provisional longer-term, large-scale wholes within which concepts have meanings. These wholes must have some claim to relative space-time autonomy and integrity ... I would call such wholes 'historical systems' ... It is a system which has a history, that is, it has a genesis, an historical development, a close (a destruction, a disintegration, a transformation ...).
>
> (1984, p. 27)

The capitalist world economy has developed through a series of secular trends, such as industrialization and the proletarianization of the mass of the population, and cyclical rhythms of economic expansion and stagnation:

> ... neither the 'development' nor the 'underdevelopment' of any specific territorial unit can be analysed or interpreted without fitting it onto the cyclical rhythms and secular trends of the world economy as a whole.
>
> (1979, pp. 73–84; and see 1987, p. 315)

The capitalist world system emerged from the uneven links of world trade which evolved from the fifteenth century onwards so that 'by the late nineteenth century, for the first time ever, there existed only one historical system on the globe' (1987, p. 316).

Within this world system, Wallerstein identified the additional stratum of the semi-periphery between metropole and satellite and the idea that, in the course of time, countries might move up or down between these three categories (1979). Countries might move from periphery to semi-periphery by, for example, aggressive state action, by taking advantage of the weakened position of core economies during the downwave of one of the periodical economic cycles, by primitive accumulation or by the intervention of multinational companies looking for opportunities to relocate their investment. Semi-peripheral countries might achieve core membership by expanding their boundaries by conquest, by the expansion of their own domestic markets or increasing export performance (1987, pp. 322–3).

While these developments make for a readier recognition of actual historical changes than was possible within Frank's dependency theory, they gravely undermine the systematic character of Frank's analysis. It becomes a matter of *ad hoc* explanations, varying with the specific historical circumstances of each specific case. When and why one society or another moves in from the periphery to the semi-periphery, or why another perhaps ceases to be part of the core, can be described in terms of the trends and cycles of World System Theory, but the conception of the system itself does not explain these trends (see So, 1990, Parts II and III). Frank has recently argued that Wallerstein's identification of the emergence of the world system with the growth of industrial capitalism confines the historical processes involved to an altogether too short a time span, and advocates refocusing analysis with a less Eurocentric perspective to include the global relations of the ancient empires of Asia (Frank and Gills, 1996; and cf. Braudel, 1976). This welcome enlargement of the historical horizon, however, does not at this stage appear any easier to confine within the analytical constraints of a systemic theoretical framework. The long centuries of the T'ang and Sung empires, the Arab conquest of Persia, the emergence of industrial capitalism in England, the rise and fall of Great Zimbabwe, for example, can be seen in a wider context, but remain to be accounted for piecemeal as before. With its extension, the concept of the world system seems to explain less and less (see Skocpol, 1977, 1979).

Convergence theory: Kerr and Galbraith

There is, of course, a perennial Marxist preoccupation with the revolutionary prospects of class conflict in the capitalist societies. Apart from that, among sociologists in the 1960s, the most widespread view of social change in technologically advanced societies was that they were converging towards a common pattern. Mass education, mass literacy, mass media, mass production and mass consumption were eroding the distinctiveness of national cultures, national idiosyncrasies of life-style and attitude, without regard to political ideology or the complexion of national governments. The industrial system, it was believed, was coming to predominate over historical cultural, political or ideological influences. For capitalist or commissar, in Kawasaki or California, the organization of industrial production presents us in all essentials with the same problems and requires the same solutions. What is true of metal manufacturing and textiles, microelectronics and food-processing is true of the service industries too. There is, at any given time, a best way of doing things, the state of the art. The logic of the industrial process knows no frontiers. If the Japanese think of a better system of inventory control, or the Swedes a better way of deploying work groups, it is likely to be adopted worldwide. After all, Lenin believed that the then new time and motion methods developed by the American Frederick Taylor should be adopted by the expanding Soviet manufacturing industry (Friedman, 1961, p. xxiii). The logic of efficient organization is the same regardless of the cultural tradition of the society that adopts it. The widening ripples of its adoption throughout every other aspect of the social structure indicated the emergence of a distinctive and convergent social configuration: industrial society.

The main difference between the theory of Industrial Society and earlier ideas, like Tönnies's concept of *gesellschaft* or the Industrial Societies of Herbert Spencer, would seem to be the latter-day emphasis on the system of interrelated and interdependent elements each intermeshing and interacting together as part of a systemic whole.

Clark Kerr and his colleagues ((1960) 1973), Wilbert Moore (1965) and Raymond Aron (1967) were perhaps chief among those who developed a systematic account of Industrial Society and identified a number of its salient features. In general terms, these involved: (a) a shift away from agricultural employment to work in the secondary, that is, manufacturing, and the tertiary or service sector of the economy; (b) an increasing differentiation of occupations and the emergence of increasing numbers of new kinds of jobs; (c) a general upgrading of occupational skill levels throughout society, with a decline in the numbers working in jobs requiring minimal educational background or little in the way of job training; and (d) a particularly marked growth in the proportion of the workforce in professional, technical and managerial employment. These changes were associated with, and to a considerable extent depended on, increasing mobility of labour and the consequent need to recruit people for their ability rather than on the basis of their social background. The theory of Industrial Society implies that all industrial societies are subject to the same demands and are, as a result, likely to become more and more alike.

In the earliest major statement of this argument, Kerr et al. set out the general structural, cultural and political characteristics of a 'pure industrial society', towards which, they indicated, the processes of industrialization would converge. To begin with, an industrial scale of production would mean that fully industrialized economies would necessarily be, or become, large scale. This relates to both the need for markets for mass-produced goods and the need to mobilize large-scale resources for productive economies of scale and to provide the means for continuing technological innovation.

The operation of industrial technology and of industrial organizations needs a highly skilled and professionally qualified labour force. There is little call for untrained hands, and the occupational structure assumes a diamond-shaped profile in place of the pyramid pattern of the less-industrialized economies. A class of highly trained technical experts, managers and administrators emerges (Kerr et al., 1973, pp. 274, 276, 288–90) to coordinate the increasingly complex system. To maintain high general levels of literacy and numeracy, but, in particular, to provide for the recruitment and training of this crucial class, an industrial society requires an open educational system. This, in turn, has further significant cultural, political and economic consequences:

> Education is intended to reduce the scarcity of skilled persons and this after a time reduces the wage and salary differentials they receive; it also pulls people out of the least skilled and

> most disagreeable occupations and raises wage levels there.
> It conduces to a new equality which has nothing to do with
> ideology.   (1973, p. 286)

So, while the traditional inequalities of class and status differences
come to count for less (1973, pp. 286–94), there is also greater
mobility so that a person's social origins will no longer prevent
abilities being matched with the organizational needs of the
developing economy. And the more meritocratic system (1973, p.
357) engenders further cultural changes. In an industrial society
the values of progress, rationality, individualism and materialism
tend to replace inherited loyalties of tradition and place:

> The industrial society is an open community encouraging
> occupational and geographic mobility and social mobility.
> In this sense industrialism must be flexible and competitive,
> it is against tradition and status based on family, class,
> religion, race or caste.   (1973, p. 35)

These values and the meritocratic social structure prevent the
polarization of class-based interests. Political confrontation gives
way to an amelioratist technical bargaining among a plurality of
differentiated, but not necessarily antagonistic interest groups:

> Class warfare will be forgotten and in its place will be the
> bureaucratic contest of interest group against interest group
> ... memos will flow instead of blood.   (1973, p. 292)

In this we can visualize the economic and structural basis of what
Bell had earlier described as *The End of Ideology* (1960) and
Fukuyama was later to claim was the *End of History* (1991). But in
Kerr's analysis these are not the result of the political exhaustion of
ideological rationalizations alone, but the product of structural
developments arising from the intrinsic technological imperatives
of industrial organization itself. Not as a result of the oppression of
one class by another. but because of the far-reaching and interrelated
decisions that are involved in its management, the state itself
inevitably becomes increasingly involved in every aspect of this
complex system. With strong echoes of Comte's third stage, in Kerr's
Industrial Society:

> The negotiator takes the place of the prophet ... industrial
> society must be administered; and the administrators become
> increasingly benevolent and increasingly skilled.
>
> (1973, p. 288)

The interests of management and labour are no longer
fundamentally in conflict. The oppressive, exploitative state is
replaced by the welfare state managing the economy in the interests
of all (1973, pp. 31, 40–41, 273–4, 290–2).

Kerr's liberal, if utopian vision, is based on what he saw as the
iron hand of technology. Galbraith's view of the convergence process
does not differ structurally from Kerr's, but represents a more
jaundiced appraisal of its political effects (Galbraith, 1967). The
growth in the scale of economic activities and the closer interlocking
of the different sectors of the economy in the attempt to control
market forces increasingly encroaches upon the responsibilities
which governments have assumed for such matters as education and
social welfare, defence strategy, regional development and
international relations, as well as the more obviously economic
questions of trade policy and employment services. In all these areas
the system operates through a myriad of technical decisions each
made in the context of all the others, with responsibility almost
impossible to pin on any identifiable shoulders. The system itself,
which Galbraith describes as 'the technostructure', dominates the
New Industrial State. Given the logic of industrial growth, for all
practical purposes the idea of a ruling class has become redundant.
It is the same for capitalist as well as socialist societies. Both are
subject to the effective power of the technostructure. There are
echoes here of Burnham's managerial revolution and Weber's
bureaucratic state, as well as the more optimistic earlier visions of
Comte and St Simon. The new and distinctive element is the view
of industrial society as a self-sustaining system towards which the
industrialized countries were irresistibly converging.

The later eclipse of this theory of convergence owed much of its
effect to John Goldthorpe's widely influential view: firstly, that it
could not be assumed that communist and western societies were,
in fact, becoming, or would become, more alike; and secondly,
that there were no signs that industrial societies were becoming
less unequal (Goldthorpe, (1964) 1968). The first strand in
Goldthorpe's critique is based on the rejection of Kerr's structural
determinism in favour of a greater influence for purposive action,

values and ideology (1968, p. 659; see also Goldthorpe, 1966, p. 191). In short, his argument was that the industrial process was not the primary determining factor in shaping social structures, though perhaps the political system was. Since then, the collapse of the Soviet system, the rejection of communism in Eastern Europe and the marketization of the economy in the People's Republic of China under Deng Xiao Ping and his successors, have all been attributed to the incompatibility of centralized and comprehensive state planning and economic growth (see, e.g., Goldman, 1983; Goldman, 1992; Aganbeygan, 1990). Goldthorpe's own later research, too, has done more than any other to undermine his earlier arguments about social mobility trends (e.g. Erikson and Goldthorpe, 1993). But it is not, and never was the case that:

> ... industrial society appears to be growing significantly *less* open than it once was.
>   (Goldthorpe, 1968, p. 654; and see Payne, 1990)

Even without the benefit of 35 years of hindsight, however, it is clear that Goldthorpe misrepresented Kerr as a simple, one-track evolutionist (1968, p. 659). Kerr, however, offered a more pluralistic view of the converging paths industrial societies would follow:

> The place the society starts from and the route it follows are likely to affect its industrial features for many years, ... Not one, however, but several roads lead into this new and ultimate empire.   (1973, p. 46)

Of course, time has moved on and events have overtaken many generalizations, and sociologists are now writing about globalization and postmodernity, but, looking back, it seems Kerr's position may be more consistent with the situation in both the 1960s and the 1990s than his critics'.

How much more than the sum of its parts?

Apart from their common basic assumption of the interrelatedness of social systems, the principal systems theorists discussed in this chapter between them explore most of the other theoretical possibilities. We can represent this schematically in a diagram. As

Figure 3 shows: (a) all three are essentially Rationalist; but (b) only Parsons, with his emphasis on the determining role of values, offers an Idealist theory. Frank's Dependency Theory and Kerr's Convergence Theory both stress material factors as central to the systems they outline; (c) while Frank is openly ideological in his approach, both Parsons and Kerr argue for the contribution of their theories to a scientifically objective account of society; (d) all stress the determining role of system properties and none, therefore, are methodological individualists; but (e) where Parsons and Kerr focus on consensus and unifying system processes, Frank emphasizes the conflict of interests as the foundation of economic dependency; (f) Parsons and Frank both regard the systems they describe as subject to major change only under the impact of external factors, while Convergence Theory emphasizes the internal, endogenous dynamics of industrialism; (g) at the same time, Kerr shares with Frank a clearly historicist view of the future which, as we found, was absent in Parsons; and, finally, (h) Parsons and Frank are aligned in their concern with existing systems, while Kerr and his colleagues were describing an evolving system which would only fully mature at some time in the future.

Characteristics of three systems models

	Parsons	Frank	Kerr
Rationalist	+	+	+
Idealist	+	-	-
Ideological	-	+	-
Methodological/ Individualist	-	-	-
Consensus Orientated	+	-	+
Change Exogenous	+	+	-
Historicist	-	+	+
System still to Mature	-	-	+

Lately many of the ideas of both the Convergence/Industrial Society
theorists and the World Systems developments of Dependency
Theory have been incorporated in Globalization Theory (see, e.g.,
Giddens, 1999; Robertson, 1992; Sklair, 1991; Waters, 1995;
Ritzer, 1991). These discussions address the impact of computers
and information technology on world trading, particularly through
the TNCs, the financial and intergovernmental integration through
the internationalization of the major stock markets in Tokyo,
Frankfurt, London and New York, and the growth of supranational
governmental organizations like NATO, OECD, the World Bank
and so forth. The growing integration and speed of transport and
communications has a particularly marked impact on international
cultural homogenization via the mass media, world sporting events
and the mass marketing of products like Coca Cola, leisure
clothing, Walkmans and McDonald's or KFC fast food. However,
this preoccupation with technological, economic and mass
consumption trends so far offers little new thinking on why, and
how far, such changes are likely to develop.

Systems theories begin with the common-sense observation that
everything seems to connect with everything else and treat it
seriously, exploring its logical and structural properties. Some
specify how the connections work (e.g. Kerr et al. and Frank),
while others are more general, simply examining what the
connections must necessarily be given the basic assumptions (e.g.
Parsons). Describing an organization or a whole society as a system
sounds very analytic, exact and scientific, but it isn't. Like any
other way of conceptualizing what happens to us all in society, the
crucial thing is the set of assumptions we make about what is
important, and there is a great deal of judgement, even guesswork
or prejudice, that goes into that. The basic premises of systems
theory, however, are quite simple, and should be questioned more
often and more aggressively. To start with, the idea that all the
important things are related to all the others in a regular and
predictable way is either a truism (i.e., only the things that are
interrelated are important) or makes an act of faith (an axiom) of
what may be open to question (cf. Lockwood). In other words,
societies might, at least sometimes, be a good deal more disjointed
and unpredictable than systems models allow for. Secondly, to the
extent that the regularity and predictability of the interactions
among the component parts of the system may be variable, then
such models are theoretically weak. That is, they may provide us

with a vocabulary for describing events, but they can, in fact, explain very little. Convergence Theory looks more empirically plausible than Dependency Theory; and both can be more readily appraised as either true or false as accounts of the world outside the lecture room than Parsons's infinitely flexible functionalist taxonomy. All, however, are vulnerable to the accusation of reifying the processes they describe, making the system something with purposes of its own, acting independently, and almost regardless of the intentions and the understanding of the people involved. At the end, like the organic analogy, the system analogy should not be taken too literally either. Social processes are too open-ended. The meaningful, creative, unreliable and incompetent, self-seeking and inexplicably heroic actions of individuals throw too many spanners into the intricate works of any systems model. That is not to reject the argument that society *is* more than the sum of its parts. It is only to recommend caution in assuming what that 'more' is, to be open minded about what we might find when we begin to explore the relationships between things.

9

Modernity, Postmodernity and Postmodernism

Modernity, crisis and change

The theory of Industrial Society which we looked at in Chapter 8 emphasized the system of industrial production and the widening repercussions of its practical needs. Theories of modernity and postmodernity, which have preoccupied social theorists in the last quarter of the twentieth century, have more directly followed Parsons's emphasis on the key role of core values in determining the social order. They have generally dealt with social change as an essentially cultural process, and have had relatively little to say about its material conditions or specifically social structural effects.

The first two theorists I want to consider, Jürgen Habermas and Daniel Bell, from respectively neo-Marxist and non-Marxist points of view, are both concerned with the crucial importance of social values in sustaining the cohesiveness of the social order. Both identify a critical challenge to the legitimacy of established society in the value conflicts which have emerged in Western capitalist societies in the course of the twentieth century. Both theorists share the belief that the continuity of the prevailing system is seriously threatened because large numbers among the general population are no longer motivated by its central values and therefore no longer accept it as legitimate. In the one case, Habermas foresees the eventual democratic transformation of an unjust capitalist system, in the other, Bell envisages the disintegration of industrial capitalism unless a new consensus around a more liberal social compact can be constructed. Giddens's account of modern society, however, which we turn to next, anticipates no similar discontinuity in the future, but argues that modernity represents a radical departure from the traditional cultures of the past and, in contrast with everything that has gone before, is highly dynamic, in permanent flux and continually generating novel cultural and institutional forms. The postmodernists, discussed later in the chapter, have extended the identification of cultural crisis and the perennial challenge to established, even recently established, values in modern society into a more far-reaching critique of all values and meaning systems, cognitive as well as normative. The postmodernists live in a world where there is a hypertrophy of information, where the endless proliferation of ungrounded images generated in the electronic media has begun to subvert our sense of reality itself. In a world of virtual reality and image manipulation, spin doctoring and news management, rational action has become an ultimately incomprehensible ideal.

Jürgen Habermas: the legitimation of capitalism

Habermas's wider concern is with the possibility of defending a rational individualism in a world verging upon chaos. He seeks to confront the challenge derived from the philosopher Nietzsche's argument (1901) that it is no longer possible to sustain a belief in objective truth because all we really have is a set of alternative evaluations, none of which can justify its priority over all the others. Habermas does not resolve this problem, but that is to anticipate the more general issues of what has come to be described as postmodernism, which we will look at briefly later in the chapter. In Habermas's view capitalism has reached a crisis and, as a result, western society is verging upon anomie (1976, p. 118). Though drawing upon a Marxist analysis of capitalist society, Habermas's critical theory locates the fault lines, along which the social order will fracture, not in the material conflict of the relations of production, but in the domain of cultural values. Modern societies have developed, he argues, beyond the stage of market-orientated liberal capitalism described by Marx. As a result, a new kind of analysis is appropriate. The determinist view of society as economic base and politico-cultural superstructure of conventional Marxism needs to be replaced by a systems-model, drawing to a considerable extent on Parsons's view of the social system outlined in the last chapter (1976, p. 5). The economic and political subsystems coexist with a sociocultural life-world, in which overall system integration is achieved through the prevailing values. Changes may originate in any of these subsystems, but their impact elsewhere, and the responses they induce, are contained and given an order of relative importance by the system of values shared through the system as a whole.

In late capitalist societies the growth of monopolies and the concentration of capital has reduced the role of purely market forces. Continued management of the economy has increasingly come to rely on intervention by the state, just as Galbraith argued in his *The New Industrial State* (1967). Like Galbraith, Habermas also believes that *laissez-faire* is no longer an adequate guarantee of effective and profitable growth. In what he calls 'organized or state-regulated capitalism' (1976, p. 33), too much is at stake to allow the uncertainties and inevitable failures of market determined outcomes to dictate the allocation of the massive capital resources of the modern economy. Instead the state has come to have an important role in regulating the business cycle, in funding research and development, in the encouragement of long-term investment and the maintenance of overall levels of demand. The state has also come to assume responsibility for the stability of the economy, for unemployment rates, and through government contracts, loans, subsidies, spending on armaments, regional investment programmes, transport and environmental infrastructure, health, education and welfare expenditure (1976, pp. 33–5), it becomes identified with every aspect of social wellbeing. In recent years we have seen governments blamed when criminals commit more crimes, when more marriages fail, or when there are floods or droughts. As Habermas observes, with regard to the economy:

> The state apparatus no longer, as in liberal capitalism, merely secures the general conditions of production ... but is now actively engaged in it.   (1976, p. 36)

In this way: '... the state actually *replaces* the market mechanism whenever it creates and improves conditions for the realization of capital' (ibid., p. 35).

The power of the state is such that it is able to deal with most of the crises endemic in the economic system of liberal market capitalism, but it must also deal with the '... competing imperatives of steady growth, the stability of the currency, full employment and the balance of foreign trade' (ibid., p. 35). Social system integration is maintained in this balancing of priorities and competing demands through the shared values which provide the legitimation of the system as a whole. This is founded on the ostensible democracy of the political system, which mobilizes the consent of the citizens in the rational pursuit of system goals. But this is a capitalist system, where the interests of capital have an overriding priority in ordering the system.

The virtual fusion of economic and political subsystems in state-regulated capitalism creates new problems for integration in the sociocultural life-world. Values which prioritized action and response in formerly discrete spheres have to be reconciled, and what might once have been a matter of expediency becomes an issue of legitimacy. What were formerly purely technical matters of better or worse commercial management have become value-loaded issues of political principle in terms of right and wrong. Thus as every issue becomes a political issue, the continuing problems of running the economy in the interests of capital exposes the ideology of democratic participation as a sham, and exposes the system as a whole to challenge from those whom it deludes and exploits (cf. O'Connor, 1973). In nineteenth-century capitalist societies, the struggle for democratic parliamentary representation and the cycle of economic boom and slump were apparently quite unrelated matters. The ups and downs of the business cycle appeared to be wholly independent of anybody's political will or any party's responsibility, almost as though they were unavoidable natural phenomena. Conflicts between competing social objectives would, in those days, be dealt with in the ordinary course of affairs, in accordance with the priority they had in terms of life-world values. Questions relating to free-trade, social welfare, political enfranchisement and reform, industrial and commercial innovation and enterprise were all dealt with piecemeal and, as far as possible, separately. Any conflict of objectives could be addressed on an *ad hoc* basis. But by involving the state directly in the economy, all these questions of policy priorities have been made into matters of political principle:

> Because the economic system has forfeited its functional autonomy *vis-à-vis* the state, crisis manifestations in advanced capitalism have also lost their nature-like character.
>   (ibid., p. 92)

Economic problems, problems of poverty, unemployment, education and the environment have become crises of legitimacy for the political order as a whole:

> If government crisis management fails, it lags behind programmatic demands that it has placed on itself. The penalty for this failure is the withdrawal of legitimation. (ibid., p. 69)

In organized capitalism there is a system contradiction between the imperatives of capitalist profit and the myths of democratic legitimation. They want us to believe it is democratic, but the expropriation of surplus value at the heart of the capitalist system means that, in the end – for all the finely worded constitutional rights – it cannot be so, and in present times more and more are coming to realize this. In his *Legitimation Crisis*, Habermas argued that the crisis facing contemporary capitalism was that nobody believed in it any more. It is clear that Habermas has synthesized elements of Marxist and Parsonian theory within his analysis. His position differs from classical Marxism in identifying the contradiction that will lead to the end of capitalism as a cultural crisis rather than one in the arena of material production. He differs from a Parsonian position in identifying the source of transformation as endogenous. For Habermas, that is to say, change is generated by the inherent contradiction within the system itself. He wrote that:

> Crises in social systems are not produced through accidental changes in the environment but through structurally inherent systems imperatives that are incompatible *and cannot* be hierarchically integrated.   (ibid., p. 2)

Thus, though like Parsons he regards values as playing a critical part in the integration of society; in contrast, he emphasizes that they can also be incompatible with one another and lead to the overthrow of the established system. It is only fair to remember, however, that Parsons was primarily interested in the conditions of social order and continuity, whereas Habermas has been mainly interested in the conditions for its transformation. Thus Parsons's neglect of contradictions may be attributed to his preoccupation with the conditions for equilibrium. Habermas's focus on the failure of capitalism to appeal to the faith and the idealism of its citizens retained a high level of plausibility into the cynical 1990s. It is set, however, at such an abstract level of generality that, as it stands, it would be difficult to rebut on empirical grounds. But, before asking what evidence there might be for the state of pro- or anti-radical or conservative sentiment in the population at large, or in particular vocal and activist sections of it, there is a more immediate issue which this theory raises. This is simply the question of whether Habermas (and Parsons) are justified in assuming that belief in the system really is indispensable to its continuing survival. We will return to this question after discussing our next theorist, Daniel Bell.

Daniel Bell: cultural contradictions

In an examination of the political predicament of modern society and culture, Daniel Bell argued that in western industrial societies of the present day, '... the consumer-oriented, free-enterprise society no longer morally satisfies the citizenry as it once did' (1979, p. 251). There is a general crisis of belief (1979, p. 244 ff.) and, as a consequence, 'a long era is coming to a slow close' (ibid., p. xxix). Perhaps not a violent upheaval then, but certainly a major transformation is taking place. The key to this is the simultaneous death of two major, but antithetical value systems. The Protestant work ethic and the complex of bourgeois values that are associated with it, on the one hand, and, on the other, the cultural movement of modernism which has dominated the arts since the last century are both played out. In neither case is there any prospect of a revival of their former vitality (1979, p. 7). If the Protestant ethic of work is essential to the continuing viability of industrial society as a productive system, '... what is striking today is that the majority has no intellectually respectable culture of its own' (1979, p. 41). That is to say, either as a puritan calling or as a more moderate 'business as usual' pragmatism, it has no voice in literature or the other creative arts, and no continuing expression in sophisticated philosophical theory as it had in, say, nineteenth-century evolutionism or Utilitarianism. And if the work ethic is mute, the historically all too vocal artistic *avant-garde* has nothing to say. The prevalent view in the arts throughout their modernist period has been that creativity could only express itself in opposition to bourgeois culture (1979, pp. 19–20). As the high culture of the artistic elite, modernism has been a consistently iconoclastic movement challenging all tradition, all established institutions and values. The conventions of social life, business for profit and personal self-control are all seen as unauthentic and incompatible with the full realization of human potential. A more hedonistic ethic of liberation, self-expression, eroticism and the idealization of spontaneity (1979, pp. 52–3) is opposed to the stuffy, middle-class puritanism of bourgeois society.

But this anti-establishment perspective has now become the established mainstream in literature and the visual arts. Though remote from the tastes of the philistine majority, the *avant-garde* have become the cultural establishment in capitalist societies, the professors in the art schools, the gallery directors, the members of grant-awarding committees, the judges of the literary competitions. In the abstract and conceptual arts, whose point eludes almost everybody, in fiction and poetry that makes little sense to anybody, in music that few listen to, the aesthetic ideas and cultural values of the modernist movement nevertheless have a pervasive influence. Increasingly, through the mass media and pop culture, through life-style journalism and fashion images, they have become the common currency of a wider range of taste amongst what Bell terms the 'cultural mass', that is, the rest of us. But the culture of modernism is exhausted, the creative impulse is moribund. The conventions and traditions it attacks have no living substance and were, in reality, overthrown long ago. Pickled sheep and piles of bricks in 1990s arts galleries scarcely cause a shrug. After all, Marcel Duchamp was making an original statement when he put a urinal in an exhibition of modern sculpture, but that was in 1917 (Tomkins, 1997). And the once startling cubist pictures of Braque and Picasso were painted before the First World War. Modernism today has ceased to surprise us. The representational realist art and the bourgeois values that were the targets of the Dadaists and Surrealists in the 1920s are no longer given any creative expression. One might make the same case with reference to sculpture and literary fiction, poetry, theatre or orchestral music. All have sought to shock, to challenge. That is the cultural crisis facing present-day society:

> ... the social order lacks either a culture that is a symbolic expression of any vitality or a moral impulse that is a motivational or binding force. What, then, can hold society together?   (Bell 1979, p. 84)

Modernism, Bell argues, is essentially nihilistic. The cultural crisis which its rejection, not only of the work ethic but of all socially integrating values, has brought about is a spiritual one, an absence of faith in anything at all. 'Lacking a past or a future, there is only a void' (1979, p. 28). Without a sustaining culture of belief, without a moral order of priorities, the conflicts between economic, political and cultural objectives have become almost irreconcilable.

Bell's analysis is not just another diatribe against the meretricious absurdities of the contemporary *avant-garde* or a rejection of the genuine achievements of the twentieth-century arts. Bell argues that our perception of reality has changed. Formerly, the imperatives of the natural world and, with the coming of the industrial revolution, the objective world of technology dominated the consciousness of thoughtful people. But in the modern world, with the apparent triumph of technology over nature, and then the rapid obsolescence of technical skills with the increasing pace of technological innovation, a more interpretative, or phenomenological, consciousness has come to dominate our subjective experience:

> Now reality is becoming only the social world, excluding nature and things, and experienced primarily through the reciprocal consciousness of others, rather than some external reality. Society increasingly becomes a web of consciousness, a form of imagination to be realized as a social construction.
>   (1979, p. 149)

In his analysis of this sociocultural system, Bell proposes a disarticulated or pluralist model, explicitly in contrast with Marxist and Functionalist views. Among the many other things they have in common, those theoretical perspectives both assume a unified system of structural and cultural components combining together within a single coherent totality (1979, p. 10). For Marxists and neo-Marxists like Habermas, contradictions occur within this social system, mode of production or whatever, and bring about its transformation since the system cannot survive the internal inconsistency. Functionalists, similarly, see all the persisting elements of the social system tending toward the maintenance of an ongoing equilibrium. In contrast with these single-system models, Bell proposes three more or less autonomous realms; the productive economy; the political system; and the cultural realm of moral, ethical and aesthetic values, beliefs and customs. These 'are ruled by contrary axial principles' (1979, p. xxxi). The 'axial principle', or fundamental rationale of the economy, is efficiency. In the politics of western industrial societies, the issue of equality has in modern times been the governing principle. And the predominant cultural value of the past 150 years or so, Bell argues, has been self-realization (or in less indulgent terms, self-gratification). Economic, political and cultural developments are largely autonomous: 'They are not congruent with one another and have different rhythms of change; they follow different norms which legitimate different and even contrasting types of behaviour. It is the discordances between these realms which are responsible for the various contradictions within society' (1979, p. 10).

This view of 'the disjunction of realms' (ibid., p. 14) is an original, important and distinctive feature of Bell's view of society. It opens up a much more open-ended prospect for social change than almost all the other theories that have been proposed since the evolutionary models of the mid-nineteenth century. It notably contrasts with the system models discussed in the last chapter. Even theories of endogenous revolutionary change or system contradiction portray society as generally more coherent, with a tendency at each stage of development toward an internal consistency or, when that cannot be maintained, undergoing a necessary transformation. Bell's view of society, in contrast, appears to be one of *enduring*

disjointedness and unpredictability, and has obvious implications for both political action since it rules out the possibility
of utopian politics, and for sociological analysis since it means
that all structures must necessarily be unstable and temporary.
Bell does not, perhaps, fully develop the exciting possibilities
this opens up. His specific analysis of the present-day
predicament of capitalist society is that without a set of
meaningful values to motivate its members, the institutional
order based on instrumental rationality and the work ethic will
break down and, sooner rather than later, will no longer
function at all.

There are a number of reasons for questioning this view.
Firstly, the cultural challenge to industrial society can be traced
back to the beginnings of industrialization and yet it still
expands (Kumar, 1978; Williams, 1961). Political radicalism,
iconoclastic modernism in the arts, in literature and the life-
styles of the *avant-garde* is a continuation of the movement
which had its origins in the Romantic moral and intellectual
reaction to early-nineteenth-century social change. Romanticism and its present-day derivatives were and are a rejection
and, at the same time, the creation of industrial society. The
ideology of individual freedom and unrestricted experience has
been used to overcome traditionalist opposition to capitalist
development (see, e.g., Gellner, 1983), as well as to criticize
the regimentation of factory employment and the spread of
urbanization. The cultural rejection of industrial capitalism in
not exclusively a late-twentieth-century response to its maturity,
but is as old as the thing itself. How few have been the artists
or writers who have ever celebrated industrial society! The
reaction against it was its birth twin.

On the other hand, the importance of the Protestant Ethic in
sustaining capitalism also seems to be vastly exaggerated. It is
true that its decline has been widely held responsible for
modern ills (e.g., Landes, 1998). Wiener, in his influential
*English Culture and the Decline of the Industrial Spirit, 1850–
1980* (1981), attributes the loss of the industrial pre-eminence
that Britain enjoyed in the 1850s to the spread of an aristocratic
hostility to business via the private sector public schools which
educated the gentrified offspring of the original entrepreneurs.
D. W. Rubinstein (1993), however, has shown that, in fact, the
business class was not assimilated with the landed gentry in

nineteenth- and early-twentieth-century Britain. Only a very small minority of the English middle class was educated in the public schools in the late nineteenth century. Cultural hostility to industrialization was far stronger both from the revolutionary left and the reactionary right in Germany, France, Japan and even the USA, but that did not succeed in stifling their development. Wiener's argument, then, is both selective and unjustified. Maybe, therefore, culture is not the final determinant of economic performance. One does not need to believe in capitalism to practice it. Empirically, Nicholls found the businessmen he surveyed to be entirely free of ideology, they just got on with making money, and Bendix remarked on the striking lack of interest on the part of entrepreneurs in any ideas. Their single-minded concern with business expediency was 'the most fundamental contrast to ideology' (Nicholls, 1969; Bendix, 1966, p. 88). Business is just business.

Engaging in trade or commerce, like most human activities, is not a deeply reflective theoretical activity. For most of those who are actively involved in market relationships, any philosophical rationale or moral justification for what they are doing is likely to be only of cosmetic rather than of fundamental importance. As John Hall observes, 'capitalism was accepted pragmatically because it delivered the goods' (1986, p. 173). This may be more in tune with Bell's notion of the disjunction of realms than his own inference of a growing cultural crisis. Be that as it may, he argues that the lack of belief in the social order of industrial capitalism is of critical significance for modern society. The cultural contradiction of modern capitalism is that no-one any longer believes in the values necessary to sustain it. No-one answers the challenge of the *avant-garde* because no-one cares. In contrast, the legitimation crisis identified by Habermas is the result of people still believing the promises in the political manifestos and feeling betrayed when they are not kept. For Bell, the rational bourgeois values of capitalist society have slowly and silently vanished away. In Habermas's view these democratic values are intact and it is their betrayal in the exploitative inequities of capitalism that engenders the outrage amongst the deceived faithful. Thus Habermas's legitimation crisis is one of disappointed values, while Bell's cultural contradiction is one of the absence of legitimating values themselves. For Habermas, the crisis entails the inevitable transformation of capitalism foreseen by Marx so as finally to realize the democratic values the bourgeois order currently only pretends to stand for. In Bell's more loosely integrated model of society, there is both more scope for tempering, or compensating for, the critical cultural values by political action but, at the same time, also scope for a more uncertain outcome, as a result of the basically more unpredictable relationships amongst the different elements of the sociocultural system and, we might add, due to the problem of finding any structural basis upon which such action might be founded. Even so, like Habermas, Bell's analysis hinges on the assumption that congruent beliefs and values are an indispensable element in the continuity of the social order and that values have causal potency in themselves.

In the work of the third theorist of modern society I shall discuss, Anthony Giddens, it is less clear why and how change takes place. For Giddens, the present stage of late modernity represents a radical break from the past and, we must infer, therefore past change has been discontinuous, but the modern era itself is one of perpetual change, continually transforming society and the life-worlds of the individuals who constitute it. The consequences of modernity are the consequences of continual change. It is mainly on these grounds that he rejects the idea that we have arrived at a new postmodern state of affairs (1990, p. 51).

Anthony Giddens: consequences of modernity

Giddens appears to believe that sociology is 'not a generic discipline to do with the study of human societies as a whole' (1984, p. xviii), but is concerned specifically with the advanced or modern societies. Because modern institutions differ from all preceding forms of social order (1991, p. 1), the ideas of the classical sociological theorists, that is Marx, Weber, Durkheim and the rest, should either be abandoned as obsolete (1981, pp. 18, 105) or radically overhauled if they are to be of any use in making sense of present-day society (1979, p. 1). Giddens's account of late modernity is hard to pin down since he identifies its dimensions as a set of paradoxes, opposing and contradictory pairs of principles which intersect so as to define the particular quality of our contemporary experience. He does not specify the conditions in which an individual or any particular social practice, or yet larger social systems such as a nation-state, will tend toward one extreme or the other, nor how, for any of them, the tensions between these contradictory principles might be balanced or contained. However, that may not have been his intention. Giddens's discussion of modernity may be regarded as significant mainly in drawing our attention to its qualitative or phenomenological tendencies. His focus upon later or mature modernity represents these tendencies in their most fully realized form. But as Ian Craib argues: '... it is not a theory aimed at telling us what happens in the world, or explaining what happens' (Craib, 1992, p. 6). This may seem a charitable view of social theory, and of Giddens's contribution to it in particular, but it is consistent with what I have argued in earlier chapters, when discussing theorists who have sometimes proved to be manifestly wrong in their empirical pronouncements, but whose contribution to our stock of ideas has nevertheless been valuable. What is more, it will, I hope, make it easier to understand the lack of precision in some of Giddens's arguments if, as Craib implies, they were not aiming at that anyway.

Giddens is unwilling to go all the way with the postmodernists in their belief that we have moved beyond the rationality of the modern world, and therefore modernist rational theoretical models should be left behind with it (1990, pp. 47–51). For all the accelerating, widening and deepening changes taking place around us, Giddens believes these are an acceleration, a widening and deepening of essential modernist tendencies. It is not so much that his own ideas break new ground, or lead us in new directions, as that he has attempted to present his 'overhaul' of existing or classical perspectives within a more all-embracing conceptual framework, with a possibly distinctive emphasis on human agency and its phenomenological consequences. So, for instance, his discussions of the perplexity of the individual in the modern world echo earlier concerns with the dilemma of rational agency and the functional rationality of the iron cage of bureaucratized society, or the structural determination of the categories of thought in Weber and Durkheim respectively. And whether, on particular issues – such as globalization, nationalism and the nation-state or individual existential insecurity – he leaves us much the wiser than those earlier theorists did, readers can judge for themselves (see, e.g., Mêstròvic, 1998). But his concern to relate them within a common framework of ideas might be regarded as an important test case for the possibilities of a synthesizing social theory, even one which is primarily sensitizing rather than explanatory.

He argues that in late or mature modernity, we are moving into a period: 'in which the consequences of modernity are becoming more radicalized and universalized that before' (1990, p. 3), without explaining why that should have happened just now, except perhaps by implication that modernism inherently tends toward extremes. The most conspicuous features of this radical modernity are, on the one hand, 'the disappearance of historical teleology' (1990, pp. 52–3), that is to say, the loss of a sense of summation, of a past cumulating in an intelligible way to bring about the present state of things and, on the other, of a sense of destiny or purpose. This absence of a sense of past and future is partly a consequences of the loss of Western world leadership which had endowed the social theory produced hitherto in the advanced capitalist countries with a sense of direction and privileged destiny in the unfolding of historical progress. At the same time, this disorientation reflects the growth of a more reflexive mode of thought, in which we have become aware of the historical conditions of our own self-consciousness. This has led to 'a new and disturbing universe of experience' (1990, p. 53). This universe he describes in terms of four dialectically related paradoxes.

a. Displacement and Re-embedding: the intersection of estrangement and familiarity.
b. Intimacy and Impersonality: the intersection of personal trust and impersonal ties.
c. Expertise and Reappropriation: the intersection of abstract systems and day-to-day knowledgeability.
d. Privatization and Engagement: the intersection of pragmatic acceptance and activism.

(1990, p. 140).

These 'intersections', where apparently contradictory trends cross, illustrate Giddens's view of modernity as a paradoxical conjunction of disparate tendencies. Where in Tönnies, for example, the displacement of particularistic intimacy by universalistic impersonality as *gemeinschaft* is progressively replaced by *gesellschaft* relationships, was an 'either/or' choice; Giddens's view of late modernity is more complex because he recognizes that it is not a matter of either one thing or its opposite, but that, instead, we confront a 'both/and' situation, where apparent incompatibilities must somehow be negotiated. 'Disembedding' is a process intensified by globalization, the scale of organizations and modern systems of communication. It means that social relations are increasingly uprooted from the multivalent connections that occur in delimited local contexts, and are reconstructed in more functionally specific low-density networks distributed across indefinite spans of time and space (1990, p. 21):

> ... in conditions of modernity, larger and larger numbers of people live in circumstances in which disembedded institutions linking local practices with globalized social relations, organize major aspects of day-to-day life.   (1990, p. 79)

Within these de-localized contexts, however, new possibilities have emerged providing individuals with new kinds of 're-embedding' within identities and social locations independent of geographical, or even temporal, proximity. Who we are is no longer a function of where we are. Our closest social ties, those which give us our sense of who we are, may be with people geographically far away whom we all too seldom see face to face, while we live surrounded by people we hardly know. This is closely related to the paradox of intimacy and impersonality. Much of our social interaction with others in modern society is on an impersonal plane on the basis of their and of our functional position within some organizational structure. But the liberation from the ascribed relationships of the traditional community makes it possible to explore and discover more selective, more intimately satisfying relationships based on personal trust rather than on the prescribed patterns of traditional roles. The highly trained expertise required for the operations of the abstract systems of coordination and service provision, as well as the technical systems of production and communication in the modern world, seem to exclude the direct participation of the non-specialist amateur majority (1991, p. 22). At the same time, however, the very complexities themselves make possible the reappropriation of lay knowledge. As consumers, clients, and so on, we come to know the systems we enter and whose operations we seek to benefit from. We learn the ropes, can judge a good or poor performance on the part of the expert, we can sometimes work the system in our own favour or make our own adaptations to the carefully engineered product or service we are supposed to passively enjoy.

In Giddens's account it is axiomatic that we are not passive victims, but <u>active agents in the systems</u> we confront and which, by our conformity or innovatory response, we sustain and create. Pragmatic acceptance of the way things work on the larger scale, while retreating into our own private preoccupations, is one kind of response. But modernity also makes all kinds of social and political activism, for instance joining in campaigning movements to bring about change, a significant option and a major feature of modern social consciousness. So, for Giddens, there is not an opposition in the duality of individual and society. The identity of both crystallize where action and historical social processes intersect. And, although he is less than clear about this relationship (Scott, 1995, p. 226), we can allow that Giddens is sensitive to its ambiguities. On the one hand, his emphasis on reflexivity sometimes makes it all seem a highly conscious, even deliberate matter. Thus he argues, '... the production and reproduction of society ... has to be treated as a skilled performance on the part of its members' (1991, p. 168). And as skilled social performers therefore, the members of society must be purposive, making judgements in a rational and effective way. On the other hand, and apparently in spite of his emphatic antithesis between modernity and tradition (e.g. 1990, pp. 36, 109), he has also noted, '... the habitual, taken-for-granted character of the vast bulk of the activities of day-to-day social life; the prevalence of familiar styles and forms of conduct ...' (1984, p. 376). Human agents can relax a little, perhaps we ordinary mortals don't have to be reflexive all the time. Of course, Giddens is right to remind us of both these aspects of our everyday conduct, what he fails to do, however, is to analyse the conditions in which we find ourselves switching from one mode to the other. It may be that we are not altogether free agents when it comes to that. But if that were so, we would need to question his view of society as a skilled performance.

There is a further degree of ambivalence or vagueness in Giddens's position *vis-à-vis* the issue of individual agency and social constraint. Thus, '... the overriding emphasis of modernity', he insists, ' is on control – the subordination of the world to human control' (1991, p. 144). But that means not just the physical world, but would include human society too. Control therefore involves both control by human agency and control over (other) human agents. This is achieved by means of the characteristic social forms of modernity: the nation state and the organization. These institutional forms represent the practical means of establishing and operating industrialization and the capitalist economy; the surveillance or control and supervision of subject populations; and the control of the means of violence, that is to say, the military in the era of industrialized total war (1991, p. 15). At one point, he compares modernity to the juggernaut – a monstrous, unsteerable engine sweeping us all along in its mad career or crushing those who get in its way beneath its wheels (1991, p. 28). This is very hard to reconcile with his emphasis on human agency and his view of social structure as a skilled and therefore rational, self-aware, in other words, reflexive performance on the part of its members (see Mêstròvic, p. 155). Modernity in this image is portrayed as a demi-urge, the *zeitgeist* with its own push potential.

Without making very clear, either, the circumstances in which the one outcome might prevail over the other, Giddens reminds us of yet another of the paradoxes of agency and constraint in his delineation of modern society:

> Holding out the possibility of emancipation, modern institutions at the same time create mechanisms of suppression rather than actualization of the self.   (1991, p. 6)

The distributive processes of class, gender and ethnicity, he suggests, 'can be partly *defined* in terms of differential access to forms of self-actualization and empowerment'. If the juggernaut – that is, the nation state and its organizations – is *other people*, and globalization, time and space distantiation, institutional disembedding and re-embedding and so forth are the choices they, the influential ones at least, are making, then why are they making those choices at this time? I think he should tell us. But none of the institutional forms of social practices is stable as a result of:

1. The separation of time and space whereby the geographically remote may be instantaneously accessible while the nearby can be virtually unknown;
2. the disembedding of social institutions and;
3. the characteristic reflexivity of modern social life whereby our knowledge about the social situation regularly becomes a factor in its organization and transformation (1991, p. 20); the pace, scope and profoundness of social change are all greater than in any prior time (1991, p. 16).

This results in another, indeed the greatest, of the paradoxical circumstances of late modernity. In spite of the unprecedented measures and resources devoted to achieving control, the condition of modernity is beset by unprecedented uncertainty and risk. At the level of the system as a whole, given the almost limitless resources involved and the global integration of systems, transmitting consequences ever more rapidly and ever more widely, the consequences of error in economic, ecological, military or political miscalculation are permanently potentially catastrophic. But at the level of individual agency, the consequences of action are also ever more incalculable.

> The reflexivity of modern social life consists in the fact that social practices are constantly examined and reformed in the light of incoming information about these very practices, thus constitutively altering their character.   (1990, p. 38)

But, as Bertens observes, this is the beginning of an infinite regress, 'modernity has turned its critical rationality upon itself' (Bertens, 1995, pp. 241, 247). The constant monitoring of our own behaviour undermines both spontaneity and unself-conscious habit. But deliberate calculations of the consequences of individual action, or, indeed, confident long-term planning on the part of collective agencies, becomes more difficult rather than less. The intensifying, intricate interconnections between political, economic, technological, cultural and ecological processes summarized under the term 'globalization', the sheer scale and complexity of the legal, financial, administrative and technical systems, which affect us all in our daily lives, are beyond anybody's individual capacity to understand. Computerized information systems may help locally in reducing the tidal wave of information, but, in their turn, they also add a further dimension of complexity to our bewildered incomprehension. Giddens's analysis reminds one of the classic view of sociology as the science of unanticipated consequences, except that in his case, the consequences are defined as unforeseeable in principle.

What is the rational response to this situation? Giddens sums up our dilemma: 'an indefinite range of potential courses of action (with their attendant risks) is at any given moment open to individuals and collectivities' (1991, pp. 28–9). Modern life is thus inherently problematic, all activity is associated with risk, all assumptions merely provisional, all objectives questionable. As a consequence, at the level of individual experience, he concludes, 'personal meaninglessness becomes a fundamental psychic problem in late modernity' (1991, p. 9): at the level of the nation-state, there is a need to repair 'damaged solidarities', democracy has come to suffer from apathy and cynicism as a result of the reflexive questioning of all values (1994, p. 13). If this sounds like Durkheim, Giddens's suggested solution reminds us of Comte's programme for the cultural crisis of the nineteenth century. There is a need, Giddens urges, for the 'reinvention of traditions' (ibid.). Modestly, he leaves the identity of the potential inventors unspecified, and the means by which their prescriptions might be adopted remains far from clear.

The many intersecting contradictory tendencies of modern society define its specifically paradoxical character. If Habermas and Bell described modern capitalist society as on the brink of crisis and radical transformation, in Giddens's account of modernity we find perpetual transformation in full swing. There are no longer any certainties. Though he does not offer us any explanations for these proliferating perplexities, this is perhaps because there are none to be looked for. Giddens's social theory is not really explanatory but hermeneutic, that is to say, it is

interpretative

an attempt to sensitize us to the complex overlapping and contradictory currents in the continuing torrent of social and cultural change. If he portrays modernity as endless, accelerating, intensifying change, at least he indicates that it might be approached in terms of an intricately intersecting web of rationally intelligible tendencies. In postmodernist theory, the rationalism of this sort of model is itself challenged. In postmodernism the carpet, too, really seems to be moving under you. Not only is there doubt about our present capacity to make sense of the social and cultural world, there is also the suggestion that reality itself is fugitive and that the solidity of any theory, in fact of all theorizing whatever, is therefore questionable.

Postmodernity, postmodernism and after

The literature of postmodernist theory relates to a broad range of discourse beyond sociological theory alone, embracing architectural, literary, aesthetic and metaphysical issues, *avant-garde* and popular culture, feminism and radical politics. Indeed, in many respects the postmodern resembles a social and cultural movement with a new 'transformative political vision' (Laclau and Mouffe, 1987, pp. 79–106; Mouffe, 1988) rather than a specific theory (see Nicholson and Seidman, 1995). One could look at it as, in itself, an expression of social and cultural change, a symptom or emblem of the situation in the last years of the twentieth century. It is, furthermore, debateable whether it makes sense to look for a postmodernist analysis or explanation of the state of things (see Waugh, 1992, p. 3), since at least some postmodernists reject the possibility of validly explaining anything in any case.

The term 'postmodern' itself, describing present times in terms of what they no longer are, reveals a little of the uncertain, ambiguous nature of the contemporary situation as perceived by postmodernist theorists. These are uncertain and ambiguous times. It seems almost impossible just to keep up with the pace and complexity of current social, cultural and political change, let alone make any sense of it all. Whole communities, and the ways of life they sustained based on once staple industries, have declined; traditional loyalties and respect have eroded; at the same time, there are the endlessly astonishing repercussions of digital technology in industry, financial services, leisure, travel, surveillance and social control; there is the new world of the global geopolitical balance of power, with the collapse of old political certainties and the constant emergence of new threats; there is the increased urgency of ethnic, feminist and ecological issues, the irresistible influence of the mass media; changes in moral values and new boundaries of moral awareness. Confronted with all of these simultaneous transformations, reason itself seems hardly adequate, science too slow-footed, imagination sorely stretched. The theories of modern society – that once appeared to explain the sort of world we lived in – now seem too tied to the circumstances of their time and perhaps to the propagandist interests of their original promoters. A new postmodernist awareness of the limitations of the old ideas of modernity, a postmodernist critical willingness to expose the fundamental assumptions of existing knowledge so as to grasp the challenging possibilities of this new era has emerged.

There is, by now, a well-entrenched, in some spheres virtually hegemonic, commitment to postmodernist theory (see Bertens, 1995). This is hard to pin down, to describe in simple terms. If modernity, as Comte, Weber or Giddens for instance, might have claimed, was essentially about the replacement of the superstition and unquestioned traditions that preceded it by the application of science and systematic reason; in the postmodern world science and reason can no longer offer any sense of confident certainty. They are no more than rather tepid versions of the truth competing to be heard amongst the babble of vociferous alternatives. Baumann has described postmodernity 'as a re-enchantment of the world that modernity tried hard to *disenchant*' (1993, p. x). That is, however, too neatly simple a reversal. Postmodernity, on the contrary, is disenchanted with everything, including disenchantment itself.

There is an ambiguity we need to be clear about, at least at the outset of this exploration of some of these ideas. The basic distinction we need to keep in mind, however difficult it may be in practice to disentangle as the discussion proceeds, is the question of whether we are discussing the substantive issue of *postmodernity*, the emergence, that is to say, of the postmodern era in history, the claim that, as a matter of fact, life in present-day societies has changed to such an extent that it no longer corresponds to what used to be described as the 'modern' pattern. Featherstone, for example, argues that:

> Postmodernism has to be understood against the background of a long-term process involving the growth of a consumer culture and expansion in the number of specialists and intermediaries engaged in the production and circulation of symbolic goods. It draws on tendencies in consumer culture which favour the aestheticization of life, the assumption that the aesthetic life is the ethically good life and that there is no human nature or the self, with the goal of life an endless pursuit of new experiences, values and vocabularies.
>
> (1991, p. 126)

This focus on the narcissistic culture of consumerism represents the major strand in postmodernity. Another more political aspect was voiced in the 1950s when C. Wright Mills argued that 'the Modern Age is being succeeded by a postmodern period.' The distinctive character of this new epoch was that '...the ideas of freedom and of reason have become moot; ... increased rationality may not be assumed to make for increased freedom' (1959, pp. 166–7), an anxiety which we may recall had very much preoccupied Max Weber. The postmodernism referred to by Featherstone, of course, reflects the consumer society of the late twentieth century, whereas Mills was writing at the height of the Cold War in the middle of the century, but, while substantive concerns may have changed, pessimism about the future of freedom and reason clearly has a long pedigree. And with the unexpected collapse of Soviet Communism in Eastern Europe in 1989, the emergence of new economic powers in East Asia, the globalization of consumer cultures (Ritzer), as well as the questioning of established practices and institutions in the more immediate life-worlds of people's experience of work and family life, people who liked to think they understood what was going on began to lose confidence. Feminist critique, multicultural diversity and ecological anxieties have all added further impetus to the delineation of the world as fundamentally changed. So the modern industrial society, in which people saw out a lifetime of work in the technologies and crafts in engineering, mining or manufacturing, has been replaced by patterns of flexible employment in the 'post-Fordist', information-dominated service economy (Sennet). Or the modern family, typically a nuclear household of married couple and their children, it is said, has been swept away in a diversity of life-styles and less than lifelong relationships, with no single prescriptive pattern or institutional coherence (Cheal). For Touraine (1988), for instance, the ceaseless change, the constant revolutionizing of the means of production and social forms have become increasingly difficult to reconcile with the central principles of rational progress which had defined modern society up to now. The consequent dislocation of consciousness brought about by this crisis of modernity amounts to the transition from one culture to another, from the modern to the postmodern, to an era in which the old certainties no longer apply.

On the other hand, apart from the question, that is, of a transformed reality, there is the issue of whether we are instead concerned rather with the exploration of *postmodernism* as a new critical mode of theorizing about the nature of experience and the possibilities of thought (see Kumar, 1995, p. 172). As a new epistemology, postmodernist thinking challenges the rational, or causal, explanatory structures of earlier theories. Instead it draws on that widespread aestheticization of experience referred to by Featherstone in the quotation above. The personal subjectivity and incommensurable diversity of such experience, and whatever reflection it gives rise to, implies a general relativization of thought. That is to say, postmodernist theorists argue that what we think depends on who we are and that the notion of a general truth, equally valid for everyone, is wholly untenable and always was, even if in times past we deluded ourselves to the contrary. The deceptively simple key to this argument is the principle succinctly summarized by Patricia Waugh in the Introduction to her useful *Reader*.

> Postmodernism ... implies that there can be no position outside culture from which to offer a critique of it.   (1992, p. 8)

The formidable implications of this apparently downright obvious point challenge the possibility of any consensus of rational thought, any constructive dialogue or any progress in understanding. But we will return to this more general point later in the chapter and in the next.

Obviously, none of us could ever wholly detach ourselves from all the influences of the culture and society in which we have become what and who we are; we could never manage to be wholly culture-free even if we should, or indeed could, ever want to be. Every word we speak, every thought that we have, ✳ originates and derives its meaning within the echoing labyrinths of inherited ideas, cultural allusions, moral and emotional commitments we have explored in the course of our lives, and which we still inhabit. In his later philosophy Ludwig Wittgenstein ((1953) 1967) argued that thought is determined within what he described as 'language games', rule-governed self-contained systems of meaning within which the significance of words or signs are prescribed by an underlying set of semantic and syntactical rules or assumptions. Each language game; cynical and political, earnest and businesslike, reverential and theological, frivolous and flirtatious or speculative and scholarly, has its own rules of procedure, its own loading of familiar terms, its own conventions and practices. Apparently similar terms carry different meaning and have different consequences in each sort of 'game'. They are rather like the different sets of rules that allow us to play whist or poker with the same pack of cards. None of them have a settled value until we have agreed upon the game we are playing. Outside a given language game, words might mean anything or nothing, they have no particular intrinsic meaning and no communication between people is possible until they realize the rules of the game they are involved in. As a consequence, therefore, no explanation, no opinion or analysis can transcend the terms of the discourse within which it is framed. And the appropriateness of each language game and the rules that govern it are culturally prescribed. Indeed, they define a culture as such. They are simultaneously the power that culture has over us and constitute all the possibilities it has to offer us for thought and action (Foucault, (1966) 1973).

For postmodernists, the notion of the determining role of language on thought reinforces those derived from Marxist views about the necessarily ideological character of ideas in capitalist society, on the one hand (Lukács, Mannheim), and the perspectivist arguments derived from Friederick Nietzsche and Martin Heidegger, on the other. For Nietzsche, since nothing could be said except from within a particular perspective bounded by our culture, history, social class, language and the like, then there was no way we could rationally justify a preference for one set of values over any other ((1901) 1964). To him, so-called objective truth was merely the currently conventional view. Every age and every society had its own beliefs and it is impossible to prove the superiority of those that happen to prevail in this particular culture. Similarly, Heidegger ((1927) 1962) questioned the traditional separation of the knowing subject and the inert object of knowledge. Our knowledge of the world and of other people is the result of our interest in and our feelings about them. How we perceive things is a function of who we are as much as an intrinsic property of the thing in itself. The inference drawn from all this by postmodernists is that therefore there can be no objectively true picture of reality and that all views are alike in their relativism. Each and every argument is only a particular way of looking at things.

It may help to bring out the way these two strands in postmodern theory – the epistemological and the substantive – intertwine, if we consider the work of two major figures in the development of postmodernist theory. While Lyotard emphasized the epistemological thrust of postmodernism, but attributes it in part to the material conditions in which knowledge is produced, Baudrillard began with a focus on the social order of postmodernity with the advent of consumerism, and the effects of the increasingly predominant cultural media on the transformation of consciousness. For Baudrillard, the consequences of postmodernity are ontological as well as epistemological. In other words, it isn't just a matter of what we can know about the social world. That in itself changes the nature of the thing. As a result of the impossibility of a knowable truth, there is not only a final decoupling of our individual experience from any objectively grounded 'reality' whatsoever. More radically still, he argues, reality itself is dead.

Jean-François Lyotard: language and paralogy

Lyotard (1924–1998) was mainly preoccupied with the epistemological dimension of postmodernism. That is to say, his major contribution to the development of postmodernist thinking was addressed to the relativization of knowledge. He approached this question from two different directions, firstly through an examination of the material and structural context within which knowledge is produced which implicates it in the social practices of the powerful pursuing their own sectional interests. In short, he argued that the creation of knowledge, including scientific knowledge, is ineradicably ideological. Secondly, following Wittgenstein's argument, any kind of meaning at all, he argued, is in any case only intelligible within the rules of discourse of a given 'language game' and it is not possible to demonstrate that any form of discourse, even scientific discourse has an overriding validity as against any other. There can therefore be no way anyone could make a final statement about anything which was true once and for all, however logical it might seem in terms of a given set of assumptions. Those whose starting points are different will reach different, but no less valid, conclusions.

In his influential study, *The Postmodern Condition: A Report on Knowledge* (1984), first published in 1979, Lyotard argued that in the advanced societies, education has abandoned such academic values as the liberation of the individual through reason or the pursuit of knowledge as an end in itself, but has come to be concerned primarily with the acquisition of marketable qualifications, skills-training and predominantly economic goals. He noted the way in which the high costs of scientific research and scholarship are provided for. Grants from foundations, government funding or research contracts mean that research today is no longer a disinterested scholarly pursuit of truth, but has itself become big business, deeply involved either with the powerful agencies of the state, defence, law and order, social policy and health care, and so on, or with the sectional interests of private sector commercial and industrial concerns. When the latest findings on the effects of smoking or the benefits of nuclear energy are published, we want to know who paid for the research. Scientists are no longer trusted to be independent of their financial backers. Like every other kind of activity, the value of science has been reduced to its effectiveness in optimizing the efficiency of the system's performance (1984, p. xxi). Science has become an instrument in the hands of power (1984, p. 46) and, as a consequence of this complicity, any claim on behalf of science to a universal validity is clearly fraudulent. Thus, since research is expensive, and money equals economic power, science cannot be detached and objective, but reflects the structured power of an unequal society.

But regardless of the contaminating influence of ideological interests, the development of science is, anyway, an inherently profoundly social process. Following Thomas Kuhn's account of the history of scientific thought (Kuhn, (1962) 1970), Lyotard reminds us that new ideas, new knowledge, emerge not as the product of a rational and linear process of development but as an unpredictable succession of paradigm shifts. A paradigm, in this sense, consists of the basic set of concepts which identify and organize a given subject, the taken-for-granted way of thinking about it within which 'normal science' deals with questions of apparent fact. Paradigm shifts occur when scientists adopt a new way of thinking about their subject which raises more interesting questions for them, whilst offering a new way of tackling issues which had seemed to be insoluble before. There is a close parallel here with Wittgenstein's language games or Foucault's later concept of discourses. The sciences, the arts, architecture, literature, philosophical and political discourse, each have their own distinctive cognitive and normative systems of meaning. It is difficult for anyone unversed in their basic assumptions or fundamental values to cross the boundaries between them. Artists in different genres are scarcely intelligible to one another. Even the sciences are fragmenting into mutually incomprehensible specializations. In all these areas, work goes on within each field, but there are no general values or congruences of approach which unify them all in a common culture. Neither is there any organic growth or pattern of rational progress. Instead each field of activity displays an irregular series of disconnected or 'paralogical' transitions to new concepts, abandoning existing paradigms, and without any common ground of shared beliefs or understandings. General ideas like progress, enlightenment or the rational pursuit of truth and freedom no longer have any unifying power to frame and give a more universal meaning to the activities of writers and thinkers.

In premodern societies the religious or foundation myths, like the Bible stories or the Hindu Bhagavad Gita, served to make sense of the world. The displacement of these traditional narratives of origin and destiny by the ideas of social progress and rational enlightenment, or the ordered march of history, was the essential foundation of modernity. In modern thinking the legendary traditional narratives were replaced by metanarratives – organizing ideas in which historical events could be rendered intelligible as taking their place within a larger and meaningful pattern. What has beset us in the late twentieth century is that these metanarratives, in their turn, have lost all credibility. They have come to be seen for what they are – myths serving the interests of the powerful, language games or intellectual paradigms which serve the purposes of the prevailing system, but without any ultimate validity. No-one any longer believes in a greater scheme of things. History has no pattern: events play no role in anything that could be called a meaningful process. Lyotard distilled the essence of his argument in a phrase that has become an emblem for the postmodernist point of view: 'I define postmodern as incredulity towards metanarratives' (1984, p. xxiv).

Lyotard believed that the 'incredulity towards meta-narratives', the prevailing postmodern scepticism towards all general theory, was not only inescapable but, for those inclined to be critical of the current social order, was also a disabling condition. The fragmentation of meaning follows from the realization that knowledge can never be certain. But it is also the outcome of the way 'the system' has undermined all potentially autonomous social and cultural bases for individual or collective resistance. He noted (1984):

> ... the course that the evolution of social interaction is currently taking: the temporary contract is in practice supplanting permanent institutions in the professional, emotional, sexual, cultural, family and international domains, as well as in political affairs.

All is provisional, temporary and, in the even slightly longer run, uncertain. The erosion of independent institutions and traditions, which once provided a secure basis for personal and collective action, has put us all at the mercy of the dominant social processes of our time. These institutional trends, on the one hand and the cognitive, semiotic and cultural relativism Lyotard outlines, on the other, point in similar disturbing

(margin handwritten note: proximity → chaotic in nature drives production of history)

directions. They are both profoundly pessimistic. They challenge both the empirical and the logical possibility of individual freedom of thought and action. They destroy our confidence in the truth of what we know and in the validity of our ultimate values. However, the relationship between these evidently empirical institutional trends and the supposedly demonstrable philosophical relativism is not closely examined. Whether Lyotard discerns a causal connection between them in one direction or the other, or merely a mutually reinforcing congruence between the intellectual critique and the social structural analysis he does not make clear.

In brief, as far as Lyotard is concerned, there are only two sorts of knowledge about the world. There is either rational, validly certain knowledge or, instead, the myths and illusions offered by competing cultural ideologies. Since, as he has shown, certainty is impossible, what is left is relativism. However, we should beware that binary contrasts of this kind tend to be misleading. The reduction of complex issues to the confrontation of two irreconcilable opposites is seldom an adequate way of dealing with them. Dividing all the diverse possibilities between just two alternatives generally produces only half-truths. Thus Lyotard's critique of rationalist theory might look irresistible, except for the empiricist objection that, for instance, he need not have started out believing it was the only way to understand things in the first place. There are other ways of doing theory. It may also be objected that Lyotard not only expects us to be persuaded by the general argument he presents, but, in his account of the way the system of power distorts the production of knowledge in its own interests, he appears to retain a politics of prescriptive humanist values in the face of the cultural dilemmas and social structural processes he had diagnosed. In other words, he does not apply his arguments to himself. Perversely and paradoxically, he writes as though he expected other people to be persuaded that what he says is true. In the end, then, it looks as though he himself was less postmodern than one might have supposed. And if he eluded the condition himself, then the persuasiveness of his generalizations about knowledge and beliefs, as applied to the rest of us, may be thought to be compromised.

Jean Baudrillard: postconsumerism and hyperreality

One writer whose own postmodernism cannot be doubted is Baudrillard To begin with he had argued that the structural basis of postmodernity was the growth of consumer society. The emergence of the postmodern era came about at the point where the priority of commodity production in capitalist society was overtaken by the priority of the creation of demand. The main problem for modern society had been the production of goods. Productivity was the ultimate creation of modern rationality. In the postmodern period, however, the key role has passed from the producer to the consumer. The critical issue for the system is not how to produce more and more, but how to ensure that the level of demand will be there to match the level of output necessary to maintain profitability. This imperative displaces the question of rational resource allocation. Baudrillard rejects the common assumption that the system exists to serve primordially essential human needs. On the contrary, he argues, all needs are generated by the system itself. The guarantee of continued growth, indeed, of the continued survival of the system, has come to depend on the motivational management of the consumer. The introduction of electronic, digital technology was more than just an improvement in the means of production of marketable commodities. It is a medium for the manipulation of information. Advertising, marketing and the mass media have become central to the stimulation of demand through the continual invention of new wants. The images and identities they disseminate promise satisfactions earlier generations never dreamed of. They suggest life-styles of endless acquisition and inexhaustible glamour, which can be had at the pleasurable price of merely buying more and more. In terms reminiscent of Durkheim's description of the anomic society (see Chapter 7 above), Baudrillard argues that:

> Work, leisure, nature and culture, all previously dispersed, separate, and more or less irreducible activities that produced anxiety and complexity in our real life, and in our 'anarchic and archaic' cities, have finally become mixed, massaged, climate-controlled and domesticated into the simple activity of perpetual shopping.   (1970)

Consumption has become the medium and substance of social interaction, of cultural meaning and personal identity. The things people buy become a system of signs, a sort of coded meaning, through which they express themselves and make sense of the social world around them. We not only categorize and classify other people in terms of their consumption patterns, the clothes they wear, their preferred holiday destinations, the things in their supermarket trolley, the music and the films they like. Through the things we spend our own money on, and in terms of what we wouldn't be seen dead wearing, we define and reaffirm our own identity (cf. Douglas, 1996). Thus style comes to replace utility, the non-rational prevails over the rational and image counts for more than substance.

Instead of the standardized product and standardized solidarities of industrial mass production, we are now bombarded by diversity, ephemeral innovations and infinities of information. According to Douglas Kellner, Baudrillard believes that:

> we have entered a new stage in history, in which sign control is almost complete and totalitarian. Signs, simulations and codes have become the primary social determinants, and supposedly follow their own logic and order of signification.
>
> (Kellner, 1989, p. 50)

New information technology has transformed manufacturing, commercial activity and leisure. Its impact has not only been on the speeding up of communications and the handling of vastly greater amounts of data than before. Its qualitative effects on how we perceive and judge the world about us, how we comprehend things, are impossible to exaggerate and it has not all been enlightening. Baudrillard argues that 'ordinary language is linear but digital language provides for the perpetual irradiation of meaning' (1996, p. 53). Instead of a knowable concrete reality we are now confronted with a knowledge overload, a seeming transparency of virtual truths that constitute what Baudrillard describes as 'hyperreality'. How can we cope with this? Instead of illumination, the availability of apparently unlimited knowledge only reveals the infinite choices to be made. The availability of a boundless ocean of seeming facts and the endless interpretations of what they might mean reduces everything to a common level of insignificance:

> All the great humanist criteria of value, the whole civilization of moral, aesthetic and practical judgement are effaced in our system of images and signs. Everything becomes undecidable...   ((1976) 1993)

Instead of being the instrument of enlightenment, the sheer overwhelming profusion of information has made it the solvent of meanings instead of their catalyst. As a result, in the postmodern world truth itself has been usurped by a confused babble of disparate views and opinions about the state of things. There is no such thing any more as 'objective reality'. The mass media tell us what is supposed to have happened, what the views of the majority apparently are, and imply what are the appropriate standards we should apply in each case. As consumers and voters, our opinions may be canvassed, our preferences courted, but the appearance of democratic participation is illusory. In the postmodern era opinions are constructed and manipulated by media presentation, and by the questions posed and alternatives given in the polls and the market research that ostensibly seem to reveal them: 'Today, the real and the imaginary are confounded in the same operational totality ...' (1993, p. 146). Objectivity is only a politically convenient, but fraudulent myth serving the interests of the currently dominant system of discourse and power. All we really have, in practice, is a choice of simulations generated by the educational system and the other agencies of cultural manipulation. These simulations are not mere illusions, however. Illusion presumes some hidden truth. Baudrillard argues that there is no core of truth behind the appearances. Like an onion, the skin peeled away reveals only another skin underneath. Undetected illusions obviously are taken for the truth, but once exposed, of course, are illusions no longer, only another skin peeled away. Our beliefs about what the world is like are best described as *simulacra*. We necessarily take these to be the truth as we know it. But whatever simulacrum of reality we currently accept cannot with any final certainty be shown to be any less an illusion than the one we have just seen exposed as false turned out to be. There can be no warrant for the idea that there is anything deeper than our simulations. When the last onion-skin is peeled away there is nothing. Whereas the modern scientific approach aimed to reveal the underlying truth beneath the surface of experience, post-modernism instead draws our attention to, and celebrates, the simulacra – it exposes the appearances behind reality.

Baudrillard's later work concerns this world of appearances, the simulacra generated through the mass media and especially television and now, I suppose, the Internet. Our experience is no longer a matter of concrete situations we have lived through – as past generations endured the great depression of the 1930s or suffered the occupation or the bombing during the Second World War. Now our knowledge of the wider world is mostly vicarious. What we have access to are no more than simulacra; not illusions exactly, but a virtual reality, representations we take to be the truth. We have no direct and independent means of testing them. If no camera was there to film, no reporter present to tell us what to feel, we would know nothing of what goes on anyway. But how can you tell that what you see on the TV screen or read in the paper really happened? How can we be sure those starving children, those soldiers, those massacred seal pups were photographed where and when we are told they were? One burning tank looks much like another, this year's third-world refugees are hard to tell apart from the refugees of five years ago. If it wasn't on television, for most of the rest of the world it never happened. If it was on television, should you believe it anyway? Baudrillard's ironic scepticism about the 1990 Gulf War as a purely media contrivance, his claim (in 1996) that reality itself has been murdered may overstate, but only a little, the anxieties many feel in a media dominated world. The death of reality itself, blown away in the hyperreality of media images where there are no facts only news values, is the perfect crime because there is no incriminating corpse, the victim has vanished, the transparency of the deed has left no clues and no-one is any longer in a position to prove that it ever took place. And yet he goes on writing about it:

The absolute rule of thought is to give back the world as it was given to us – unintelligible. And, if possible, to render it a little more unintelligible.   (1996, p. 105)

Postmodernist theory and continuing change

With reference to the other general issues for theory set out in Chapter 1, the postmodernist perspective has a distinctive signature:

a. In strong contrast with Giddens's emphasis on reflexive human agency, Bertens describes postmodernism's hostility toward the individual as subject and refers to the absence of any theory of agency in postmodernist theory (1995, p. 207: fn.). For postmodernists, individual identities are tentative and derivative, localized reflexivities within the simulacra, the varying versions of hyperreality. Both the substantive argument that structures have become more fluid or indeterminate, on the one hand, and the methodological claim that they are in any case only figments of discourse, on the other, are sociologically realist positions. Even Baudrillard's claim that 'the image masks the absence of a basic reality' (1988, p. 170), amounts to a paradoxical sociological realism because it is the web of meanings, the code of seeming, that is the focus and grounding of analysis and not the interpreting, initiating individual.

b. In postmodernist theorizing mundane experience, such as watching television or buying a pair of trousers, is rendered esoteric. It becomes an ambiguous involvement in the virtual reality of sign systems, which has to be interpreted for us all by an intellectual elite, self-certified as alone able to appreciate and explicate its ironies (see Calinicos, 1990; Gellner, 1992, p. 66; Baumann, 1993, p. 24). The hyperreal seems to be unconstrained by material factors. It does not appear to be related in any obvious way to the scarcity or abundance of commodities, the distribution of personal power or economic resources. Notwithstanding Lyotard's concern with the funding of research and, in his earlier writings, Baudrillard's concern with the operation of 'the system' (presumably the capitalist system), postmodernist argument represents an essentially sociological realist idealism.

c. But unlike the Systems Theories we considered earlier, the key theme of postmodernist scepticism towards all metanarratives

embraces a number of essentially relativist axioms. It denies the
possibility of an objective truth accessible to scientific
investigation. The emptiness of representation as a mode of
thinking about the external world means that there can be no
external legitimation of belief. Since postmodernists believe there
is no independent and objective truth against which our beliefs
can be validated, then for them all legitimation is de-
authenticated. Science itself is relativized and postmodernist
discourse becomes, in the later work of Baudrillard for example,
essentially poetic in content if not in form.

d. The absence of legitimate, or for that matter illegitimate,
objective structures, logically and practically entails a decentring
of power. It also precludes the possibility of consensus, and
implies a residual and decentred conflict model of society. This
is one, however, in which the prospects for coherent political
action are at best pessimistic (Laclau and Mouffe), more so than
in the theories of modernity, even Giddens's version, which we
considered earlier.

e. What I have called substantive postmodernism bases its account
of present-day society on the identification of a number of changes
which have overtaken modern society. Change has accelerated to
such an extent that the old certainties no longer apply, and once
well-understood patterns of cause and effect can no longer be
relied on. Crook and his colleagues have argued that:

> Postmodernization is characterized by an unprecedented
> level of unpredictability and apparent chaos. Action is
> divorced from underlying material constraints ... and enters
> the voluntaristic realm of taste, choice and preference. As it
> does so the boundaries between social groups disappear.
>   (Crook et al., 1992, p. 15)

The postmodern world, as Baumann says, is 'irreducibly and
irrevocably pluralistic, split into a multitude of sovereign units
and sites of authority, with no horizontal or vertical order,
either in actuality or potency' (1988, p. 799). This unpredictability and disorder entail the disappearance of even the
possibility of structured social relationships. Boundaries blur,
patterns dissolve, social customs and established practice no

longer offer any guide to what might be expected. This all may seem to demand the historical emergence of a methodological postmodernism as the relativist theory of an incoherent era. However, the connection between them is by no means necessary or, indeed, without its contradictory aspects.

f. The doctrine of the exhaustion of metanarrative paradoxically lodges methodological postmodernism within a rationalist paradigm of theoretical discourse. Postmodernists reach their pessimistic and relativistic conclusions deductively from the death of metanarrative, and the consequent destruction of the axiomatic assumptions which alone could validate their interpretation of events. Empiricists never relied upon metanarratives anyway. As we saw in Chapter 1, they based their suggested explanations inductively on experiential data. The question of the logical validity of knowledge doesn't arise for them. Baconian empiricists acknowledge the tentative or provisional nature of all knowledge of the observable world, but nevertheless regard it as grounded in experience of an objective and independent reality (Rorty, 1985, pp. 161–75; Kumar, 1995; and see Chapter 1 above). Postmodernist uncertainty is therefore of a very different kind. The logical result of critical rationalist analysis turned back upon its own basic assumptions has led to the vertiginous situation where no account of the social can have any defensible claim to superiority over any other.

10

Continuing Change and Continuing Theory

We have now examined the main theories of structural social change. It is clear that as the phenomenon itself continues, possibly at an accelerating pace, so attempts to explain it or to explore its consequences continue to proliferate. Recent theorists have shown an increasingly self-conscious awareness of the intimate interrelationships between the ideas they propose and the changing cultural context which they claim to articulate. Their view of society as a system of discourse heightens the role they attribute to social theory (and theorists) as constitutive factors and, at the same time, emphasizes theory's vulnerability as an essentially situation-determined form of expression. Earlier theorization had aimed at a more context-free validity, but the mere aspiration to such virtue has come to be questioned. Relativism, however, becomes auto-destructive and present theory gives no pointers to what might be expected in the future, either in substance or of theory.

This study has not been a comprehensive history of sociological thought, and therefore theories and traditions which have not addressed the issue of social change have been omitted. Interactionist theories, ethnomethodology and phenomenological perspectives, for instance, which have mainly been concerned with the minutiae of interaction and questions of identity, action and structure, have not been included. Nor am I aware of any specifically feminist theory of structural social change so that another major element in the recent theoretical literature of sociology has not been included either. Nevertheless, the discussion does suggest the possibility of some wider generalizations about the existing diversity and the further development of sociological theory. Those theories we have considered do not add up to a cumulative series in which the more recent supersede and improve upon the earlier. The appearance of the various arguments has no doubt been influenced by the historical circumstances in which they were conceived, and this may very well continue to be so. But, for us, they provide a repertoire of ideas and arguments which are all still relevant to our present theoretical needs and interests. It is not like the development of engineering science, in which, antiquarian interest apart, the productive potential, convenience, economy and reliability of the latest products far surpass the crude if ingenious inventions of the early pioneers. The history of social theory is more like the history of music, in which the eighteenth or nineteenth centuries may still offer as much for our inspiration or delight as even the finest work from the twentieth.

Inspiration or delight might be asking a lot, but it would also be misguided to look forward to any general consensus emerging in the future. Old ideas sometimes become fashionable again, new ideas occasionally surface. But there will be no ultimate common agreement because there is no common ground upon which it could be built. Any descriptive account of what is going on is determined not just by what may take place in the external world, but by the basic theoretical, that is, ontological and epistemological assumptions about what is of significance, whether there is a larger pattern to events, whether we are concerned primarily with humanly meaningful reasons for action or with the largely impersonal causes of behaviour, and about what sort of statements, deductive or inductive, logically certain or provisional, would serve to satisfy our curiosity. As we have seen, there are two or more possible answers to all these questions, and no final resolution to any of them. Part of the diversity of social theory is the result of different theorists clutching at different straws in the wind of historical change. Theory has not in the past contained, nor could it ever in the future pursue, some broad convergence of ✳ view. On the contrary, arguments about the causes, direction and probable outcomes of change have diverged because each different account has been rooted in the different assumptions from which its authors have set out. That is true of present-day theory and of whatever will replace it.

Current theories of modernity and postmodernity alike

display a preoccupation with the cultural. The modernization theory of Giddens and the postmodernism of Baudrillard are also alike in the role they implicitly attribute to communication technology as generating the cultural effects with which they are primarily concerned. Earlier writers, Smith, the evolutionists or Marx for example, assumed that technological innovation would be part of the strategy of entrepreneurs seeking to make the most of the resources available to them, and other writers, Tönnies, Weber or the systems theorists, saw technological development as part of the wider process of rationalization. There is, that is to say, an implied reductionism in recent theory, which could indicate a pessimism about the possibility of a distinctively sociological analysis were it not for the continuing persuasiveness of those earlier points of view.

These more recent discussions of modernity and postmodernity, however, also share with the evolutionists the sense of a historical discontinuity, resulting from the transition to greater diversity and complexity, on the one hand, or to globalization and hyperreality, on the other. Modernist theorists, however, still want to retain the possibility of a rational understanding of the complex and sometimes contradictory tendencies of contemporary change; postmodernists, for the most part, argue that we are in, or are now entering, a new era which defies rational analysis and that, as a consequence, all those earlier theories that discussed the modernization of the world are no longer relevant. This follows since it is not just that the present cannot be confined within a rational explanation, but that rational analysis itself is a time-bound, class-biased, culturally relativized idea, and therefore, our understanding of the past must be as uncertain and precarious as the stories we make up about our current predicament. Where then does that leave all those attempts to make sense of social change we have just been looking at?

Can we only think about social change in snatched glimpses from within the torrent of events? A cool detachment can be misleading. The complexity, diversity and persistence of the processes of change are not well represented as a transition from *A* to *B*, as from, for example, feudalism to capitalism, Fordist to post-Fordist, traditional to modern society, and so on. The changes do not stop once the defining conditions of the *B* state are fulfilled, and historical inquiry perennially tends to cast increasing doubt on the purity and coherence of the *A* state. Binary contrasts do have a heuristic value as pointers. They are, however, misleading when ideal-typifications are taken to be historical reality. All those attempts by social theorists to contrast the society of their own times with what had gone before are flawed by the freeze-frame exclusion of the fluidity of continuing change. Modernity versus post-modernity is the latest of these attempts to capture the dynamic flux of social process within the categories of a (more or less) neat typology. The problem with substantive postmodernism, therefore, is essentially the overly-static conceptualizations from which its arguments derive. Thus the need to distinguish a new postmodern phase of history derives from the rigidities and oversimplifications of theoretical characterizations of the preceding modern phase. These have exaggerated the predominance and stability of some features, such as the nuclear family or class conflict, which were neither universal nor unchanging. Attention has now shifted to other features of the present scene, the role of cultural media or globalizing trends for example, and, in particular, to diversity and discontinuity, which earlier writers tended to ignore in their concern to describe underlying patterns and general trends. Variability and transience may or may not have become more common (Noble, 1998), but they have not replaced those continuities of power and structural constraint that had interested the sociologists of modern times (Gellner, 1992). This new focus of attention, then, is, at most, only partially the result of objective changes in society itself. It reflects, at least as much, the worthwhile realization of some of the limitations of classical theories, on the one hand, while, on the other, it reflects the perennial need of theorists to come up with something new.

There is also a contradiction between the historical claims of substantive postmodernity and what we might call methodological postmodernism, the view that 'the sociology of postmodernization must be a sociology which is itself in transition' (Crook et al., p. 236) or the still more radical argument that what passes for reality is, or has become, only a figment. Like the simplification of history which the contrast of the modern and postmodern eras entails, so the juxtaposition of postmodernist and modernist theory itself oversimplifies and over-dramatizes the theoretical disjuncture. There never was a single version of modern (pre-postmodern) sociology. Any introductory text will confront the reader with the competing perspectives of differently orientated theorists, Marxists and functionalists, interactionists, conflict and consensus theorists and so forth. On the other hand, the idea that if we are adequately to understand a changing social world, then sociological theory needs to be tentative, provisional, possibly eclectic (e.g., Crook et al., p. 236) is hardly new, but none the less very welcome. But then, we could argue, sociology should always have been like that. The paradox or self-contradiction of postmodernist theorizing should be immediately obvious. If what Lyotard or Baudrillard, for instance, argue is true – then it is true and not just another point of view. But if there is no final truth, only alternative discourses, then postmodernity is just another story with no privileged claim on our belief. There could be no reason why we should agree with it in preference to any other perspective, such as, for instance, the familiar scientific view that there is for all of us one ultimate truth if ever we could contrive to discover what it is. So the idea that life at the end of the twentieth century and beginning of the twenty-first, say, had become more culturally diverse, less structured and so forth, and the contrary kind of scepticism that nothing had fundamentally changed are both alternative ways of looking at the world about us and, for the consistently postmodernist theorists, neither could be established as objectively true. So we have to make up our minds about whether we are either presenting a new kind of sceptical epistemology or looking at something substantively new, the postmodern period of social history. These are separate arguments and neither will justify the other (cf. Featherstone, 1988; Smart, 1990).

By the late 1990s the empty promises of postmodernist theory seemed to attract fewer takers. What then follows in the shape of theory for the new century? What about post-postmodernism? Do we just give up trying to make sense of the changing social world we have somehow to cope with? The requirements of explanation vary with the nature of the problem to be understood (Boudon, 1986, p. 125) and the cognitive context within which it is to be incorporated. In other words, it may be a different matter when making sense of past trends from trying to offer a predictive model or forecast as a possible guide for policy in the making. The kinds of change we are looking at: long-term or short-term; material, cognitive, normative or institutional; face-to-face, organizational or global may be more easily understood with different kinds of theory. Different models may be helpful if we want to understand the organizational transformation of management in corporate hierarchies, the erosion of interpersonal trust on a deprived urban housing estate, second-wave industrialization in the Pacific rim, postcolonial African religious movements or the globalization of consumer footwear preferences. There is also the reflexive question of why you would want to know about such things. What would it take to make sense of the question, what sort of answers would satisfy your curiosity? The context of beliefs and understanding within which any new investigation has to be located will make some approaches seem appealing, others less so. At the same time, that doesn't mean that any old theory will do. Theories of social change need to take note of the dilemmas addressed by past theorists, their insights as well as their failings, if they are to avoid merely going over well-trodden ground.

The arguments will, and should, continue. In spite of the intellectual pessimism of postmodernists or the intellectual complacency of those who argue that major social transformations are well in the past, and history has come to a stop, the debate will never cease. Even without the inescapability of continuing change in the real world, there is no ultimate theoretical synthesis, no final distillation of a common essence at the heart of every sociological theory. The needs for understanding human society and the possibilities of creative theory are too diverse ever to be confined within any one framework of ideas. Boudon argued that '... it is always possible to find in the real world an inexhaustible supply of examples of processes capable of supporting any theory of social change' (1986, p. 189). That may be going too far. There are better and worse, more and less plausible theories, and we should be able to tell the differences between them. However, the really interesting social theorists have always had distinctive views, usually at odds with prevailing opinions, whether radical or reactionary. Sociology has always been disharmonious and is likely to remain so. We will always have to find our own way about amongst contradictory and irreconcilable perspectives.

The unifying theme here is the essential sociological problem, the issue that gave rise to the subject in the first place and which continues to make it relevant for the world at large outside the lecture room, that is, the causes and consequences of social change. Looking at the range of views which social theorists have offered on this topic, I have recommended no 'best buy', though here and there I have commented on the durability and some of the operating problems of the various models under consideration. Readers who find the question interesting are encouraged to make their own choice or, better, to begin to work out their own arguments, more relevant to these interesting times. But if they can emulate the courage and imagination with which our predecessors tried to explore and explain their changing world, we should be able to look at the sociology of the twenty-first century with some degree of hope.

Bibliography

AGANBEYGAN, A. 'Planned Market: Perestroika in the USSR', in J. Anderson and M. Ricci (eds), *Society and Social Science* (Open University 1990).

ALBROW, Martin *Bureaucracy* (Pall Mall 1970).

ALTHUSSER, Louis *For Marx* (Allen Lane 1969).

ANDERSON, Perry *Lineages of the Absolutist State* (New Left Books 1974).

ANDRESKI, Stanislav (ed.), *The Essential Comte* (Croom Helm 1974).

ARON, Raymond *Main Currents in Sociological Thought*, 2 vols (Penguin Books 1964).

ARON, Raymond *Eighteen Lectures on Industrial Society* (Weidenfeld and Nicolson 1967).

BARAN, Paul *The Political Economy of Growth* (Monthly Review Press 1957).

BARAN, Paul, and Paul SWEEZY *Monopoly Capital* (Penguin1968).

BAUDRILLARD, Jean *Consumer Society* (Sage 1970).

BAUDRILLARD, Jean (1976) *Symbolic Exchange and Death* (Sage: 1993 edn).

BAUDRILLARD, Jean *Selected Writings* (Stanford University Press 1988).

BAUDRILLARD, Jean *The Perfect Crime* (Verso 1996).

BAUMANN, Z. 'Sociology and Postmodernity', *Sociological Review*, 36, 1988, pp. 790–813.

BAUMANN, Zygmunt *Intimations of Postmodernity* (Routledge 1993).

BEETHAM, David *Bureaucracy* (Open University Press 1987).

BELL, Daniel *The End of Ideology: On The Exhaustion of Political Ideas in the Fifties* (Free Press 1960).

BELL, Daniel *The Coming of Post-Industrial Society* (Basic Books 1973).

BELL, Daniel (1976) *The Cultural Contradictions of Capitalism* (Heinemann: 1979 edn).

BELL, Norman, and Ezra VOGEL 'Introduction', in Bell and Vogel (eds), *A Modern Introduction to the Family* (Routledge 1964).

BELLAH, Robert *Beyond Belief* (Harper and Row 1970).

BENDIX, Reinhard *Work and Authority in Industry* (Wiley 1966).

BERTENS, Hans *The Idea of the Postmodern: A History* (Routledge 1995).

BLACK, Max (ed.), *The Social Theories of Talcott Parsons* (Prentice Hall 1961).

BLAU, Peter M. *Exchange and Power in Social Life* (John Wiley 1964).

BLAU, Peter M. *The Concept of Social Structure* (Open Books 1968).

BLAU, Peter M., and M. W. MEYER *Bureaucracy in Modern Society* (Random House 1971).

BLUMER, Herbert *Symbolic Interactionism* (Prentice-Hall 1969).

BOSWELL, James (1791) *The Life of Samuel Johnson* (Everyman: 1992 edn).
BOUDON, Raymond *Theories of Social Change: A Critical Approach* (Polity Press 1986).
BOURDIEU, Pierre, and J. C. PASSERON *Reproduction in Education, Society and Culture* (Sage 1970).
BOWLER, Peter *The Invention of Progress* (Basil Blackwell 1983).
BRAUDEL, Fernand (1976) *Civilisation and Capitalism*, 3 vols (Collins: 1984 edn).
BURGESS, E. W., and H. J. LOCKE *The Family From Institution to Companionship* (American Book Co. 1953).
BURNHAM, James *The Managerial Revolution* (Penguin Books 1945).
BURNS, T., and G. M. STALKER *The Management of Innovation* (Routledge and Kegan Paul 1961).
BURROW, J. *Evolution and Society: A Study in Victorian Social Theory* (Cambridge University Press 1966).
CALINICOS, Alex *Against Postmodernism: A Marxist Critique* (Polity Press 1990).
CAMPBELL, Tom *Seven Theories of Human Society* (Oxford University Press 1990).
CHEAL, David *The Family and the State of Theory* (Harvester-Wheatsheaf 1991).
COHEN, G. A. *Karl Marx's Theory of History: A Defence* (Oxford University Press 1978).
COLLINS, Randall *Conflict Sociology: Towards an Explanatory Science* (Academic Press 1975).
COMTE, Auguste (1875) *A System of Positive Polity*, 3 vols.
COSER, Lewis *The Functions of Social Conflict* (Routledge and Kegan Paul 1956).
CRAIB, Ian *Anthony Giddens* (Routledge 1992).
CROOK, Stephen, Jon PAKULSKI and Malcolm WATERS *Postmodernisation: Change in Advanced Society* (Sage 1992).
CUPPITT, Don *Taking Leave of God* (1980).
CYERT, R., and J. G. MARCH *A Behavioural Theory of the Firm* (Prentice-Hall 1963).
DARWIN, Charles (1859) *The Origin of Species by Means of Natural Selection* (Penguin: 1982 edn).
DAVIS, Kingsley *Human Society* (Macmillan 1948).
DAVIS, Kingsley 'The Myth of Functional Analysis as a Special Method of Sociology and Anthropology', *American Sociological Review*, 24, 1959, pp. 757–73.
DAVIS, Winston 'Religion and Development: Weber and East Asian Experience', in Myron Weiner and Samuel Huntington (eds), *Understanding Political Development* (Little, Brown 1987), pp. 221–79.
DAWE, Alan 'The Two Sociologies', *British Journal of Sociology*, XXI, 1970, pp. 207–18.
DAWKINS, Richard *The Selfish Gene* (Oxford University Press 1976).
DAWKINS, Richard *The Blind Watchmaker* (Oxford University Press 1986).
DEANE, Phyllis *The First Industrial Revolution* (Oxford University Press 1979).

DJILAS, Milovan *The New Class* (Praeger 1957).
DOUGLAS, Mary *Natural Symbols* (Barrie and Jenkins 1973).
DOUGLAS, Mary *Thought Styles* (Sage 1996).
DUDLEY, Leonard, M. *The Word and the Sword* (Blackwell 1991).
DUMONT, René *Homo Hierarchicus* (Paladin Books 1972).
DURKHEIM, Emile (1893) *The Division of Labour in Society* (Routledge and Kegan Paul: 1982 edn).
DURKHEIM, Emile (1895) *The Rules of Sociological Method* (Routledge and Kegan Paul: 1951 edn).
DURKHEIM, Emile (1897) *Suicide* (Free Press: 1951 edn).
DURKHEIM, Emile (1912) *The Elementary Forms of Religious Life* (Routledge and Kegan Paul: 1956 edn).
DURKHEIM, Emile *Essays in Sociology and Philosophy* (Cohen and West 1951).
DURKHEIM, Emile *Professional Ethics and Civic Morals* (Routledge and Kegan Paul 1957).
DURKHEIM, Emile *Socialism and St Simon* (Routledge and Kegan Paul 1959).
ELTON, G. R. *Reformation Europe* (Oxford University Press 1963).
ENGELS, Friedrich (1845) *The Condition of the Working Class in England* (Penguin: 1987 edn).
ERIKSON, Robert, and J. H. GOLDTHORPE *The Constant Flux* (Clarendon Press 1993).
FEATHERSTONE, Mike 'In Pursuit of the Postmodern: An Introduction', *Theory, Culture and Society*, 5, 1988, p. 205.
FEATHERSTONE, Mike *Consumer Culture and Postmodernism* (Sage 1991).
FERGUSON, Adam (1767) *Essay on the History of Civil Society* (Edinburgh University Press: 1967 edn).
FEUER, Lewis *Ideology and the Ideologists* (Blackwell 1975).
FLEW, Anthony *Thinking About Social Thinking* (Blackwell 1985).
FOUCAULT, Michel (1966) *The Order of Things* (Tavistock: 1973 edn).
FRANK, Andre Gunder *Capitalism and Underdevelopment in Latin America* (Penguin Books 1971).
FRANK, Andre Gunder, and Barry K. GILLS *The World System: Five Hundred Years or Five Thousand?* (Routledge 1996).
FRIEDMAN, Georges *The Anatomy of Work* (Heinemann 1961).
FUKUYAMA, Francis *The End of History and the Last Man* (Penguin Books 1991).
GALBRAITH, J. K. *The New Industrial State* (Houghton Mifflin 1967).
GELLNER, Ernest *Nations and Nationalism* (Blackwell 1983).
GELLNER, Ernest *Postmodernism, Reason and Religion* (Routledge 1992).
GERTH, Hans, and C. WRIGHT MILLS (eds) (1948) *From Max Weber: Essays in Sociology* (Routledge and Kegan Paul: 1967 edn).
GIDDENS, Anthony *Capitalism and Modern Social Theory* (Cambridge University Press 1971).
GIDDENS, Anthony *Politics and Sociology in the Thought of Max Weber* (Macmillan 1972).
GIDDENS, Anthony *Central Problems in Social Theory* (Macmillan 1979).
GIDDENS, Anthony *A Contemporary Critique of Historical Materialism*

(Macmillan 1981).

GIDDENS, Anthony *The Constitution of Society* (Polity Press 1984).

GIDDENS, Anthony *The Consequences of Modernity* (Polity Press 1990).

GIDDENS, Anthony *Modernity and Self-Identity: Self and Society in the Late Modern Age* (Polity Press 1991).

GIDDENS, Anthony *Beyond Left and Right* (Polity Press 1994).

GIDDENS, Anthony (1999) *Runaway World*, The Reith Lectures (www.bbc.co.uk/reith99).

GINSBERG, Morris (1916) 'Introduction', in L. T. Hobhouse, G. C. Wheeler and M. Ginsberg (eds), *The Material Culture and Social Institutions of the Simpler Peoples* (Humanities Press: 1965 edn).

GOLDMAN, M. I. *USSR in Crisis: The Failure of the Economic System* (W. W. Norton 1983).

GOLDMAN, M. I. *What Went Wrong with Perestroika* (W. W. Norton 1992).

GOLDTHORPE, J. H. 'Social Stratification in Industrial Society', *Sociological Review Monograph*, no. 8, 1964, pp. 97–122; and in R. Bendix and S. M. Lipset (eds), *Class, Status and Power* (Routledge: 2nd edn 1968), pp. 648–59.

GOLDTHORPE, J. H. 'Reply to Dunning and Hopper', *Sociological Review*, 14, 1966, p. 191.

GORDON-CHILDE, V. *What Happened in History?* (Penguin Books 1956).

GOULDNER, Alvin 'Reciprocity and Autonomy in Functional Theory', in Gouldner, *For Sociology* (Penguin Books 1973), pp. 214–17.

GRAMSCI, A. *Political Writings* (Lawrence and Wishart 1970).

HABERMAS, Jürgen *Legitimation Crisis* (Heinemann 1976).

HABERMAS, Jürgen *Moral Consciousness and Communicative Action* (Polity Press 1990).

HALL, John *Powers and Liberties* (Penguin 1986), chs 6 and 7.

HAMMERSLEY, Martin 'On Feminist Methodology', *Sociology*, 26, 1992, pp. 187–206.

HAMNETT, Ian 'Durkheim and The Study of Religion', in Steve Fenton (ed.), *Durkheim and Modern Sociology* (Cambridge University Press 1984).

HARRIS, C. C. *The Family in Industrial Society* (Allen and Unwin 1983).

HARRIS, Nigel *The End of the Third World: Newly Industrialising Countries and the Decline of an Ideology* (Penguin Books 1986).

HAWTHORN, Geoffrey *Enlightenment and Despair* (Cambridge University Press 1976).

HEIDEGGER, Martin (1927) *Being and Time* (SCM Press: 1962 edn).

HEILBRONNER, Robert *The Essential Adam Smith* (Norton 1986).

HOBBES, Thomas (1651) *Leviathan* (Penguin Books: 1968 edn).

HOMANS, George *Social Behaviour: Its Elementary Forms* (Routledge and Kegan Paul 1961).

HUME, David (1778) *History of England* (Liberty Fund: 1983 edn).

HUNTINGTON, Ellsworth *Mainsprings of Civilisation* (John Wiley 1945).

KELLNER, Douglas *Jean Baudrillard: From Marxism to Postmodernism and Beyond* (Polity Press 1989).

KERR, Clark, J. T. DUNLOP, F. H. HARBISON and C. A. MYERS (1960) *Industrialism and Industrial Man: The Problems of Labour and*

Management in Economic Growth (Penguin: 1973 edn).

KEYNES, J. M. *The General Theory of Employment, Interest and Money* (Macmillan 1936).

KOHN, Melvin 'Bureaucratic Man: A Portrait and an Interpretation', *American Sociological Review*, 36, 1971, pp. 461–74.

KROPOTKIN, Pyotr (1902) *Mutual Aid* (Penguin Books: 1939 edn).

KUHN, Thomas, S. (1962) *The Structure of Scientific Revolutions* (University of Chicago Press: 1970 edn).

KUMAR, Krishnan *Prophecy and Progress* (Penguin Books 1978).

KUMAR, Krishnan *From Post-Industrial to Post-Modern Society: New Theories of the Contemporary World* (Blackwell 1995).

LACLAU, Ernesto *Politics and Ideology in Marxist Theory* (New Left Books 1977).

LACLAU, Ernesto, and Chantal MOUFFE 'Postmarxism Without Apologies', *New Left Review*, 166, 1987, pp. 79–106.

LANDES, David *The Wealth and Poverty of Nations* (Little, Brown 1998).

LASLETT, Peter 'Size and Structure of the Households in England over Three Centuries', *Population Studies*, 23, 1969, pp. 199–223.

LASLETT, Peter *Family Life and Illicit Love in Earlier Generations* (Cambridge University Press 1977).

LAYDER, Derek *Understanding Social Theory* (Sage 1994).

LENIN, V. I. (1917) *Imperialism* (Progress Publishers: 1966 edn).

LENSKI, Gerhard 'History and Social Change', *American Journal of Sociology*, 82, 1976, p. 548–64.

LENSKI, G., and J. Lenski *Human Societies: An Introduction to Macrosociology* (McGraw-Hill 1987).

LINTON, Ralph *The Study of Man* (Appleton-Century-Crofts 1936).

LIST, Friedrich (1885) *National Political Economy* (Kelley: 1977 edn).

LOCKWOOD, David 'Social Integration and System Integration', in G. Zollschan and W. Hirsch (eds), *Explorations in Social Change* (Routledge 1964), pp. 244–56.

LUKÁCS, Gyorgy (1923) *History and Class Consciousness* (Merlin Press: 1971 edn).

LYOTARD, Jean-François (1979) *The Postmodern Condition: A Report on Knowledge* (Manchester University Press: 1984 edn).

MACFARLANE, Alan *The Origins of English Individualism* (Basil Blackwell 1978).

MACFARLANE, Alan *The Culture of Capitalism* (Basil Blackwell 1987).

MACHIAVELLI, G. (1513) *The Prince* (Everyman: 1992 edn).

MACKINNON, Malcolm H. 'Calvinism and the Infallible Assurance of Grace: The Weber Thesis Reconsidered', *British Journal of Sociology*, XXXIX, 1988.

MANNHEIM, Karl (1936) *Ideology and Utopia* (Routledge: 1960 edn).

MARCH, J. G., and J. P. OLSEN *Ambiguity and Choice in Organisations* (Universitets Forlaget, Bergen 1976).

MARCUSE, Herbert *One Dimensional Man* (Penguin Books 1964).

MARX, Karl *The Economic and Philosophical Manuscripts of 1844* (International Publishers 1964).

MARX, Karl (1843) 'On the Jewish Question', in David McLellan (ed.),

Karl Marx: Selected
Writings (Oxford University Press: 1977 edn).
MARX, Karl (1845) 'Theses on Feuerback', in T. B. Bottomore and
   Maximilian Rubel (eds), *Karl Marx: Selected Writings in Sociology and
   Social Philosophy* (Watts 1957).
MARX, Karl (1847) *The Poverty of Philosophy* (Progress Press: 1955 edn).
MARX, Karl (1852) 'The Eighteenth Brumaine of Louise Bonaparte', in
   Selected Works (Lawrence and Wishart: 1950 edn).
MARX, Karl (1857) *Grundrisse: Foundations of the Critique of Political
   Economy* (Penguin Books: 1973 edn).
MARX, Karl (1859) *Contribution to the Critique of Political Economy*
   (Lawrence and Wishart: 1971 edn).
MARX, Karl (1865) 'Value, Price and Profit', in *Selected Works* (Lawrence
   and Wishart: 1950 edn).
MARX, Karl (1867) *Capital*, vol. 1 (Penguin Books: 1976 edn).
MARX, Karl, and Friedrich ENGELS (1846) *The German Ideology*
   (Lawrence and Wishart: 1970 edn).
MARX, Karl, and Friedrich ENGELS (1848) *The Communist Manifesto*
   (Penguin Books: 1967 edn).
MATTHIAS, Peter *The First Industrial Nation* (Oxford University Press:
   2nd edn 1983).
MCLACHLAN, John *The Divine Image* (Lindsey Press 1972).
MEAD, George Herbert (1934) *Mind, Self and Society* (University of
   Chicago Press: 1962 edn).
MÊSTRÓVIC, Stepan G. *Anthony Giddens: The Last Modernist* (Routledge
   1998).
MINTZBERG, H. *Power in and Around Organisations* (Prentice-Hall 1983).
MOORE, Wilbert *The Impact of Industry* (Prentice Hall 1965).
MOSCA, Gaetano (1896) *The Ruling Class* (McGraw-Hill: 1939 edn).
MOUFFE, Chantal *Universal Abandon? The Politics of Postmodernism*
   (Edinburgh University Press 1988).
NEEDHAM, Joseph *Science and Civilisation in China*, vol. 1 (Cambridge
   University Press 1954).
NICHOLLS, Theo *Ownership, Control and Ideology* (Allen and Unwin
   1969).
NICHOLSON, Linda, and Steven SEIDMAN *Social Postmodernism*
   (Cambridge University Press 1995).
NIETZSCHE, Friedrich (1901) *The Will to Power* (Russell and Russell: 1964
   edn).
NIMKOFF, M. F., and R. MIDDLETON 'Types of Family and Types of
   Economy', *American Journal of Sociology*, 66, 1960, pp. 215–25.
NISBET, Robert *The Sociological Tradition* (Basic Books 1966).
NISBET, Robert *Social Change and History* (Oxford University Press 1969).
NOBLE, Trevor 'Postmodernity and Family Theory', *International Journal
   of Comparative Sociology* , XXXIX, 1998, pp. 257–77.
O'CONNOR, James *The Fiscal Crisis of the State* (St Martins Press 1973).
OLIVER, Ian 'The Limits of the Sociology of Religion: A Critique of the
   Durkheimian Approach', *British Journal of Sociology*, 27, 1976, pp.
   461–73.

PAINE, Tom (1794) *The Age of Reason* (Watts: 1956 edn).

PARETO, Vilfredo (1916) *Mind and Society: A Treatise on General Sociology* (Dover: 1963 edn).

PARKIN, Frank *Marxism and Class Theory: A Bourgeois Critique* (Tavistock 1978).

PARSONS, Talcott *The Structure of Social Action* (Free Press 1937).

PARSONS, Talcott *The Social System* (Free Press 1951).

PARSONS, Talcott *Essays in Social Theory* (Free Press 1954).

PARSONS, Talcott *Structure and Process in Modern Societies* (Free Press 1960).

PARSONS, Talcott 'An Outline of the Social System', in Parsons et al. (eds), *Theories of   Society* (Free Press 1961).

PARSONS, Talcott *Societies: Evolutionary and Comparative Perspectives* (Prentice-Hall 1966).

PARSONS, T. 'Some Considerations on the Theory of Social Change', in S. N. Eisenstadt (ed.), *Readings in Social Evolution and Development* (Pergamon 1970), pp. 95–130.

PARSONS, Talcott *The System of Modern Societies* (Prentice-Hall 1971).

PARSONS, Talcott, and Robert BALES *Family, Socialisation and Interaction Process* (Routledge 1956).

PARSONS, Talcott, and Edward SHILS *Towards a General Theory of Action* (Free Press 1951).

PARSONS, Talcott, and Neil SMELSER *Economy and Society* (Free Press 1956).

PARSONS, Talcott et al. (eds.), *Theories of Society* (Free Press 1961).

PAYNE, Geoff 'Social Mobility in Britain: A Contrary View', in Jon Clark, Celia and Sohan Modgil (eds), *John H. Goldthorpe: Consensus and Controversy* (Falmer Press 1990), ch. 18.

PEEL, J. D. Y. *Herbert Spencer* (Heinemann 1971).

PEEL, J. D. Y. 'Two Cheers for Empiricism', *Sociology*, 12, 1978, pp. 347–59.

PIRENNE, Henri *Mediaeval Cities* (Princeton University Press 1925).

POLLARD, Sidney *The Idea of Progress* (Penguin 1968).

POPPER, Karl *The Open Society and its Enemies*, 2 vols (Routledge 1945).

POPPER, Karl *The Poverty of Historicism* (Routledge 1957).

POULANTZAS, Nicos *Political Power and Social Classes* (New Left Books 1973).

PROUDHON, P.-J. (1840) *What is Property?* (Reeves n.d.).

RAPHAEL, D. D. *Adam Smith* (Oxford University Press 1985).

RIESMAN, David *The Lonely Crowd: A Study in the Changing American Character* (Anchor Books 1966).

RITZER, G. *The McDonaldization of Society* (Sage 1991).

ROBERTSON, Roland *Globalization: Social Theory and Global Structure* (Sage 1992).

ROBINSON, John *Honest to God* (Penguin 1963).

RORTY, Richard 'Habermas and Lyotard on Postmodernity', in Richard Bernstein (ed.), *Habermas and Modernity* (Polity Press 1985), pp. 161–75.

ROSTOW, W. W. *The Stages of Economic Growth* (Cambridge University

Press 1960).
ROUSSEAU, Jean-Jacques (1762) *The Social Contract* (Dent: 1973 edn).
RUBINSTEIN, W. D. *Capitalism, Culture and Decline in Britain, 1950–1990* (Routledge 1993).
RUNCIMAN, W. G. *Max Weber: Selections in Translation* (Cambridge University Press 1978).
RYAN, Alan *Philosophy of the Social Sciences* (Macmillan 1970).
SAHLINS, Marshall, and E. SERVICE (eds), *Evolution and Culture* (University of Michigan Press 1960).
SCHULTZ, T. W. (ed.), *Economics of the Family* (Chicago University Press 1974).
SCHUTZ, Alfred *The Phenomenology of the Social World* (Heinemann 1972).
SCOTFORD ARCHER, Margaret *Culture and Agency* (Cambridge University Press 1988).
SCOTT, John *Sociological Theory: Contemporary Debates* (Edward Elgar 1995).
SENNET, Richard *The Corrosion of Character* (Norton 1998).
SHILS, Edward *Tradition* (Chicago University Press 1981).
SIMON, H. A. 'Decision Making and Administrative Organisation', in R. K. Merton et al. (eds), *Reader in Bureaucracy* (Free Press 1952), pp. 185–94.
SKLAIR, Leslie *Sociology of the Global System* (Harvester Wheatsheaf 1991).
SKOCPOL, T. 'Wallerstein's World Capitalist System: A Theoretical and Historical Critique', *American Journal of Sociology*, 82, 1977.
SKOCPOL, T. *States and Social Revolutions* (Cambridge University Press 1979).
SMART, Barry 'Modernity, Postmodernity and the Present', in Bryan S. Turner (ed.), *Theories of Modernity and Postmodernity* (Sage 1990).
SMELSER, Neil 'Toward a Theory of Modernization', in Amitai Etzioni and Eva Etzioni (eds), *Social Change* (Basic Books 1964), pp. 268–84.
SMITH, Adam (1759) *The Theory of Moral Sentiments* (Oxford University Press: 1969 edn).
SMITH, Adam (1776) *An Inquiry into the Nature and Causes of the Wealth of Nations* (Random House: 1994 edn).
SMITH, Adam *Lectures on Jurisprudence* (Oxford University Press 1970).
SO, Alvin *Social Change and Development* (Sage 1990).
SPENCER, Herbert (1862) *First Principles* (Watts: 1937 edn).
SPENCER, Herbert (1865) *Principles of Biology* (Williams and Norgate: 1865 edn).
SPENCER, Herbert (1873) *The Study of Sociology* (Kegan Paul: 1873 edn).
SPENCER, Herbert (1898–9) *Principles of Sociology*, 3 vols (Macmillan: 1969 edn).
SPENGLER, Oswald (1918) *The Decline of the West* (Alfred Knopf: 1939 edn).
STINCHCOMBE, Arthur *Constructing Social Theories* (Harcourt Brace 1968).
STUART-HUGHES, H. *Consciousness and Society* (Random House 1958).

TAWNEY, R. H. *Religion and the Rise of Capitalism* (Penguin Books 1975).
TIMASCHEFF, N. S. *History of Sociological Thought* (Van Nostrand 1957).
TIVEY, L. *The Politics of the Firm* (Martin Robertson 1978).
TOMKINS, Calvin *Marcel Duchamp* (Chatto 1997).
TÖNNIES, Ferdinand (1887) *Gemeinschaft and Gesellschaft [Community and Association]* (Routledge and Kegan Paul: 1955 edn).
TOURAINE, A. 'Modernity and Cultural Specificities', *International Social Science Journal*, 40, 1988.
TOYNBEE, Arnold *A Study of History* (Oxford University Press: 1961 abr. edn).
TREVOR-ROPER, Hugh *Religion, The Reformation and Social Change* (Macmillan 1972).
TURNER, Bryan S. (ed.) *Theories of Modernity and Postmodernity* (Sage 1990).
VEBLEN, Thorstein (1915) *Imperial Germany and the Industrial Revolution* (Viking: 1942 edn).
VOGEL, Ezra 'Kinship Structure, Migration to the City, and Modernisation', in R. P. Dore (ed.), *Aspects of Social Change in Modern Japan* (Princeton University Press 1967), pp. 91–111.
WALLERSTEIN, Immanuel *The Capitalist World Economy* (Cambridge University Press 1979).
WALLERSTEIN, Immanuel 'Underdevelopment Phase B: Effects of the Seventeenth Century Stagnation on Core and Periphery of the European World-Economy', in W. L. Goldfrank (ed.), *The World-System of Capitalism: Past and Present* (Sage 1979), pp. 73–84.
WALLERSTEIN, Immanuel *The Politics of the Capitalist World Economy* (Cambridge University Press 1984).
WALLERSTEIN, Immanuel 'World-System Analysis', in A. Giddens and J. H. Turner (eds), *Social Theory Today* (Stanford University Press 1987).
WARREN, Ben *Imperialism: Pioneer of Capitalism* (New Left Books 1980).
WATERS, Malcolm *Globalization* (Routledge 1995).
WAUGH, Patricia *Postmodernism: A Reader* (Edward Arnold 1992).
WEBER, Max (1904) *The Protestant Ethic and the Spirit of Capitalism* (Allen and Unwin: 1974 edn).
WEBER, Max (1905) *The Protestant Ethic and the Spirit of Capitalism* (Scribner's: 1958 edn).
WEBER, Max (1906) *The Methodology of the Social Sciences* (Free Press: 1949 edn).
WEBER, Max (1917) *The Religion of India* (Free Press: 1958 edn).
WEBER, Max (1920) 'Politics as a Vocation', in Hans Gerth and C. Wright Mills (eds), *From Max Weber: Essays in Sociology* (Routledge and Kegan Paul: 1958 edn).
WEBER, Max (1920) *General Economic History* (Free Press: 1954 edn).
WEBER, Max (1922) *Economy and Society* (Bedminster Press: 1968 edn).
WEBER, Max *The Religion of China: Confucianism and Taoism* (Free Press 1957).
WEBER, Max 'Science as a Vocation', in H. Gerth and C. Wright Mills (eds), *From Max Weber: Essays in Sociology* (Routledge and Kegan Paul 1967).

WHITELOCK, Dorothy *The Beginnings of English Society* (Penguin 1952).
WHYTE, W. F. *The Organisation Man* (Simon and Schuster 1956).
WIENER, Martin J. *English Culture and the Decline of the Industrial Spirit,*
     1850–1980 (Cambridge University Press 1981).
WILLIAMS, Raymond *Culture and Society 1780–1950* (Penguin Books
     1961).
WILSON, E. O. *Socio-Biology: The New Synthesis* (Harvard University Press
     1975).
WINCH, Donald *Adam Smith's Politics* (Cambridge University Press 1978).
WITTFOGEL, Karl *Oriental Despotism* (Yale University Press 1957).
WITTGENSTEIN, Ludwig (1953) *Philosophical Investigations* (Blackwell
     1967).
WONG, Siu-Lun 'The Applicability of Asian Family Values to Other Socio-
     Cultural Settings', in P. L. Berger and Hsiu-Huang Michael Hsiao (eds),
     In Search of an East-Asian Development Model (Transaction 1988), pp.
     134–54.
WORLD BANK *The East Asian Miracle* (Oxford University Press 1993).
WRIGHT MILLS, C. *The Sociological Imagination* (Oxford University Press
     1959).

Index

Aganbeygan, A., 198
agency, 5, 10, 22–3, 112–4, 159,
  201, 214–18, 235
Albrow, M., 141
alienation, 34, 60, 97–98, 220
Althusser, L., 92, 98
altruism, 46
Anderson, P., 95
Andreski, S., 43
anomie, 154–5, 203, 220
Aron, R., 11, 194
authority, 134–8

Bacon, F., 15
Bales, R., 178
Baran, P., 187
Baran, P. and Sweezy, P., 96
Baudrillard, J., 8, 226, 231–4, 240,
  242
Bauer, B., 75, 86, 161
Bauman, Z., 222, 235, 236
Beetham, D., 137
behaviourism, 12
Bell D., 53, 196, 202, 207–13, 220
Bell, N. and Vogel, E., 181
Bellah, R., 164
Bendix, R., 212
Bertens, H., 219, 222, 235
Black, M., 184
Blanqui, A., 76
Blau, P., 12
Blau, P. and Meyer M., 141
Blumer, H., 11
Boswell, J., 20
Boudon, R., 242–3
Bourdieu, P., 86
Bowler, P., 7

Braudel, F., 11, 95, 97, 193
bureaucracy, 58, 136–8, 141–2,
  196, 214
Burgess, E. and Locke, J., 182
Burnham, J., 93, 197
Burns, T. and Stalker, G., 142
Burrow, J., 7

Calinicos, A., 235
Campbell, T., 20
capitalism,
  and class in A. Smith, 30–5,37–
    8
  conservative criticism, 101,
    105–6, 116–7
  development, and, 67–9,188–97
  Marx's critique, 77–94
  value conflicts of, 187–8, 202–
    13, 215–16
  Weber and rationalism of, 123–
    5, 138–44
caste, 7, 133, 196
cerebral hygiene, 46
charisma, 135–6, 140, 144
Cheal, D., 224
class
  convergence, 194–7
  dialectical relations of, 72–3,
    77–91, 96–97, 190
  distributive process of, 125–6,
    132–4, 218
  division of labour and, 20–1,
    26–34, 152–3
  social evolution and, 42, 54, 67
Cohen, G., 84, 91
collective representations, 159,
  168–71

255

Collins, R., 6
Comte, A., 7, 41, 48, 55, 57, 72,
    77, 100, 178, 196, 220, 222
conflict, 72, 78–83, 99, 110–11,
    143, 153, 171, 185, 196–7, 203
    and consensus, 6–7, 47, 64,
    117, 171, 199
conscience collective, 147–57,
    162–70
consumers, consumption, 27–8,
    69–70, 89, 133, 139, 155, 195,
    200, 207, 231–2
convergence theory, 175, 194–201
Coser, L., 185
Craib, I., 214
critical theory, 86
Crook, S., Pakulski, J. and Waters,
    M., 236, 241, 242
Cuppitt, D., 165
cyclical change, 1, 7–8. 66, 112–
    17, 193
Cyert, R. and March, J., 142

Darwin, Darwinism, 7, 36, 41, 51,
    54, 60
Davis, K., 11
Davis, W., 127
Dawe, A., 13–14
Dawkins, R., 6, 36
Deane, P., 95
dependency theory, 174–5, 187–
    93, 199–201
dialectics, 7, 73–5, 78–83, 88–91,
    99
disjunction of realms, 210–11
division of labour, 24–31, 34–5,
    38, 145–55, 163, 168, 173, 195
Djilas, M., 93
Douglas, M., 63–4, 232
Dudley, L., 11–12
Dumont, R., 7
Durkheim, E., 3–4, 9, 17, 129,
    145–71, 213, 220, 231

education, 34–5, 86, 145, 155–6,
    195–6, 197, 204
elites, 46–47, 67, 111–17, 190,
    207–9, 235
Elton, G., 130
empiricism, 5, 15–16, 31, 39, 48,
    56, 117, 144, 237, 242–3
endogenous change, 5–7, 39, 47,
    53, 65–70, 99, 117, 143, 175,
    199, 206, 210
Engels, F., 71, 75–7, 97, 128
Erikson, R. and Goldthorpe, J. H.,
    198
evolutionary theories, 36, 39, 40–
    56, 86, 100, 117, 160, 199, 208
exchange theory, 12
exogenous change, 5–6, 53–4, 64,
    68, 175, 183, 185, 199

Featherstone, M., 223, 242
Ferguson, A., 18, 23, 172
Feuer, L., 47
Feuerbach, L., 75, 86, 161
Flew, A., 13
Ford, H. and Fordism, 26–7, 223–
    4
Foucault, M., 225, 228
Frank, A. G., 174–5, 187–93, 199
Frank, A. G. and Gills, B., 193
Frankfurt School – *see* critical
    theory
Friedman, G., 194
Fukuyama, F., 7, 196
functionalism, 9–10, 53–4, 61–5,
    84, 145, 160–1, 173–5, 178–87,
    201, 210

Galbraith, J. K., 175, 197, 204
gemeinschaft und gesellschaft,
    102–8, 150–1, 194, 216
Gellner, E., 211, 235, 241
gender, 13–14, 218
Giddens, A., 10, 42, 200, 202–3,
    213–20, 222, 235, 240

Ginsberg, M., 58
globalization, 56–8, 62–3, 190–3,
    200, 218–20, 240, 243
Goffman, E., 9
Goldman, M., 198
Goldthorpe, J. H., 197–8
Gordon-Childe, V., 11
Gouldner, A., 186
Gramsci, A., 86

Habermas, J., 202–7, 212–3, 220
Hall, J., 81, 212
Hammersley, M., 13
Hamnett, I., 165
Harris, C., 182
Harris, N., 192
Hawthorn, G., 15
Hegel, G., 7, 12, 73–6
Heidegger, M., 225–6
Heilbronner, R., 33
historicism, 8, 47, 54, 64, 99, 116–
    7, 171, 183, 199
Hobbes, T., 6
Homans, G., 12
hunters and gatherers, 25–6, 37, 58
Huntington, E., 11
hyperreality, 203, 232–3

ideal-types,
    bureaucracy, 137–8
    criticisms of, 116, 142–4, 174
    puritans, 121–2, 128
    social structure, 103–4, 146,
        150–1, 171
idealism and materialism, 5, 10–
    12, 47, 55, 65, 73–5, 98–9,
    116–7, 143–4, 171, 199
ideology,
    class and, 32–3, 64, 67, 85–6,
        107, 110–11, 205, 212
    objectivity and, 5, 12–14, 39,
        55–6, 99–100, 116–17, 161,
        168, 171, 199
industrial society, *see* convergence

theory
inherited property, 38, 42, 79–80,
    89–90, 133, 152–3
invisible hand, 36–7
    see also unintended
    consequences

Johnson, S. *see* Boswell

Kant, I., 122, 168
Kellner, D., 232
Kerr, C., 175, 194–200
Kohn, M., 141
Kuhn, T., 228
Kumar, K., 8, 15–16. 211, 224, 237

Laclau, E., 189
Laclau, E. and Mouffe, C., 221,
    236
Lamarck, J.-B., 41, 60
Landes, D., 211
landowners, 31–2, 79, 110, 115
Laslett, P., 182
law, 29, 38, 145, 148–9
law of three stages, 43–7
law of historical development,
    72–6, 92
    see also materialist conception
    of history
Layder, D., 10
Lenin, V. I., 71, 92, 187
Lenski, G., 59
Lenski, G. and Lenski J., 42
Linton, R., 61
lions and foxes, 112–16
    see also elites
List, F., 95
Lockwood, D., 185–200
Lukács, G., 168, 225
Lyotard, J.-F., 8, 226–30, 235, 242

Machiavelli, N., 6
Macfarlane, A., 124, 130, 148, 182
MacKinnon, M.,129

Mannheim, K., 168, 225
March, J. and Olsen J., 142
Marcuse, H., 98
markets, 27–30, 51, 85, 203–5
Marx, K., 3, 7, 9, 17, 19, 54, 71–
    100, 110, 128–31, 154, 161,
    168, 189, 191, 203, 210, 213
mass media, 194, 200, 203, 208,
    231–4
materialism, *see* idealism and
    materialism
materialist conception of history,
    7, 76–83, 128
Matthias, P., 95
McLachlan, D ., 165
Mead, G. H., 9, 11, 22
Mêstròvic, S., 215, 218
metanarratives, 5, 8, 228–9, 235,
    237
methodological individualism, 5,
    9–10, 12, 117, 118–22, 143,
    150, 158, 199
militant societies, 48, 55
Mintzberg, H., 142
mode of production, 78–83, 94,
    100, 184, 188, 191
modernity, 4, 56, 58–64, 105–8,
    117, 138–40, 202–21, 239
Montesquieu, C.-L., 8, 11
Moore, W., 194
Mosca, G., 115–6
Mouffe, C., 221

Needham, J., 29
neo-evolutionist theory, 56, 57–
    70, 199
Nicholls, T., 212
Nicholson, L. and Seidman, S.,
    221
Nietzsche, F., 225–6
Nimkoff, M. and Middleton, R.,
    182
Nisbet, R., 11, 154
Noble, T., 64, 241

O'Connor, J., 205
Oliver, I., 165
organic analogy, 53, 147, 151, 173

Paine, T., 161
paralogy, 227–8
Pareto, V., 3, 6, 108–17, 129
Parkin, F., 92
Parsons, T., 10, 60–4, 106, 176–87,
    199, 200–1, 204, 206–7
pattern variables, 60–1, 106, 176–
    8
Payne, G., 198
Peel, J. D. Y., 13, 51
Pirenne, H., 95
Pollard, S., 41
Popper, K., 8, 9
positivism, 43–8
postmodernist theories, 2, 4, 8,
    56, 168, 171, 214, 221–37,
    239–42
postmodernity, 4, 171, 214, 221–
    37, 240–1
Poulantzas, N., 92
progress, 3, 5, 7, 40–2, 43, 50–1,
    54–6, 100–1, 224, 229
    see also law of three stages, law
    of historical development
Proudhon, P.-J., 76–7
puritans, 122, 125–8, 138–9, 207

Raphael, D., 24
rationalisation of the world, 7, 44–
    5, 74–5, 101, 106, 138–40,
    143–4, 210, 212, 224
rationalism, 5, 15–16, 48, 56, 64,
    91, 99, 108, 115, 116, 119–20,
    124–5, 138–9, 144, 168–9, 199,
    219, 237
    see also empiricism
religion, 20, 22, 44, 87, 114, 125,
    181
    Durkheim on, 129, 161–7

in Marxist Theory, 84, 86, 128–9
in Weber's Theory, 126–130
residues, 109–113, 117
revolutionary theory, 3, 71–100,
    101, 111, 153–4, 184, 191,
    194, 210
Ritzer, G., 200, 223
Robertson, R., 200
Robinson, J., 165
Rorty, R., 16, 237
Rostow, W., 65–70, 95
Rousseau, J.-J., 6
Rubinstein, D. W., 211–2
Runciman, W. G., 122
Ryan, A., 13

Sahlins, M. and Service, E., 58–9
St Matthew, 128
St Simon, H., 7, 11, 42, 45, 72, 76,
    153–5, 197
Schultz, T., 181
Schutz, A., 9, 11
Scotford Archer, M., 10
Scott, J., 10, 143, 217
Sennett, R., 224
Shils, E., 11, 178
Simon, H. A., 142
simulacra, 233–5
Sklair, L., 200
Skocpol, T., 93
slavery, 40, 50, 79, 90, 93
Smart, B., 242
Smelser, N., 59–60, 178, 182
Smith, A., 2, 3, 17–39, 72, 75, 97,
    172, 240
So, A., 193
socialism, 6, 8, 73, 76, 82–3, 92–3,
    99, 101, 140, 153–4, 188, 191,
    197
social mobility, 50, 92, 105, 111–
    12, 130, 152–3, 196, 197–8
sociological realism, 5, 9–10, 12,
    47, 55, 64, 83–4, 99, 116, 158,
    171, 199, 235

Spencer, H., 7, 41–2, 48–56, 57,
    59, 77, 150, 194
Spengler, O., 8
stages of development, 37–8, 43–
    5, 47, 50–1, 61–3, 65–70, 77–
    82, 146–9, 160–1, 173, 213–5,
    222–3, 236, 240–1
Stinchcombe, A., 183
Stuart-Hughes, H., 139
systems theories, 4, 172–201, 203–
    4, 210–11, 235, 240

Taylor, F., 26–7, 194
technological change, 11–12, 26–
    7, 89, 181–2, 194–5, 240
teleological explanation, 8, 182–3,
    215
third world, 57, 60, 66–9, 91–2,
    174–5, 187–91
Timascheff, N., 46
Tivey, L., 181
Tomkins, C., 208
Tönnies, F., 3, 60, 102–8, 116–17,
    150, 194, 216, 240
Touraine, A., 224
Toynbee, A., 7
Trevor-Roper, H., 130

unintended consequences, 20, 23,
    30–1, 36–7, 158, 172–3, 220

value relevance, 14, 119
Veblen, T., 53
Vogel, E., 64

Wallerstein, I., 192–3
war, 6, 11–12, 49–50, 54, 59, 66–7,
    69
Warren, B., 191
Waters, M., 200
Waugh, P., 221, 224
Weber, M., 3–4, 9, 14, 66, 103,
    106, 117–144, 158, 176, 182,
    197, 214, 223, 240

wergeld, 148
westernisation, 58–9
Whitelock, D., 148
Whyte, W. F., 106
Wiener, M., 129, 211–12
Williams, R., 211
Wilson, E. O., 6

Winch, D., 34
Wittfoge,l K., 81
Wittgenstein, L., 225, 227
Wong, S.-L., 64
World Bank, 192, 200
Wright Mills, C., 223

Printed in the United States
101399LV00002B/66/A